DEPRESSION
Second Edition

Depression
Second Edition

Constance Hammen
University of California, Los Angeles

Edward Watkins
University of Exeter, UK

Psychology Press
Taylor & Francis Group

HOVE AND NEW YORK

First published 2008 by Psychology Press
27 Church Road, Hove, East Sussex BN3 2FA

Simultaneously published in the USA and Canada
by Psychology Press
270 Madison Avenue, New York, NY 10016

Psychology Press is an imprint of the Taylor & Francis Group, an Informa business

Typeset in Palatino by Garfield Morgan, Swansea, West Glamorgan
Printed and bound in Great Britain by TJ International Ltd, Padstow, Cornwall
Cover design by Jim Wilkie

British Library Cataloguing in Publication Data
A catalogue record for this book is available from the British Library

Library of Congress Cataloging-in-Publication Data
Hammen, Constance L.
   Depression / Constance Hammen and Ed Watkins. – 2nd ed.
       p. ; cm.
   Includes bibliographical references and index.
   ISBN 978-0-415-41972-7 (hbk) – ISBN 978-0-415-41973-4 (pbk.) 1. Depression,
Mental. I. Watkins, Ed, 1971- II. Title.
   [DNLM: 1. Depressive Disorder. 2. Depression. WM 171 H224db 2008]
   RC537.H297 2008
   616.85'27–dc22
                                                                2007027005

ISBN: 978-0-415-41972-7 (hbk)
ISBN: 978-0-415-41973-4 (pbk)

Contents

Series preface

Clinical Psychology: A Modular Course was designed to overcome the problems faced by the traditional textbook in conveying what psychological disorders are really like. All the books in the series, written by leading scholars and practitioners in the field, can be read as standalone text, but they will also integrate with the other modules to form a comprehensive resource in clinical psychology. Students of psychology, medicine, nursing, and social work, as well as busy practitioners in many professions, often need an accessible but thorough introduction to how people experience anxiety, depression, addiction, or other disorders, how common they are, and who is most likely to suffer from them, as well as up-to-date research evidence on the causes and available treatments. The series will appeal to those who want to go deeper into the subject than the traditional textbook will allow, and base their examination answers, research projects, assignments, or practical decisions on a clearer and more rounded appreciation of the clinical and research evidence.

Chris R. Brewin

Other titles in this series:

Depression, First Edition
Constance Hammen

Stress and Trauma
Patricia A. Resick

Childhood Disorders
Philip C. Kendall

Schizophrenia
Max Birchwood and Chris Jackson

Addictions
Maree Teesson, Louise Degenhardt and Wayne Hall

Anxiety
S. Rachman

Eating and Weight Disorders
Carlos M. Grilo

List of tables
and figures

Defining and diagnosing depression 1

Lew takes one look at me and says that he doesn't even need to ask how I'm doing. I pour it all out to him: I can't sleep. I can't eat. I can't read or talk or concentrate for more than several seconds. The force of gravity around me has tripled. It takes so much effort just to lift an arm or take a step. When I am not curled up in a ball on the couch, I pace. I rock desperately in my rocking chair. I wring my hands.

I try to go to my Saturday morning meditation group. I park the car but almost turn back two or three times before I get to the front door . . . I try to listen and add something, but I can hardly follow the conversation. I can't even fake it anymore. At the break I excuse myself with a lie that I have to get to Keara's softball game. I know that I can't make it through forty-five minutes of silent meditation. I come home crying. More empty tears to God about why this is still happening. Tears for an end to it. Tears for mercy.

The house is deserted. I search for things to do. It is all I can do just to empty the dishwasher and sweep the floor. Then I lie on the couch and stare into space, vacant and deadened. I have a haircut appointment that I am already dreading, even though it's three hours away. How will I keep up a conversation with my effusive hairdresser? It will be a monumental effort just to move my lips into a smile. My face is simultaneously waxy and frozen. The muscles have gone on strike.
Martha Manning (1994, p. 104, pp. 106–107), *Undercurrents: A Therapist's Reckoning With Her Own Depression.*

[By October] the fading evening light . . . had none of its autumnal loveliness, but ensnared me in a suffocating gloom . . . I felt an immense and aching solitude. I could no longer concentrate during those afternoon hours, which for years had been my working time . . .

Soon evident are the slowed-down responses, near paralysis, psychic energy throttled back close to zero. Ultimately, the body is affected and feels sapped, drained . . . I found myself eating only for subsistence [and] exhaustion combined with sleeplessness is a rare torture . . . What I had begun to discover is that, mysteriously and in ways that are totally remote from normal experience, the gray drizzle of horror induced by depression takes on the quality of physical pain . . . it is entirely natural that the victim begins to think ceaselessly of oblivion.

William Styron (1990), *Darkness Visible*.

The words of these two modern writers capture vividly the experience of depression, but its themes have also been echoed in ancient texts of the Bible, Greek, Roman, and Chinese classics—as well as Shakespearean plays and Russian novels. Depression is a universal, timeless, and ageless human affliction. Among those who first described the features of depression in modern clinical terms was Kraepelin (1921, p. 76), the German scholar who helped establish a classification system for mental disorders:

Mood is sometimes dominated by a profound inward dejection and gloomy hopelessness, sometimes more by indefinite anxiety and restlessness. The patient's heart is heavy, nothing can permanently rouse his interest, nothing gives him pleasure . . .

He feels solitary, indescribably unhappy, as a "creature disinherited of fate"; he is skeptical about God, and with a certain dull submission, which shuts out every comfort and every gleam of light, he drags himself with difficulty from one day to another. Everything has become disagreeable to him; everything wearies him, company, music, travel, his professional work. Everywhere he sees only the dark side and difficulties; the people round him are not so good and unselfish as he had thought; one disappointment and disillusionment follows another. Life appears to him aimless, he thinks that he is superfluous in the world, he cannot restrain himself any longer, the thought occurs to him to take his life without his knowing why. He has a feeling as if something had cracked in him.

While the personal experience of depression is profoundly painful, it is often misunderstood by others. The experience of depression often seems paradoxical: a new mother gets depressed after a much-wanted birth of a child; an executive slips into a depression following a successful effort to achieve a higher position; a widow seems more depressed when her dog dies than she did when her husband of many years died. Moreover, most individuals in Western societies are raised to expect to have considerable control over moods, and are exhorted not to let themselves suffer from depression. Thus, it is distressing to others when a loved one or friend does not "snap out" of depression, and the hopeless, helpless, and self-hating attitudes expressed by depressed individuals often seem illogical and irrational, as if the depressed person willfully and perversely holds onto unreasonable moods and beliefs.

As this book hopes to explore, depression is neither uncommon nor particularly paradoxical—nor is it a failure of willpower and motivation. It is enormously impairing—and even deadly—and its effects on both the afflicted person and his or her family can be profoundly negative. Yet, we also have a number of effective treatments for depression, and science is gaining considerable insight into the processes underpinning depression.

Phenomenology of depressive experiences

The term *depression* is used in everyday language to describe a range of experiences from a slightly noticeable and temporary mood decrease to a profoundly impairing and even life-threatening disorder. When used to describe a mood, the term conveys a temporary state of dysphoria that may last a few moments, hours, or even a few days. As such, it is usually a normal reaction to an upsetting event, or even an exaggerated description of a typical event ("this weather is depressing," or "I've gained a few pounds. How depressing!"). A young man might feel sad for a few days following a romantic disappointment, or a woman might be discouraged for a few days on being passed over for a job. Such experiences are not the topic of this book. Instead, the term "depression" as described in the book refers to a constellation of experiences including not only mood, but also physical, mental, and behavioural experiences that define more prolonged, impairing, and severe conditions that may be clinically diagnosable as a syndrome of depression.

The descriptions at the beginning of the chapter differ from one another, but they share features of the syndromes of depression. Each one has some features from the four different domains that define depressive disorders. Depressed people may differ from one another by the number, unique patterns, and severity of the symptoms. The four general domains are *affect, cognition, behaviour,* and *physical functioning*.

Affective symptoms.   Depression is one of several disorders generically called affective disorders, referring to the manifestations of abnormal affect, or mood, as a defining feature. Thus, depressed mood, sadness, feeling low, down in the dumps, or empty are typical. However, sometimes the most apparent mood is irritability (especially in depressed children). Moreover, not all depressed people manifest sadness or depression as such. Instead, they may report feeling loss of interest or pleasure, a feeling of "blah", listlessness, apathy. Nothing seems enjoyable—not even experiences that previously elicited positive feelings, including work and recreation, social interactions, sexual activity, and the like. Pastimes are no longer enjoyable; even pleasurable relationships with one's family and friends may no longer hold appeal or even be negative, and the individual may find it hard to think of things to do that might help to relieve the depression even temporarily. Even when he or she accomplishes an important task, there is little sense of satisfaction. Some severely depressed people have described the loss of pleasure as seeing the world in black, white, and gray with no colour. The experience of loss of interest or pleasure, called anhedonia, is one of the most common features of the depression syndrome, according to many studies of depressed adults and teenagers, from many different countries (reviewed in Klinger, 1993).

> George, a middle-aged man of apparent good health, has felt listless and bored for a few weeks. His favourite television programmes no longer interest him in the evenings, and on weekends he can't think of anything to do that he imagines would be pleasurable—in contrast to his formerly active and fun-seeking self. He says his pals are "boring" and his attitude about seeing his girlfriend is that she doesn't interest him anymore. Fortunately, she is astute enough to suspect that he became depressed ever since someone else got the promotion at work that he hoped for—though George himself would deny that he is depressed.

Cognitive symptoms. Some have called depression a disorder of thinking, as much as it is a disorder of mood. Depressed people typically have negative thoughts about themselves, their worlds, and the future. They experience themselves as incompetent, worthless, and are relentlessly critical of their own acts and characteristics, and often feel guilty as they dwell on their perceived shortcomings. Low self-esteem is therefore a common attribute of depression. Individuals may feel helpless to manage their lives or resolve problems. They may view their lives and futures as bleak and unrewarding, feeling that change is not only pointless but essentially unattainable. Cognitions reflecting hopelessness about one's ability to control desired outcomes may be common, and the resulting despair may also give rise to thoughts of wanting to die or to take one's own life.

> Annette has been increasingly depressed since her boyfriend went off to the university. Although he keeps in touch with her, she is consumed with the thoughts that he is trying to meet other women, that she's not good enough to sustain his interest—and that indeed, why would anyone ever love her. At work she imagines that she is doing a poor job and expects to be fired—despite her boss's praise for her achievements. When her girlfriends ask her to go out with them she believes that they don't really want her company and are only feeling sorry for her that her boyfriend is away. As she becomes more and more depressed, she believes herself to be a horrible person; tasks at work seem more and more overwhelming so that she believes that she is incompetent and utterly helpless to figure out how to manage projects she used to do with ease.

The cognitive features of depression have been given particular emphasis by some investigators, who note that thinking in such grim and self-critical ways actually makes people more depressed or prolongs their depression. The negativistic thinking is commonly irrational and distorted, and represents very different interpretations of the self and the world during the depressed state than an individual would typically display when he or she wasn't depressed. This observation gave rise to Aaron Beck's cognitive model of depression (A. T. Beck, 1967, 1976), that hypothesizes an underlying vulnerability to depression due to tendencies to perceive the self, world, and future in negative ways. Somewhat similar models of depression emphasizing self-esteem (Crocker & Wolfe, 2001; J. E. Roberts & Gotlib, 1997; J. E. Roberts & Monroe, 1994) and hopelessness (Abramson, Metalsky, & Alloy, 1989; Alloy et al., 1999) are discussed in a later chapter.

In addition to negativistic thinking, depression is often marked by difficulties in mental processes involving concentration, decision making, and memory. The depressed person may find it enormously difficult to make even simple decisions, and significant decisions seem beyond one's capacity altogether. Depressed patients often report problems in concentrating, especially when reading or watching television, and memory may be impaired (Tarbuck & Paykel, 1995; Watts, 1993). Memory problems, in fact, often lead depressed people to worry further that their minds are failing, and in older depressed individuals what is actually a treatable memory deficit due to depression may be misinterpreted as a sign of irreversible dementia. Experimental studies suggest that deficits in cognitive initiative are implicated in the impaired memory and concentration observed in depression: when the memory task requires participants to focus attention on the to-be-remembered material, depressed participants perform as well as nondepressed participants (Hertel & Rude, 1991). Thus, it appears that some of the cognitive-functioning problems found in depression are due to distraction by irrelevant (depressive) thoughts (Hertel, 1998), and others are due to difficulties in mobilizing cognitive resources (Hertel, 2000).

Behavioural symptoms. Consistent with the apathy and diminished motivation of depression, it is common for individuals to withdraw from social activities or reduce typical behaviours. In severe depression, the individual might stay in bed for prolonged periods. Social interactions might be shunned, both because of loss of motivation and interest, and also because depressed people perceive, fairly accurately, that being around them may be aversive to others.

Actual changes in motor behaviour are often observed, taking the form either of being slowed down or agitated and restless. Some depressed individuals may talk and move more slowly, their faces showing little animation with their mouths and eyes seeming to droop as if weighted down, all of which are labeled psychomotor retardation. Their speech is marked by pauses, fewer words, monotone voice, and less eye contact (Perez & Riggio, 2002; Sobin & Sackeim, 1997). Other depressed people display psychomotor agitation, indicated by restlessness, hand movements, fidgeting and self-touching, and gesturing.

Psychomotor agitation may be more commonly observed in depressed people who are also experiencing anxiety symptoms, while psychomotor retardation is thought to be more typical of "pure" depression. Psychomotor retardation may also be more common in males and patients under the age of 40, whereas psycho-motor agitation is more common in females and patients over the age of forty. Interestingly, presence of psychomotor retardation has been found to be a good predictor of a positive response to antidepressant medication (Joyce & Paykel, 1989; Sobin & Sackeim, 1997).

Physical symptoms. In addition to motor behaviour changes that are apparent in some depressed people, there may also be changes in appetite, sleep, and energy. Reduced energy is a very frequent com-plaint. Depressed patients complain of listlessness, lethargy, feeling heavy and leaden, and lacking the physical stamina to undertake or complete tasks.

Sleep disturbance is a particularly important symptom of depres-sion, with the majority of unipolar depressed patients reporting poorer quality of sleep, experienced as a loss of restfulness and/or a reduced duration of sleep (Benca, Obermeyer, Thisted, & Gillin, 1992; Kupfer, 1995). Sleep changes can take several forms: difficulty falling asleep, staying asleep, or too much sleep. Depressed people some-times experience what is called "early morning awakening," a prob-lem of waking an hour or more before the regular awakening time, usually with difficulty falling back asleep.

The relationship between sleep disturbance and depression is a complex one, with a close correspondence existing between regulation of mood and regulation of sleep (Lustberg & Reynolds, 2000). As well as being an important consequence or complication of depression, impaired sleep is also a vulnerability factor for further relapse and recurrence, and an indicator of future prognosis and treatment outcome, often preceding the onset of an episode of major depression (N. Breslau, Roth, Rosenthal, & Andreski, 1996; Riemann & Voderholzer, 2003).

Patients with depression also experience changes in appetite, typically in the form of decreased appetite with corresponding weight loss. However, some depressed people eat more when depressed, with this pattern often associated with increased sleep. This combi-nation of increased appetite (hyperphagia) and increased sleep (hypersomnia) within depression has been labeled *atypical depression* (Davidson, Miller, Turnbull, & Sullivan, 1982; Matza, Revicki, Davidson, & Stewart, 2003).

Implications. The multiplicity of symptoms of depression means that depressed people differ one from another in the manifestations of their disorder. Such differences may reflect variability in the severity of the depression, as well as suggesting that there may be different forms of depression that have different causes and treatments. The diagnostic systems in use today define several categories that cut across these variabilities, and that represent the major forms of the disorder that are the basis of most research and clinical categorization.

Diagnosis of depression

The first diagnostic distinction to be made is the difference between *unipolar* depression and *bipolar* disorder. Unipolar depression, which is the focus of this book, includes only depressive conditions occurring in the absence of current or past mania or hypomania. *Mania* is defined as a distinct period of abnormally and persistently elevated, expansive, or irritable mood lasting at least 1 week, in combination with at least three of the following symptoms: inflated self-esteem or grandiosity, decreased need for sleep, increased talkativeness, flight of ideas or racing thoughts, distractibility and poor concentration, increase in goal-directed activity or psychomotor agitation, and excessive involvement in pleasurable but risky activities such as overspending or sexual indiscretions. *Hypomania* is a milder form of mania, lasting 4 days or more. Thus, like an episode of depression, an episode of mania or hypomania involves an abnormal pattern of affective, cognitive, behavioural, and physical symptoms. However, whereas depression is typically characterized by reduced arousal and reduced sensitivity to reward and pleasure, mania is typically characterized by increased arousal and increased sensitivity to reward and pleasure.

Bipolar disorder is diagnosed when an individual has at least one lifetime manic episode and, as such, the diagnosis does not require the individual to have had an episode of depression. Nonetheless, the majority of individuals with bipolar affective disorder experience cycles of both depression and mania/hypomania, with a subset of 20% to 30% of individuals with bipolar disorder not experiencing depression (Kessler, Rubinow, Holmes, Abelson, & Zhao, 1997b). Bipolar affective disorder is a chronic problem of recurrent symptoms, often marked not only by extreme mood swings but even by psychotic experiences including delusions and hallucinations. Psychotic features are relatively common in the manic phase of bipolar disorder, with rates as high as 65% (Coryell, Leon, Turvey, Akiskal, Mueller, & Endicott, 2001).

Episodes of depression within bipolar disorder (bipolar depression) appear to be similar to episodes of unipolar depression with respect to symptoms, biological features, course, and psychosocial antecedents, although bipolar depression is associated with more frequent episodes and more abrupt onsets of depression than unipolar depression, suggesting greater dysregulation of mood in bipolar depression (Cuellar, Johnson, & Winters, 2005). Because unipolar and bipolar depressions may be similar, diagnostic errors occur when bipolar disorder is mistaken as unipolar depression. Nonetheless, individuals with bipolar disorder are considered to have an etiologically different disorder with a different course from unipolar depression, and to require different types of treatment. Thus, a researcher or clinician must carefully evaluate not only the current symptoms but also the individuals' personal and family history of mood disorders, bearing in mind that research has found that a significant minority of initially depressed people go on to develop bipolar episodes (Angst, Sellaro, Stassen, & Gamma, 2005; Goldberg, Harrow, & Whiteside, 2001).

> Ronald has just been hospitalized for severe depression and suicidality. Nearly unable to get out of bed, he is dishevelled, weeping, and moaning about wishing he were dead. The examining psychiatrist at the hospital determines, however, that in the months before the depression Ronald was extremely euphoric and overactive. He believed he had achieved a breakthrough in his business ideas, and had borrowed huge sums of money to finance new ventures that in retrospect had little chance of success. Sleeping only 2 or 3 hours a night, he had worked feverishly on his projects, jumping from one to another without completing any—and had talked incessantly to anyone he could find about how great his ideas were and how important he was about to become. Information from Ronald's family members revealed that he had experienced several such cycles of mania and depression since his early 20s. He was given a diagnosis of bipolar disorder, and treated with lithium as well as an antidepressant medication.

Bipolar I disorder typically includes a history of episodes of depression and mania, while depression with a history of hypomania is called Bipolar II disorder. The case above illustrates Bipolar I disorder, because of relatively clear patterns of severe mood disturbance, but Bipolar II is relatively more difficult to detect if the hypomania is more subtle or brief. An additional diagnostic problem is that sometimes there is no history of previous mania or hypomania but the person is nonetheless suffering from bipolar disorder. Longitudinal studies find that over time a significant proportion of diagnoses of unipolar depression are converted to a diagnosis of bipolar disorder as a consequence of the later occurrence of a manic or hypomanic episode. Note that it is the diagnosis that changes—not the underlying disorder, which goes unrecognized until mania or hypomania are observed. It is estimated that for each year since the original diagnosis of depression, there is an additional 1% chance of the diagnosis switching from depression to bipolar disorder; for example a 10% chance after 10 years (Angst et al., 2005). The rates of diagnostic conversion are even higher when the initial diagnosis of depression occurs in adolescence or young adulthood, particularly when the initial episodes are severe and/or involve psychotic symptoms. For example, a 15-year follow-up of young depressed inpatients found that 15% were rediagnosed as Bipolar I and 26% as Bipolar II over time (Goldberg et al., 2001).

According to the *Diagnostic and Statistical Manual of Mental Disorders*, which is a set of agreed guidelines for diagnosis, and that is now on its 4th edition, revised (*DSM-IV-TR*; American Psychiatric Association, 2000), unipolar depressions basically take one of three forms: major depressive episode, dysthymic disorder, or "depression not otherwise specified" (including several forms of briefer or milder periods of depression). These conditions are briefly described.

Major depressive episode. The diagnostic criteria for major depression are very similar for both the *DSM-IV-TR* and for the *International Classification of Disorders–Version 10* (ICD-10; World Health Organization, 1993). Table 1.1 indicates diagnostic criteria for *ICD-10*. Acknowledging the heterogeneity of depressive presentations, these systems permit individual variability so long as essential features are shared. Within the *DSM-IV-TR* these essential features include seriously compromised mood (continuous depressed mood or loss of interest/anhedonia) and at least four additional cognitive, behavioural, or physical symptoms. Note that individuals must show the symptoms all or most of the day, nearly every day for at least 2 weeks. Also, in order to be diagnosed, the episode must be clinically significant in terms of causing distress or impaired functioning in the person's typical social or occupational roles. Furthermore, alternative causes for the symptoms such as bereavement or the direct physiological effects of medical illness (e.g., hypothyroidism), medications, and substance misuse need to be ruled out before a diagnosis of a major depressive episode can be reached.

TABLE 1.1

Diagnostic criteria for depressive disorders: *International Classification of Disorders* (*ICD-10*: **World Health Organization, 1993**)

Note: general diagnostic criteria and clinical features are specified, but the following are the more precisely defined diagnostic criteria for research (for depressive episode and dysthymia).

Depressive episode

A   Symptoms must be present for at least two weeks; the person did not meet criteria for mania or hypomania at any time.

B   a) depressed mood most of the day and almost every day, uninfluenced by circumstances
    b) loss of interest or pleasure in activities that are normally pleasurable
    c) increased fatiguability or decreased energy

C   a) loss of confidence or self-esteem
    b) unreasonable feelings of self-reproach or excessive and inappropriate guilt
    c) recurrent thoughts of death or suicide, or any suicidal behaviour
    d) complaints or evidence of diminished ability to think or concentrate, such as indecisiveness or vacillation
    e) change in psychomotor activity, with agitation or retardation (either subjective or objective)
    f) sleep disturbance of any type
    g) change in appetite (decrease or increase) with corresponding weight change

Note: Depressive episodes may be diagnosed as: *Mild* (at least 2 from B plus at least 2 from C, for a total of at least 4); *Moderate* (at least 2 from B plus 3 or 4 from C for a total of at least 6); *Severe* depressive episode without psychotic features (all 3 from B plus at least 4 from C, for a total of at least 9—no hallucinations, delusions, or depressive stupor).

Dysthymia

A   There must be a period of at least 2 years of constant or constantly recurring depressed mood. Intervening periods of normal mood rarely last for longer than a few weeks, and there are no episodes of hypomania.

B   None, or very few, individual episodes within the 2-year period are sufficiently severe or long-lasting to meet criteria for recurrent mild depressive disorder.

C   During at least some of the periods of depression at least 3 of the following should be present:
    a) reduced energy or activity
    b) insomnia
    c) loss of self-confidence or feelings of inadequacy
    d) difficulty in concentrating
    e) frequent tearfulness
    f) loss of interest in or enjoyment of sex and other pleasurable activities
    g) feeling of hopelessness or despair
    h) a perceived inability to cope with the routine responsibilities of everyday life
    i) pessimism about the future or brooding over the past
    j) social withdrawal
    k) reduced talkativeness

World Health Organization (1993). *The ICD-10 Classification of Mental and Behavioural Disorders: Diagnostic Criteria for Research*. Geneva: WHO. Reproduced by permission of the World Health Organization.

Dysthymic disorder. In contrast to a distinct period of marked symptom-atology, some individuals display milder but chronic symptoms (see Table 1.1). Dysthymic disorder would be diagnosed if symptoms persisted for at least 2 years (although there might be brief periods of normal mood lasting no more than 2 months). Additionally, in order to be diagnosed, dysthymic disorder must be seen to cause significant distress or disruption in the person's significant areas of functioning.

The subcategory of "early-onset" dysthymia, referring to presence of the disorder before age 21, appears to mark an especially severe form of the disorder that occurs in approximately two thirds of presentations. Early-onset dysthymic patients have significantly higher rates of personality and substance abuse disorders, a signifi-cantly longer index major depressive episode, and also higher rates of past major depressive episodes than later-onset dysthymic patients, even with both groups experiencing concurrent major depression (D. N. Klein, Taylor, Dickstein, & Harding, 1988a; D. N. Klein et al., 1999). Longitudinal studies indicate that dysthymia is a chronic condition with a protracted course and a high risk of relapse, with nearly all individuals with dysthymia eventually experiencing at least one superimposed episode of major depression (D. N. Klein, Schwartz, Rose, & Leader, 2000; D. N. Klein, Shankman, & Rose, 2006). This superimposition of a major depressive episode on dysthymia is known as "double depression." Double depression is particularly pernicious in its course and associated impairment (D. N. Klein, Taylor, Harding, & Dickstein, 1988b; Leader & Klein, 1996). Even in untreated community samples, the co-occurrence of major depression and dysthymic disorder is common, as indicated in interview surveys of both adults and adolescents (Lewinsohn, Rohde, Seeley, & Hops, 1991). When individuals have histories of both disorders, dysthymia typically precedes the depression.

Other depression diagnoses. When depressive features are present but do not fit the criteria for major depressive episode or dysthymic dis-order, they may fit one of several possible residual categories of "depression not otherwise specified." These include *premenstrual dysphoric disorder (PMDD)*, which is defined as the presence, during most menstrual cycles in the last year, of five or more of the symptoms of depression, with these symptoms emerging during the last week of the luteal phase of the menstrual cycle (premenstruation) and remitting a few days after menstruation. PMDD appears to be a relatively stable disorder, distinct from diagnoses of depression, which occurs in between 3% and 8% of women (Endicott et al., 1999;

Wittchen, Becker, Lieb, & Krause, 2002). One potentially important difference between PMDD and major depression is the differential response to selective serotonin reuptake inhibitor (SSRI) antidepressant medication. In PMDD, SSRIs work substantially faster and are still effective when administered intermittently only during the premenstrual phase (Steiner, 2000), suggesting that PMDD has a biological basis distinct from major depression. There is some debate as to whether PMDD is best classified as a mood disorder, anxiety disorder, or distinct entity (Hartlage & Arduino, 2002; Landen & Eriksson, 2003). *Minor depressive disorder* includes at least 2 weeks of symptoms but with fewer than the five required for major depressive disorder. *Recurrent brief depression* refers to episodes lasting 2 days to 2 weeks, occurring at least once a month for 12 months.

Diagnosis of depression in children and adolescents

Although the emphasis of the book is adult depression, there has been considerable interest in child and adolescent depression following the "discovery" that such conditions could be diagnosed in children using virtually the same criteria as for adults.

> Barney is a 10-year-old boy whose irritability and temper tantrums are evident both at home and at school. With little provocation he bursts into tears and yells and throws objects. At home he has been sleeping poorly, and has gained 10 pounds over the past couple of months from constant snacking. At school he seems to have difficulty concentrating and seems easily distracted. Increasingly shunned by his peers, he plays by himself—and at home, spends most of his time in his room watching television. The school psychologist talked with him, and she reports that he is a deeply unhappy child who expresses feelings of worthlessness and hopelessness—and even a wish that he would die. These experiences probably began about 6 months ago when his father—divorced from the mother for several years—remarried and moved to another town where he spends far less time with Barney.

This case illustrates three key issues about the diagnosis of depression in youngsters. One is that the essential phenomenological features of the depression syndrome are similar in both children and adults (Carlson & Cantwell, 1980; Kovacs, 1996; Lewinsohn, Pettit, Joiner, & Seeley, 2003; Mitchell, McCauley, Burke, & Moss, 1988; J. E. Roberts, Lewinsohn, & Seeley, 1995b). Second, because children's externalizing or disruptive behaviours attract more attention or are more readily expressed, compared to internal, subjective suffering, depression is sometimes overlooked. It may not be recognized, or it might not be assessed. Childhood depression has a high level of co-existing disorders, especially involving conduct problems and other disruptive behaviours; such patterns gave rise to the erroneous belief that depression is "masked." Third, there are a few features of the syndrome of depression, such as irritable mood, that are more likely to be typical of children than of adults, leading to age-specific modifications of the diagnostic criteria.

Major depression, therefore, would be diagnosed with adult criteria as in Table 1.1, but permitting irritability instead of depressed mood. Dysthymia in children must persist at least 1 year (in adults duration is at least 2 years). Dysthymic disorder in children seems to differ from major depression primarily in the emphasis on gloomy thoughts and other negative affect, with fewer symptoms such as anhedonia, social withdrawal, fatigue, and reduced sleep and poor appetite.

Developmental considerations should be taken into account when assessing for depression in children. For instance, irritability may be substituted for depressed mood because it is recognized both that irritability is a common expression of distress in depressed young-sters—as shown in the case of Barney—and that young depressed children may not express subjective negative affect. When minor modifications to diagnostic criteria are made to reflect age-appropriate presentations, such as assessing irritability, major depression can be sensitively discriminated even in preschool children (Egger & Angold, 2006; Luby et al., 2003; Luby, Heffelfinger, Mrakotsky, Hessler, Brown, & Hildebrand, 2002).

It has been argued that developmental level could potentially influence the presentation of depression in children and adolescents by (1) altering the expression of essential symptoms; (2) altering which symptoms characterize depression in different developmental groups (B. Weiss & Garber, 2003). First, the same underlying symptom may manifest itself in different ways for different developmental groups. For example, subjective dysphoria and hopelessness are not reported by young depressed children, especially preschoolers and preadoles-cents, who instead "look" depressed in facial expression and posture, whereas in adolescence, depressed mood is more commonly reported (e.g., Birmaher et al., 2004; Luby et al., 2003; Ryan et al., 1987).

Second, particular depressive symptoms, such as hopelessness, guilt, and low self-esteem may depend on important cognitive developments, such as the advent of abstract thinking and a stable sense of self, which do not occur until middle-to-late childhood (Cicchetti & Toth, 1998). Thus, these symptoms might not be so apparent in young children.

The debate as to the nature and extent of developmental differences in the presentation of depression has not yet been resolved, with a number of studies reporting few differences between children and adolescents (Birmaher et al., 2004; Lewinsohn et al., 2003). Nonetheless, there is some evidence that adolescents with depression report more hopelessness, hypersomnia, suicidality, and weight changes than children with depression (Yorbik, Birmaher, Axelson, Williamson, & Ryan, 2004), whereas younger depressed children are more likely to have physically unjustified or exaggerated somatic complaints and greater irritability (Kovacs, 1996; Luby et al., 2003).

A number of studies have compared the symptoms of depressed youngsters and adults. Most studies find little relationship between age and presentation of depression (Haarasilta, Marttunen, Kaprio, & Aro, 2001; Kovacs, 1996; Lewinsohn et al., 2003; J. E. Roberts et al., 1995b).

In addition to presentation of depressive symptoms, patterns of comorbidity are also likely to be somewhat different at different ages. For instance, depressed children (and young adolescents) are more likely than depressed older adolescents to display separation anxiety disorders, while adolescents report more generalized anxiety disorders, eating disorders, and substance use disorders (e.g., Yorbik et al., 2004).

There are several other symptoms frequently seen in children and adolescents, including social withdrawal, excessive worrying, and other anxiety symptoms, somatic symptoms and bodily complaints, and problems with self-esteem. These symptoms parallel the symptoms found in adult depression. In addition, there is high comorbidity with conduct disorder and other disruptive behaviour disorder diagnoses (Kovacs, 1996).

Suicidal thoughts and attempts are among the diagnostic criteria for major depression. Suicidal ideation is quite common in depressed youngsters: with rates ranging from 41% to 68% in children and adolescents (e.g., Kovacs, Goldston, & Gatsonis, 1993; Lewinsohn, Rohde, & Seeley, 1998; Ryan et al., 1987). Actual rates of suicide attempts range from 24% by age 17 (Kovacs et al., 1993) to 39% of the preadolescent and adolescent patient samples of Mitchell et al. (1988), with 6% to 12% of the Ryan et al. (1987) child and adolescent samples making moderate or severe attempts. Suicidality is not restricted to depressed youth, however: Suicide is the third leading cause of death in 10- to 19-year-olds, with suicide-attempt rates within unselected community samples around 4% (Borowsky, Ireland, & Resnick, 2001; Glowinski et al., 2001). Substance use disorders and impulsive behaviour disorders increase the rates of suicide, particularly when comorbid with depression. The best predictor of suicidal behaviour is a previous suicide attempt. Other important predictors of suicidal behaviour in youth include a family history of suicide, increased hopelessness, low self-esteem, high levels of risky behaviour (including alcohol and substance use, smoking, sexual activity, violence), exposure to suicide through a friend's death or media reports, and same-sex romantic attraction (e.g., Borowsky et al., 2001; Cerel, Roberts, & Nilsen, 2005; Fergusson, Horwood, & Beautrais, 1999; Hallfors, Waller, Ford, Halpern, Brodish, & Iritani, 2004; Nock & Kessler, 2006; also see review by E. Evans, Hawton, & Rodham, 2004).

Subtypes of depression

In addition to the more formal diagnostic subtypes of depression currently included in the *DSM-IV* that are defined by severity or duration, there is an enormous need to consider the possible qualitative distinctions in depressions. As indicated by the heterogeneity of expressions of the features of depression, some seem more "biological" in presentation while others are more "psychological." Also, the depressions may vary considerably in their possible etiological factors, including both biological and psychological origins. It is hardly surprising, therefore, that considerable effort has been devoted to the search for depression subtypes.

Unfortunately, the research on subtypes has been considerably confused by mixing severity, type of symptoms, diagnostic criteria, and presumed etiology. Historically, research has focused on the neurotic–psychotic, reactive–endogenous, and endogenous–nonendogenous subtype distinctions, but the terms *psychotic* and *endogenous* have variously and confusingly referred to severity or qualitative distinctions, or to absence of precipitating stressors, often with different investigators using the same term with different operational criteria. A theme cutting across the search for subtypes has been the idea that there are "biological" (endogenous) depressions that are diseases arising in the absence of environmental precipitants vs. "psychological" depressions that stem from personality or situational factors. Labels for "endogenous" depression have included vital, severe, major, incapacitating, psychotic, primary, retarded, melancholic, autonomous, and endogenomorphic, while "nonendogenous" depressions have been variously termed neurotic, reactive, characterologic, atypical, secondary, mild, psychogenic, situational, and nonmelancholic (Zimmerman, Coryell, Stangl, & Pfohl, 1987).

To date there is little evidence for subtypes of depression that are qualitatively and etiologically distinct (e.g., Harkness & Monroe, 2002; Kendler, 1997; Leventhal & Rehm, 2005). Indeed, so-called endogenous depression is often preceded by negative life events and childhood adversity (Harkness & Monroe, 2002; F. Keller, Spiess, & Hautzinger, 1996; Mundt, Reck, Backenstrass, Kronmuller, & Fiedler, 2000). Furthermore, there is still an ongoing debate as to the predictive and prognostic validity and utility of putative subtypes, i.e., do the proposed subtypes help to predict different courses of depression and different treatment responses? For example, a number of studies find little difference in the course of depression (Joyce et al., 2002a; Kessing, 2003; Mulder, Joyce, Frampton, Luty, & Sullivan, 2006) or treatment response between melancholic versus nonmelancholic depression (M. Fava, Uebelacker, Alpert, Nierenberg, Pava, & Rosenbaum, 1997; Joyce et al., 2002b). Nonetheless there is some evidence indicating that there may be distinct patterns of symptom clusters within unipolar depression that vary in the presentation and nature of physical and biological symptoms. The most researched distinct symptom profiles for depression are *atypical depression* and *melancholic depression*, whose features and correlates will be described later.

Diagnostic "specifiers." By using the term "specifiers" to define descriptively important distinctive features of a depressive episode, the *DSM-IV-TR* avoids the implication that these are specific subtypes understood by their etiological and prognostic features. The main purpose of using the specifiers with *DSM-IV* diagnoses is to more precisely define patients groups for research or treatment purposes.

Melancholic features include loss of pleasure in all or almost all activities, lack of reactivity to pleasurable stimuli such that even good events, funny stories, or enjoyable experiences do not elicit any (or only a small amount) of positive reaction. Also, depression is regularly worse in the morning than evening (diurnal variation), the person shows excessive or inappropriate guilt, early morning awakening, marked psychomotor change (retarded or agitated), significant loss of appetite and weight loss (D. F. Klein, 1974; Rush &

Weissenburger, 1994). Supportive of the melancholic subtype, a taxometric analysis to determine the latent structure of symptoms suggests a discrete endogenous subtype (Haslam & Beck, 1994). Individuals who display the melancholic subtype tend to show similar features during subsequent episodes (Coryell, Winokur, Shea, Maser, Endicott, & Akiskal, 1994b). Furthermore, there are consistent abnormal biological functions associated with melancholia, such as motor disturbances, changes in sleep brain activity patterns, and alterations in response to different pharmacological-hormonal tests (Leventhal & Rehm, 2005; Rush et al., 1997). However, as noted earlier, melancholic and nonmelancholic depression cannot be distinguished on etiology, psychosocial, or developmental factors (Harkness & Monroe, 2002; Kendler, 1997; Mundt et al., 2000), course of the depression (Joyce et al., 2002a; Kessing, 2003; Mulder et al., 2006), or treatment response to pharmacotherapy (M. Fava et al., 1997; Joyce et al., 2002b). These findings have led some researchers to propose that whilst melancholia does identify a subset of distinct clinical features, melancholic depression is best conceptualized as more severe but not etiologically distinct from nonmelancholic depression (Kendler, 1997; Lafer, Nierenberg, Rosenbaum, & Fava, 1996).

Atypical features include mood reactivity in which mood improves in response to positive events, increase in appetite or weight, hypersomnia, heavy and leaden feelings in the arms or legs, and a long-standing pattern of increased sensitivity to criticism or rejection from other people (J. R. T. Davidson et al., 1982). There is some evidence that atypical depression can be discriminated from non-atypical unipolar depression in its clinical presentation and course, particularly when the biological symptoms of increased appetite and hypersomnia are used to distinguish between subtypes (Agosti & Stewart, 2001; Horwath, Johnson, Weissman, & Hornig, 1992; Kendler, Eaves, Walters, Neale, Heath, & Kessler, 1996; Matza et al., 2003; Nierenberg, Alpert, Pava, Rosenbaum, & Fava, 1998), and that atypical depression is more responsive to monoamine oxidase inhibitor (MAOI) antidepressants than to tricyclic antidepressants (Henkel, Mergl, Allgaier, Kohnen, Moller, & Hegerl, 2006; Liebowitz et al., 1988; Quitkin et al., 1993).

Seasonal pattern depressions refer to those that have an apparent regular onset during certain times of the year, and which also disappear at a characteristic time of the year. In the Northern Hemisphere, the most common pattern is Autumn or Winter depressions, remitting in the Spring. Depression with a seasonal pattern, also known as Seasonal Affective Disorder (SAD; Rosenthal et al.,

1984), has a prevalence of 1% to 3% in temperate climates, demonstrates stability in presentation across time, and is more common in women (Blazer, Kessler, & Swartz, 1998; Michalak, Wilkinson, Dowrick, & Wilkinson, 2001). Qualitatively, such depressive episodes are especially marked by low energy, more sleeping, overeating and weight gain, and craving for carbohydrate foods (Jacobsen, Wehr, Sack, James, & Rosenthal, 1987). SAD has been linked with changes in circadian rhythms, particularly those associated with the hormone melatonin, and seasonal differences in light onset (Lewy, Lefler, Emens, & Bauer, 2006; Wehr et al., 2001). SAD can be successfully treated by repeated exposure to bright light in the morning (phototherapy; Golden et al., 2005; R. W. Lam et al., 2006).

> Ellen dreads the Autumn. As the days become shorter and the weather cold and gloomy, her spirits sink. She becomes more and more lethargic, going to bed a bit earlier each night and having trouble getting up in the dark mornings. In contrast to her Summer favourites of fruits and vegetables, she finds herself eating heavier foods, with a special interest in rich, thick sauces and oily meats and breads and pastries of any kind. Often, by December she slips into a depressive episode, marked by low energy and inactivity—with sleeping and eating representing her main enjoyments. Although she believes that she will never feel good again and sometimes finds herself wishing for death, she has learned that by March or April she begins to emerge from her gloom and return to her normal life.

Depression with psychotic features is usually a severe depression in terms of the general symptoms, and includes presence of either hallucinations or delusions. Typically, such hallucinations or delusions have a depressive theme, such as guilt due to the belief that one has caused a terrible misfortune, belief that one is deserving of punishment or is being punished (e.g., voices accusing one of sins or failures), nihilistic beliefs (delusions about the world ending or that one is going to be killed or is already dead), or somatic delusions reflecting the belief that one is rotting away. Such delusions and hallucinations are described as mood-congruent since they are consistent with the negative, self-critical thinking found in depression. Less often, depressed individuals may have delusions and hallucinations that are not related to depressive or destructive themes (e.g., belief that one's thoughts are being broadcast on the radio, described as mood-incongruent). For a diagnosis of major depression with psychotic features, rather than schizophrenia or schizoaffective disorder, the delusions and hallucinations must only occur in the context of a major depressive episode. Psychotic depressions, even more than melancholic depressions, appear to be relatively stable over repeated episodes, such that if a person has a psychotic depression his or her future episodes are likely to show psychotic features (Coryell et al., 1994b, 1996). Psychotic depression is associated with severe psychomotor disturbance (agitation or retardation), increased feelings of worthlessness and guilt, more severe symptoms, increased mortality, and a more severe clinical course (Lattuada, Serretti, Cusin, Gasperini, & Smeraldi, 1999; Ohayon & Schatzberg, 2002; Thakur, Hays, & Krishnan, 1999; Vythilingam, Chen, Bremner, Mazure, Maciejewski, & Nelson, 2003). Between 14% and 20% of treated patients suffering from major depression will experience psychotic features (J. Johnson, Horwath, & Weissman, 1991; Ohayon & Schatzberg, 2002).

Postpartum depression.   Between 30% and 75% of women develop mild symptoms such as crying, insomnia, poor appetite, and mood lability in the period 3 to 7 days after giving birth; called "baby blues," these experiences are considered normal responses to the profound shifts in hormones, and typically spontaneously remit after several days. However, when a major depressive episode develops in the few weeks after delivery, it may be identified as major depression with postpartum onset. Postpartum depression is the most common complication of childbearing, occurring in between 10% and 15% of mothers (O'Hara & Swain, 1996), although this rate increases to 25% for teenage mothers. Although the prevalence of depression postpartum is equivalent to the prevalence of depression found in demographically matched nonchildbearing women (D. Murray, Cox, Chapman, & Jones, 1995; O'Hara, Zekoski, Philipps, & Wright, 1990; Whiffen & Gotlib, 1993), having a child seems to be a potentially stressful event, with the onset of depression increasing three-fold during the 5 weeks postpartum (Cox, Murray, & Chapman, 1993). Generally speaking, the symptoms of postpartum depression are not different from symptoms of major depressive episode, and, perhaps, slightly milder than nonpostpartum depressions (Whiffen & Gotlib, 1993). Premenstrual dysphoric disorder, low mood in the first 2 to 4 days postpartum, experiencing stressful events during pregnancy, low social support, and a previous history of depression all predict increased risk for postpartum depression (Bloch, Rotenberg, Koren, & Klein, 2005; O'Hara & Swain, 1996; Robertson, Grace, Wallington, & Stewart, 2004). Women who do develop postpartum-depression appear to be at increased risk for developing future depressive episodes, as indicated in a 4½-year follow-up (Philipps & O'Hara, 1991).

About 1 woman in 1000 has a psychotic postpartum depression. These severe episodes commonly involve delusions about the child ("he's the devil") that cause the woman to act in ways that endanger the child's life. Women who have had one such postpartum psychosis have an elevated risk for subsequent postpartum episodes with psychotic features. It should also be noted that such episodes are especially likely to occur among women with histories of bipolar disorder, but may also occur in unipolar depression.

Comorbidity in depression

In addition to the heterogeneity of the forms of depression, a further complication in understanding and treating depressive disorders is the problem of comorbidity. That is, depression is often accompanied by other disorders. In both the original U.S. National Comorbidity Study (NCS) and the recent NCS replication, of all the community residents who met criteria for lifetime and/or 12-month major depression, approximately 75% had at least one other diagnosis, with only a minority having "pure" cases of depression (Blazer, Kessler, McGonagle, & Swartz, 1994; Kessler, Chiu, Demler, & Walters, 2005b; Kessler et al., 2003). For patients with a diagnosis of current major depression only 40% to 45% have depression in isolation, with 60% to 65% having at least one comorbid diagnosis, with these rates consistently found across different countries (e.g., Blazer et al., 1994; De Graaf, Bijl, Smith, Vollebergh, & Spijker, 2002; Rush et al., 2005; Zimmerman, Chelminski, & McDermut, 2002).

The most common comorbid disorders are anxiety disorders (approximately 60%), particularly generalized anxiety disorder, panic disorder, social phobia, and posttraumatic stress disorders (PTSD; Mineka, Watson, & Clark, 1998). For patients with anxiety disorders, approximately 30% have a comorbid mood disorder (T. A. Brown, Campbell, Lehman, Grisham, & Mancill, 2001a). The onset of anxiety disorders typically precedes the onset of depression, with earlier-onset anxiety disorders (panic, social anxiety, and generalized anxiety disorder) predicting the subsequent first onset of depression (Andrade et al., 2003; Kessler, Nelson, McGonagle, Liu, Swartz, & Blazer, 1996; Stein, Fuetsch, Muller, Hofler, Lieb, & Wittchen, 2001). Furthermore, whereas some individuals have distinct episodes or periods of one or the other, many people have current mixtures of both anxiety and depression symptoms (Blazer, Swartz, Woodbury, Manton, Hughes, & George, 1988). Accordingly, the recent *DSM-IV-R* version contains a diagnostic category (anxiety not otherwise specified) that is a mixed anxiety–depression constellation of symptoms (M. Fava et al., 2004).

Besides anxiety disorders, substance abuse and alcoholism and eating disorders are frequently accompanied by depressive disorders, in both clinical and community samples (Rohde, Lewinsohn, & Seeley, 1991; Sanderson, Beck, & Beck, 1990; Swendsen & Merikangas, 2000). Several recent large epidemiological studies found rates of 25% to 30% for comorbid substance/alcohol abuse (Davis et al., 2005; Melartin, Rytsala, Leskela, Lestela-Mielonen, Sokero, & Isometsa, 2002).

Not only are *DSM-IV* Axis I disorders highly likely to co-occur with depression, but also *personality disorders* are more the rule than the exception with depressed patients. Personality disorders refer to a set of patterns of dysfunctional conduct and attitudes that started early in life, are persistent, and affect all areas of the person's functioning. Depending on the study, rates of personality disorders among depressed people range between 23% and 87% (Shea et al., 1990; Shea, Widiger, & Klein, 1992). Several recent studies report that around 44% to 51% of patients with major depression met criteria for a personality disorder (Brieger, Ehrt, & Marneros, 2003; Melartin et al., 2002; Russell et al., 2003). Most studies have found that personality disorders in the "dramatic/erratic" cluster (such as borderline personality disorder), and in the "anxious/fearful" cluster (such as avoidant personality disorder) predominate (e.g., Alpert et al., 1997; Brieger et al., 2003; Rossi et al., 2001; Shea et al., 1990).

Antonia is in her 20s and has been brought to the psychiatric hospital by her desperate parents. She took a nonfatal overdose of pills ("anything I could find in the medicine chest") following the break-up of her romantic relationship. She is currently extremely depressed in mood, crying and screaming about her loss. Her psychiatrist elicits a history of her adjustment, both from her parents and Antonia herself, and uncovers a complex history of drug use of various kinds since adolescence, and poor performance in school while feeling "desperately unhappy." Her history includes frequent panic attacks in which she suddenly felt like she was going to die, with pounding heart and shortness of breath for no apparent reason, and multiple brief and chaotic affairs with boys—one of which resulted in an unwanted pregnancy and subsequent abortion.

Although she is clearly depressed, her depression is only one of several problems, some of which are chronic so that if her depression is treated the other difficulties will still be there.

Mixtures of disorders raise a number of important implications. One is that much research purporting to discuss "depression" might actually be about the comorbid disorders; since investigators commonly do not report co-existing diagnoses, it is difficult to tell how much the results are influenced by the correlated problems rather than the depressive disorder itself. A second issue is that depression comorbidity raises interesting and important questions about how the comorbid conditions came about: did one cause the other, did they stem from separate but correlated risk factors, or do they reflect processes common across different disorders ("trans-diagnostic processes"; Harvey, Watkins, Mansell, & Shafran, 2004) or a common dimension of general distress (Shankman & Klein, 2003)? There is accumulating evidence that the high levels of comorbidity observed between anxiety and mood disorders may result, in part, from temperamental dimensions common across disorders. In particular, it has been proposed that individuals with anxiety disorders and mood disorders share a common temperamental feature of elevated negative affectivity/neuroticism that results in increased subjective emotional distress. Depression is further proposed to involve a distinct specific factor of low positive affectivity/extraversion (i.e., anhedonia) that distinguishes it from anxiety disorders (L. A. Clark, 2005; L. A. Clark, Watson, & Mineka, 1994; Watson, 2005; Watson, Gamez, & Simms, 2005). Thus, the personality dimension of neuroticism is strongly implicated as a vulnerability factor for both depression and anxiety, and seems to predict worse long-term outcome (Mulder, 2002).

Alternatively, the elevated comorbidity could simply be an artifact of the diagnostic system itself. For example, the overlap between the symptom criteria for major depression and several anxiety disorders (in particular, generalized anxiety disorder and PTSD) has led some researchers to suggest that there may be potential boundary problems in diagnostic classification, with all these diagnoses forming a cluster of disorders characterized by elevated distress (T. A. Brown, Di Nardo, Lehman, & Campbell, 2001b; Widiger & Samuel, 2005).

Finally, a very important implication of comorbidity of depression is that it usually implies worse functioning and a worse course of disorder than "pure" depression. For example, the presence of a comorbid anxiety disorder predicts a significantly worse course of depression and dysthymia (C. Brown, Schulberg, Madonia, Shear, & Houck, 1996; Gaynes, Magruder, Burns, Wagner, Yarnall, & Broadhead, 1999; Shankman & Klein, 2002). Likewise, a comorbid personality disorder predicts a poorer outcome (Daley et al., 1999; D. N. Klein, 2003; D. N. Klein & Shih, 1998; see review by Newton-Howes, Tyrer, & Johnson, 2006).

The continuum of depression

Although most research on depression refers to clinically diagnosed conditions, there is increasing evidence that recurrent or persistent mild, subclinical symptoms are also important. There appears to be continuity between minor, subsyndromal depression and major depression (Kessler, Zhao, Blazer, & Swartz, 1997c), with subsyndromal depression predicting the increased onset of major depressive episodes (Judd et al., 1998). A study of nearly 7000 representative U.S. adults assessed their mood and other symptoms at one point in time, and then followed them up over a period of 16 years (Zonderman, Herbst, Schmidt, Costa, & McCrae, 1993). Depressive symptoms predicted future psychiatric disorders significant enough to have resulted in hospitalization. Diagnoses included both depressive and nondepressive disorders, and higher levels of subclinical symptoms were more strongly related to eventual hospitalization. These findings have been replicated in the Baltimore Epidemiological Catchment Area Study that followed 1634 individuals over a 15-year period: Minor depression was found to predict the first onset of major depression (Fogel, Eaton, & Ford, 2006). Individuals with subclinical symptoms or dysthymia are between 4 to 5 times more likely to develop major depression than individuals without those symptoms (Fogel et al., 2006). Similarly, in a 12-year follow-up of 534 depressed patients, Judd and colleagues (1998) found that major depression, minor depression, and subsyndromal symptoms commonly alternate over time in the same patients, suggesting that all these symptom patterns reflect a single underlying dysfunction of mood with a changeable, dynamic presentation. That is, any individual presenting with subsyndromal symptoms is likely to present with full-blown depression at a later date. Depressive symptoms may thus be a marker of general risk for disorder, including presence of highly stressful environments, inadequate social supports, biological vulnerabilities, and personality predisposition to disorder and maladaptive functioning.

Besides the possibility that mild symptoms may foretell significant disorder, they may also, like major depressive disorder, result in significantly impaired functioning in daily life—a topic discussed in Chapter 2.

At the low end of the continuum of depression, there is increasing evidence for the existence of depressive personality disorder (DPD), in which an individual has stable personality traits that resemble pervasive and mild depressive symptoms. The key characteristics of DPD are: quiet, introverted, passive; gloomy, pessimistic, incapable of fun; self-critical, self-derogatory; critical of others, hard to please; conscientious, responsible, self-disciplined; brooding and worrying; preoccupied with negative events, personal shortcomings, and feelings of inadequacy (D. N. Klein & Miller, 1993). Research has demonstrated that the associations between depressive personality and major depression are fairly low, suggesting that the depressive personality disorder is not redundant with depression (D. N. Klein & Shih, 1998; McDermut, Zimmerman, & Chelminski, 2003), with up to 60% of patients with depressive personality not currently meeting criteria for major depression (Phillips et al., 1998). Furthermore, the diagnosis of DPD appears to be relatively stable over time (Laptook, Klein, & Dougherty, 2006; Phillips et al., 1998; although there was a nonreplication by Markowitz et al., 2005b). These findings provide convergent evidence supportive for a diagnosis of a depressive personality type that is distinct from depression, whilst increasing risk for major depression and subjective distress.

Assessing depression

Both clinical description and research on depression rely on two types of methods: those that measure the severity of depressive experiences, and those that measure the presence of diagnosable conditions. This section briefly describes the most frequently used procedures, acknowledging that many more exist than will be discussed.

Diagnostic methods. Applying the *DSM* or *ICD* criteria for major depression and dysthymia requires interviewing the individual (or an appropriate informant). For research purposes it is highly desirable to use standardized interviews in which the relevant questions are asked in the same way each time by each interviewer. Such procedures ensure comparability and communicability across different studies purporting to investigate similar clinical conditions.

The Schedule for Affective Disorders and Schizophrenia (SADS) was developed by Endicott and Spitzer (1978) in an attempt to increase the reliability of interviewer-derived psychiatric diagnoses based on the *Research Diagnostic Criteria*, a forerunner of the current *Diagnostic and Statistical Manual*. Different versions cover lifetime history of disorders, current conditions, and changes in disorders occurring between assessments in a longitudinal study. The SADS covers not only depression, but also such diagnostic categories as schizophrenia, anxiety disorders, and substance use disorders. Trained clinical interviewers can administer the semistructured procedure with adequate interrater reliability (Endicott & Spitzer, 1978).

In the last decade, the SADS has been superseded by an updated interview to cover the DSM diagnostic criteria, called the Structured Clinical Interview for DSM (SCID; current version, DSM-IV-R), which covers all the major diagnostic categories (Spitzer, Williams, Gibbon, & First, 1992, 1996). (A child version of the SADS, called the Kiddie-SADS continues to be widely used for juvenile populations.) The semistructured probes of the SCID are intended to cover both current and lifetime history of disorders, and clinical judgments are required so that it is assumed that interviewers have had clinical training. Field trials have indicated adequate reliability for major diagnoses. The following is an example of a probe for symptoms of major depressive episode:

> In the last month . . . has there been a period of time when you were feeling depressed or down most of the day nearly every day? (What was that like?)
> IF YES: How long did it last? (As long as two weeks?)
> During this time . . . did you lose or gain any weight? (How much?) (Were you trying to lose weight?)
> IF NO: How was your appetite? (What about compared to your usual appetite?). (Was that nearly every day?)

Likewise, the Composite International Diagnostic Interview (CIDI; Robins et al., 1988) is a standardized diagnostic interview commonly used for epidemiological research.

Assessing severity of depression. Several methods are commonly used to evaluate the severity of current depression separate from diagnosis. One approach is interview-based, such as the Hamilton Rating Scale for Depression (HRSD; M. Hamilton, 1960). It remains the most frequently used interviewer-rated measure of depression, and the original version contains 21 items covering mood, behavioural, somatic, and cognitive symptoms. By convention, only 17 of the original 21 items are typically scored. For the 17-item version, total scores of 0 to 7 indicate no depression, 8 to 17 mild depression, 18 to 25 moderate depression, and scores of 26+ indicate severe depression (guidelines for the HRSD have been produced by J. Williams, 1998). The HRSD is most commonly administered by experienced clinicians, although a number of investigators have demonstrated that laypersons can be trained in a relatively short period of time to reach acceptable levels of administration. The HRSD has been shown to be sensitive to change in the severity of depressive symptomatology over time, and consequently, is useful as a measure of the efficacy of therapy.

There are numerous self-report instruments designed to measure depression or depressed affect. Among them, the Beck Depression Inventory (BDI) is probably the most frequently used self-report method of assessing depressive symptoms. The original version consisted of 21 items selected to represent the affective, cognitive, motivational, and physiological symptoms of depression (A. T. Beck, Ward, Mendelson, Mock, & Erbaugh, 1961). In all versions, for each symptom question, the patient rates how they have been feeling for the past week on a graded series of four alternative statements, ranging from neutral (e.g., "I do not feel sad," "I don't feel dis-appointed in myself") to a maximum level of severity (e.g., "I am so sad or unhappy that I can't stand it," "I would kill myself if I had the chance"). The items are scored from 0 to 3, with the sum of the scores representing the total BDI score, which can range from 0 to 63. For the original version, a total score of 0 to 9 indicates a normal non-depressed state; 10 to 18 reflects a mild level of depression; 19 to 29 reflects moderate depression; and 30 to 63 indicates a severe level of depression (A. T. Beck, Steer, & Garbin, 1988). In response to criticism that the original BDI overemphasized subjective, cognitive symptoms to the relative neglect of somatic symptoms and did not reflect the diagnostic criteria for a major depressive episode, the BDI-II was created (A. T. Beck, Steer, Ball, & Ranieri, 1996a; A. T. Beck, Steer, & Brown, 1996b). The BDI-II updates the BDI by expanding the time frame for endorsing the items to the last 2 weeks, and by adapting the appetite and sleep items to allow report of oversleeping and over-eating as well as insomnia and loss of appetite. For the BDI-II, scores of 0 to 13 indicate no depression, 14 to 19 mild depression, 20 to 28 moderate depression, and scores of 29 to 63 severe depression.

It is important to note that the BDI, along with any other self-report questionnaire for depression, was not designed to yield a discrete diagnosis of depression; rather, it was constructed to measure depression as one single dimension of psychopathology that cuts across a wide variety of diagnostic categories. Its major focus, therefore, is on the depth or severity of depressive symptomatology. Numerous studies of its psychometric properties have been reported, indicating that it is a generally useful and valid measure of the severity of depressive symptoms (A. T. Beck et al., 1988). However, it is worth noting that the BDI taps into constructs other than depressive symptoms, such as low self-esteem, other forms of psychopathology, and the effects of personality on symptom reporting (Enns, Larsen, & Cox, 2000). A questionnaire for children and adolescents, modeled after the BDI, is the Children's Depression Inventory (CDI; Kovacs, 1985), consisting of 27 items scored 0 through 3. It is widely used in research and treatment, and has good psychometric properties (Craighead, Curry, & Ilardi, 1995; Craighead, Smucker, Craighead, & Ilardi, 1998).

Summary

- Depression ranges from a normal sad mood lasting only moments to a profoundly impairing condition that may be life-threatening.
- To be clinically significant, depression involves changes in mood, cognitive functioning, behaviour, and bodily states, and must persist over time and interfere with normal behaviour.
- A crucial distinction must be made between unipolar and bipolar depression, due to different causes, course, and treatment.
- Both children and adults may be diagnosed with major depression or dysthymia.
- Depression presents many faces, may co-exist with other disorders, and there may be different underlying subtypes with different causes.
- Different instruments are available to measure depression diagnoses and severity of depressive symptoms.

Course and consequences of depression 2

While depression has sometimes been called the "common cold" of psychological disorders, such a label is misleading because it implies that suffering from depression is merely a bothersome but brief and mild inconvenience. Unfortunately, nothing could be further from the truth. Depression may be so severe as to be lethal, and, for many if not most sufferers, it is a recurring or even chronic disorder. Moreover, its effects may be devastating to the individual—not only in suffering, but also in terms of the damaging effects on one's work, family, and marital relations. Indeed, the consequences to the lives of depressed people might even contribute environmental conditions that create the likelihood that depression will continue or recur. Therefore, in this chapter we explore the features of the course of depression, including its impairing consequences.

Course of unipolar major depressive disorder

Age of onset of depression

Depression is increasingly recognized as a disorder of relatively young onset. Previously viewed as a disorder of middle age, today's researchers observe that youth and early adulthood are the most typical periods of depression onset. Indeed, as we explore in Chapter 3, age of onset has become increasingly younger. Age 30 was reported as the median onset of major depression in a U.S. sample of adults (Kessler, Berglund, Demler, Jin, Merikangas, & Walters, 2005a), while a survey of 10 nations reported a median age of onset in the range of 20 to 25 in most countries (International Consortium of Psychiatric Epidemiology Surveys—Andrade et al., 2003), suggesting that the teenage and early adult years are periods of particular risk (see also K. C. Burke, Burke, Regier, & Rae, 1990). General trends in age of onset, however, obscure potentially important differences between groups. Recent evidence suggests that depression with onset in children, adolescents, adults, and older adults may have somewhat different implications in terms of etiology and clinical course.

Core differences between the age groups are briefly noted in this chapter and Chapter 3, but it is also acknowledged that many studies of depression reviewed in the book have not distinguished samples by onset age, and may therefore require caution in their applicability to different age-of-onset groups.

Clinical implications of age of onset. Researchers have yet to agree on a uniform definition of early onset, with studies varying between those defining early as prior to 18, before 30, before 40, or even before 60. In general, however, with exceptions to be noted, earlier age of onset of depression is associated with a worse course of depression, with greater chances of recurrence, chronicity, and impairment in role functioning (e.g., Hollon et al., 2006a; Zisook et al., 2004).

There are at least two explanations for worse outcomes. One is that earlier age of onset reflects a more severe form of depression, with greater likelihood of familial (genetic) transmission of the disorder. Several studies have reported an association between early-onset depression and depressive disorders in close relatives (e.g., Bland, Newman, & Orn, 1986; Kendler, Gatz, Gardner, & Pedersen, 2005a), with numerous studies reporting early-onset depression among off-spring of depressed parents (e.g., Hammen & Brennan, 2003; Weissman, Fendrich, Warner, & Wickramaratne, 1992; reviewed in Beardslee, Versage, & Gladstone, 1998). Whether such patterns reflect heritability of a disease or psychological factors associated with being reared among depressed family members cannot be determined from these studies.

A second hypothesis is that early onset of depression causes disruption of the process of acquiring important adaptive skills and managing life transitions. It is possible that early onset of depression interferes with healthy development and acquisition of problem-solving skills and positive views of the self and others. Such impairments may contribute to challenging life conditions (or to failure to resolve them) and to the occurrence of negative life events that the person cannot cope with effectively. Thus, depression may recur as individuals with early onset fail to manage stressors in their lives.

Duration of major depressive episodes

By definition, major depressive episodes must last at least 2 weeks to meet diagnostic criteria. Apart from this minimum, there is considerable variability in the length of depressive episodes. If one suffers from major depression, research reveals both good news and bad news. The good news is that most people recover from major depression within 3 to 6 months and eventually recover, whether treated or not. However, the bad news is that many people do not fully recover and continue to have persisting low levels of symptoms.

Not surprisingly, reports of the course of depression may vary depending on whether the studied sample is a clinical sample that typically has sought help because they have more severe and persisting problems with depression, or a community sample with random selection of participants who may or may not have depression. Despite variability, however, the findings are relatively consistent. In their classic long-term follow-up study of depressed patients, M. B. Keller, Shapiro, Lavori, and Wolfe (1982) found that 64% of patients had recovered within 6 months of entering their study, and Coryell et al. (1994a) found that 55% of patients in the 6-year follow-up NIMH (National Institute of Mental Health) Collaborative Program on the Psychobiology of Depression recovered by 6 months.

Recent studies of community samples using similar standardized assessment interviews have found similar but somewhat faster recovery times. For instance, the Netherlands Mental Health Survey and Incidence Study of 7000 people reported a median duration of major depression of 3 months, with 63% recovery within 6 months (Spijker, de Graaf, Bijl, Beekman, Ormel, & Nolen, 2002). The U.S. National Comorbidity Survey–Replication reported a mean duration of major depression of 4 months (Kessler et al., 2003), although a large U.S. survey recently reported a mean duration of 6 months (Hasin, Goodwin, Stinson, & Grant, 2005).

Predictors of duration of an episode of major depression include severity, with longer duration associated with more severe symptoms (Hollon et al., 2006a; Spijker, de Graaf, Bijl, Beekman, Ormel, & Nolen, 2004; Spijker et al., 2002). Also, these same studies agree that first episodes are typically longer in duration than recurrent episodes.

Most studies that have reported on duration of episodes and rates of recovery have commonly defined the terms by the absence of full symptom criteria for major depressive disorder, or have been cross-sectional studies that did not investigate the natural course of symptomatology over time and between depressive episodes. It has been easy to assume, therefore, that individuals not in diagnosable episodes are "free" of depression. However, such an assumption is far from accurate. As mentioned in Chapter 1, Judd and colleagues (1998) studied the weekly symptom course over a period of up to 12 years in a population seeking treatment for major depression. They found that patients were entirely symptom-free an average of only 41% of weeks of follow-up. While it is not surprising that individuals with histories of multiple major depressive episodes (MDE) or with "double depression" (MDE plus dysthymic disorder) were frequently symptomatic, even those with first-episode depression had only 54% of weeks symptom-free. Most individuals reported highly fluctuating courses over time; in and out of periods varying in symptom severity—typically below diagnostic threshold but nonetheless debilitating. Thus, for many individuals depression resembles a chronic disease with a fluctuating course but with some levels of persisting symptoms, rather than a disorder in which episodes are followed by long stretches of normal good mood.

Recurrence or chronicity of depression

Unipolar depression is increasingly characterized as a recurring or even chronic disorder. Although some individuals may experience only a single episode of major depression in their lifetimes, the majority of those who have an episode will have multiple episodes. And for a substantial minority, their depressions persist for long periods or even indefinitely—varying in severity but never going away entirely. *Relapse* is the term usually employed when individuals get worse following incomplete or only brief recovery (e.g., less than 2 months of being well), whereas *recurrence* usually means a new episode following a period of recovery lasting more than 2 months.

Recurrent episodes.   Three key points should be made about depression recurrence. First, major depressive disorder is commonly a recurrent disorder. Among patients seeking treatment for depression, longitudinal studies have reported that between 50% and 85% with one MDE will have at least one additional episode (M. B. Keller, 1985). Judd (1997), reporting on data from a longitudinal study conducted in the modern era of antidepressant medications, found that the median number of episodes reported was four.

Second, there is evidence that the risk for recurrence progressively increases with each episode of major depression—and decreases as the period of recovery is longer. For instance, D. A. Solomon et al. (2000) reported that among depressed patients followed over a

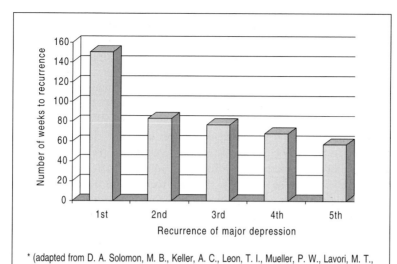

Figure 2.1.
Decreasing intervals
between successive
episodes of
depression*.

Number of weeks to recurrence

160
140
120
100
80
60
40
20
0

1st   2nd   3rd   4th   5th

Recurrence of major depression

* (adapted from D. A. Solomon, M. B., Keller, A. C., Leon, T. I., Mueller, P. W., Lavori, M. T., Shea et al. (2000). Multiple recurrences of major depressive disorder. *American Journal of Psychiatry, 157,* 229–233. Copyright by the American Psychiatric Press, Inc. Reprinted with permission.

10-year period, the probability of recurrence increased 16% with each successive episode. These investigators also found that episodes come closer together over time, as illustrated in Figure 2.1. Theories about underlying psychobiological processes potentially responsible for progressive recurrence are discussed in later chapters.

A third point is that because most depressions are recurrent, most clinical and research samples of depression contain mostly individuals who are experiencing recurrent episodes rather than first-onset episodes (e.g., Kessler, 1997). This is an important reminder, because studies that have compared predictors of first vs. recurrent episodes have generally found different predictors (e.g., Daley, Hammen, & Rao, 2000; Lewinsohn, Allen, Seeley, & Gotlib, 1999a). Post (1992) suggested, for example, that stressors are more predictive of first than later episodes of depression, reflecting a process of "sensitization." If depression is a progressive disorder as naturalistic studies have suggested, there may be neurobiological and psychological vulnerabilities that are altered with successive episodes—and which could have different treatment implications compared to first episodes (see Chapters 7 and 8). Therefore, studies that do not account for the stage of illness of participants may not result in findings that are widely generalizable.

Predictors of recurrence.   One of the strongest findings in predicting the course of depression is that past depression predicts future depression: more prior episodes predict greater likelihood of recurrence (e.g., Bockting, Spinhoven, Koeter, Wouters, Schene, & Depression Evaluation Longitudinal Therapy Assessment Study Group, 2006; Kessing, Hansen, Andersen, & Angst, 2004; Lin et al., 1998). Furthermore, as noted above, a higher number of previous episodes predicts more rapid recurrence of major depression after recovery. Similarly, recurrent depressives who were withdrawn from medication were highly likely to relapse: 70% experienced a recurrence within 6 months (Frank, Kupfer, & Perel, 1989)—a finding that has greatly affected approaches to both psychopharmacologic and psychological treatments, as discussed in later chapters.

Additional *clinical* predictors of recurrence include the occurrence of a major depressive episode superimposed on pre-existing dysthymic disorder—a condition called "double depression," which occurs in about a quarter of all depressed patients. Double depression appears to increase risk for recurrence of major depression (M. B. Keller, Lavori, Endicott, Coryell, & Klerman, 1983). Although double depressives appear to recover faster from major depression, they relapse faster and have an overall higher recurrence rate (M. B. Keller, 1988). Similarly, residual symptoms of depression and severity of depression predict recurrence (Bockting et al., 2006; Lin et al., 1998; Melartin, Rytsala, Leskela, Lestela-Mielonen, Sokero, & Isometsa, 2004). A further predictor of depression recurrence is presence of a history of some additional psychiatric disorder besides depression (Coryell, Endicott, & Keller, 1991; Melartin et al., 2004).

Studies have explored whether certain *demographic* factors may be associated with greater risk of recurrence. In general, research suggests that although women are far more likely to have first onsets of depression than men, men and women are about equally likely to experience recurrence (e.g., Coryell et al., 1991; Kessing et al., 2004). As noted above, younger age of onset is also typically associated with greater likelihood of recurrent depressive episodes.

A number of psychosocial factors such as stressful life events, personality and cognitive vulnerabilities, and poor social support have been studied as predictors of depression—mostly recurrent episodes. A full review of these factors is presented in later chapters. For instance, Chapter 5 discusses the role of stressful life events and depression recurrence, a relationship that is hypothesized to change over the course of multiple episodes.

Chronicity of depression. It has been estimated that chronic depression occurs in at least 25% of cases (e.g., Depue & Monroe, 1986). The DSM has made efforts over the years to define chronic depression in precise ways, distinguishing between dysthymic disorder (mild symptoms with a minimum of 2 years' duration in adults), chronic major depression of at least 2 years, major depression superimposed on dysthymic disorder (double depression), and major depression with incomplete recovery, among other definitions. However, two recent studies have shed doubt on the validity of such distinctions, based on comparisons among different defined chronic depression groups of patients (McCullough, Klein, Keller, Holzer, Davis, & Komstein, 2000; McCullough et al., 2003). These investigators concluded that there were insufficient differences among groups in most demographic, clinical, family mood disorder history, childhood, psychosocial functioning, and response to treatment variables to warrant the current DSM distinctions. They suggested that the clinically and etiologically important distinctions among depression groups are best characterized instead by two crossed dimensions, mild/moderate–severe and chronic/nonchronic depression. Such a classification system results in four groups: mild chronic (dysthymic disorder), moderate–severe chronic (double depression, chronic major depression, and chronic major depression with incomplete recovery), mild nonchronic (minor depressive disorder), and moderate–severe nonchronic (episodic major depression). As noted in Chapter 1, most dysthymic disorder eventually results in MDEs (e.g., Klein et al., 2000).

In general there is good agreement that chronic depression, however defined, is associated with a variety of negative features. For example, people with dysthymic disorder and double depression were found to have slow recovery and high rates of relapse or continuing symptoms over a 10-year follow-up (Klein et al., 2006). They had relatively high rates of poor-quality early home environments (Lizardi, Klein, Ouimette, Riso, Anderson, & Donaldson, 1995), and a relatively high rate of exposure to early adverse conditions including child physical and sexual abuse, as well as ongoing stressful life conditions (Riso, Miyatake, & Thase, 2002). Chronic depression is also associated with higher rates of familial depression than is episodic major depression (D. N. Klein, Shankman, Lewinsohn, Rohde, & Seeley, 2004b), potentially suggesting an etiological subtype. In view of the relatively pernicious profile, forms of treatment specifically targeted for chronic depression have been developed and will be discussed in later chapters.

Nature and course of depression in children, adolescents, and older adults

Depression is a heterogeneous disorder with different etiological and clinical features. As noted, recent research has suggested that it is important to distinguish between childhood, adolescent, and adult onset. For instance, biological and genetic contributions may be different for childhood and adolescent onset (e.g., Kaufman, Martin, King, & Charney, 2001; Silberg, Rutter, & Eaves, 2001). Silberg et al. (2001) found evidence suggesting that adolescent-onset depression is more likely associated with genetic factors, at least in females. Weissman and colleagues (Weissman, et al., 1999a, 1999b) and Harrington, Fudge, Rutter, Pickles, and Hill (1990) both reported that in contrast to the earlier assumption that childhood onset of depression likely predicted further depression continuing into adulthood, depression onset before puberty was associated with *less* continuity of depression than was adolescent onset depression. Definitive conclusions are difficult at this point, however, since many studies have included mixed samples of children and adolescents (e.g., Fombonne, Wostear, Cooper, Harrington, & Rutter, 2001), or have failed to specify the age of onset of adolescent samples.

Also, there is growing evidence that late-adult onset of depression may also reflect different etiological factors (e.g., Powers, Thompson, Futterman, & Gallagher-Thompson, 2002). Therefore, the following sections will present a few key clinical features of each age-of-onset group, mindful that new developments may increasingly alter our understanding.

Childhood-onset depression. Weissman and her colleagues (1999b) conducted one of the few long-term longitudinal studies of children with major depressive disorder followed into adulthood 10 to 15 years later. The majority of the children had adverse outcomes, with considerable psychiatric and psychosocial difficulties in adulthood. However, an especially notable result was the varied outcomes of the depressed children. The long-term study identified three possible subgroups: (1) those with apparently true early-onset depression that recurred into adulthood; (2) those who did not have further depression but did have other significant psychopathology such as conduct disorder and substance abuse; (3) those who went on to show evidence of bipolar disorder.

True childhood-onset unipolar depression is relatively rare, but appears to be associated with a high risk of recurrence; many have early-onset dysthymic disorder followed by major depression episodes (double depression), and a high degree of depressive disorders in relatives (Birmaher et al., 2004; Kovacs, Akiskal, Gatsonis, & Parrone, 1994; Kovacs, Devlin, Pollock, Richards, & Mukerji, 1997; Weissman et al., 1999b). Several studies have found a strong association between childhood anxiety symptoms and inhibited or withdrawn behaviour, and later anxiety and depressive disorders (e.g., R. D. Goodwin, Fergusson, & Horwood, 2004; similar associations have been found for adolescents: Pine, Cohen, Gurley, Brook, & Ma, 1998; Silberg et al., 2001; Stein et al., 2001; Wittchen, Beesdo, Bittner, & Goodwin, 2003). It may be speculated that these "true" depressives will have substantial risk for life-long depression.

The second group of depressed children identified in the Weissman et al. (1999b) childhood depression follow-up study appears to be those with considerable impairment and social maladjustment. Among these youngsters the initial depression may be a nonspecific response to considerable psychosocial and family adversity, such as abuse, parental disorder and criminality, and disrupted family life. The depression does not recur as such; instead it appears to foretell the emergence of a variety of other psychiatric and social problems in adolescence and adulthood (see also Hofstra, van der Ende, & Verhulst, 2000). However, children with true early-onset recurrent depression may also experience considerable psychosocial adversity (Jaffee, Moffitt, Caspi, Fombonne, Poulton, & Martin, 2002). Thus, it may be difficult to predict which depressed children will go on to experience further depression, and which ones might have no further depression but will develop substance abuse, delinquency and conduct problems, and other life difficulties. Further study is needed to help refine these depression subgroups and their predictors.

The Weissman childhood depression study also found that several of the formerly depressed children developed bipolar disorder by adulthood. Studies now indicate that a significant proportion of children diagnosed with depression in clinical settings eventually evidence the hypomania or mania that enable the bipolar diagnosis to be made (e.g., reviewed in Kovacs, 1996). For instance, Kovacs et al. (1994) found that 13% of their depressed sample "switched" to bipolar disorder. Geller and colleagues (Geller, Fox, & Clark, 1994) found that among a sample of 79 severely depressed children (ages 6 to 12), 32% switched to Bipolar I or II during a 2- to 5-year follow-up. When the same subjects were recontacted in young adulthood (mean age 21), 49% were found to have switched to bipolar disorder (including 33% with Bipolar I) (Geller, Zimerman, Williams, Bolhofner, & Craney, 2001). Although clinical predictors of switching have yet to be validated, having a family member with bipolar disorder would increase the likelihood that a child's depression may be an early manifestation of bipolar disorder. Clearly, further research is needed to help identify children at risk for recurrent unipolar or bipolar disorder, who may be targeted for different interventions to lessen the severity of illness over time.

Adolescent-onset depression. A great deal of research on adolescent depression has appeared in recent years (e.g., reviewed in Rudolph, Hammen, & Daley, 2006). Adolescent-onset depression is notable for several features. It is one of the most common periods of first onset for those who experience depression in adulthood (Burke et al., 1990). Rates of depression in boys and girls diverge sharply in adolescence, compared to their relatively similar rates in childhood (e.g., Hankin, Abramson, Moffitt, Silva, McGee, & Angell, 1998; Nolen-Hoeksema & Girgus, 1994). During this period, girls' rates increase sharply to the level of about 2:1 the rates of depression in boys. Furthermore, rates of major depression have been increasing in adolescents in recent generations (e.g., Kessler et al., 2003), with recent community studies suggesting lifetime rates of major depressive episode by age 19 between 15% and 30% (Kessler & Walters, 1998; Lewinsohn et al., 1998). Unsurprisingly, there has been considerable concern about an "epidemic" of adolescent depression.

However, just as not all childhood depressions are alike, the same is true of adolescent depression. A key factor appears to be whether adolescent depressions recur. Clinical samples suggest that about 60% or more have recurrences depending on the duration of follow-up (Emslie et al., 1997; Harrington et al., 1990; Weissman et al., 1999a). Community samples, presumably more representative of adolescent depressive experiences in general, report between 25% and 45% recurrence over varying periods of time (Bardone, Moffitt, Caspi, Dickson, & Silva, 1996; Fleming, Boyle, & Offord, 1993; Lewinsohn, Rohde, Klein, & Seeley, 1999b; Pine et al., 1998; Rao, Hammen, & Daley, 1999). In general, roughly half of adolescent depressions will portend continuity into adulthood, while the others do not recur, possibly suggesting a temporary response to the developmental challenges of adolescence. Those with recurrent depression have clinical courses and functional outcomes as described earlier in the chapter.

Late-life depression. Considerable interest in recent years has focused on characteristics of depression in the elderly that might be different from those of younger adult samples. Clinically, depression in later life may be overlooked, misunderstood, or even misattributed, because its symptoms often overlap with those of medical problems— for instance, loss of appetite and sleep problems, decreased energy, diminished pleasure and involvement, difficulties in memory and concentration. Thus, a treatable disorder like depression might be mislabeled as dementia or other chronic medical illness, or ignored altogether as less important than medical difficulties. An additional obstacle to recognition and treatment was that many epidemiological studies suggested that rates of major depression were lower after 65 years of age compared to younger adults—but such studies typically failed to sample sufficiently large numbers of the "oldest old." According to recent reviews and surveys, rates of major depression increase among those older than 80 years of age (e.g., Blazer, 2003; Steffens et al., 2000). Also many surveys had excluded those in long-term care facilities, or those hospitalized for medical and surgical services—groups in which depression diagnoses and significant symptoms are relatively high (Blazer, 2003).

In general, much of what is known or emerging about late-life depression, including diagnostic and clinical features, depends on making distinctions about whether depression occurring in late life actually first occurred in older years or whether earlier episodes in younger adulthood preceded late-life depression. While some research distinguishes between early-onset depression before age 60, and later-onset depression after 60, unfortunately many studies of depression in late life do not make a distinction about age of onset, potentially obscuring important patterns or yielding inconsistent findings.

An important implication of age-of-onset differences concerns etiological factors. Late-onset depression may often reflect the effects of vascular changes in the brain or other older age dementing disorders such as Alzheimer's disease or Parkinson's (e.g., Blazer, 2003; Powers et al., 2002), or result from biological changes associated with certain diseases, such as stroke. For instance, Van den Berg and colleagues (Van den Berg, Oldehinkel, Bouhuys, Brilman, Beekman, & Ormel, 2001) found that late-onset depressed Dutch elders had higher vascular risk factors than elderly depressed with early onset. The latter had depressions that were best predicted by stressful life events (e.g., loss of spouse, medical problems), familial history of depression, and neuroticism. Depression symptoms in older adults may in fact sometimes mark the early warning signs of dementia (Blazer, 2003). Some investigators have noted subtle differences in presentation of symptoms in older depressed patients compared with younger ones, including more withdrawal, apathy, and "depletion" (Newman, Engel, & Jensen, 1991), less anxiety, irritability, and less negativism about themselves or the future (Husain et al., 2005). Depression occurring in the context of vascular and brain changes may be accompanied by more cognitive impairment, psychomotor slowing, and reduced interest in typical activities (Blazer, 2003).

Late-life depression, whether with early- or late-onset, often occurs in the context of co-existing medical problems, and increased use of medical services (e.g., Husain et al., 2005)—a topic addressed in later sections. Among the minority of individuals who experience significant depression in old age, the problems tend to be chronic or recurrent (Beekman et al., 2002; Blazer, 2003), likely reflecting the impact of adverse life conditions such as medical disability and social isolation. Rates of suicide among older white males are higher than any other age or gender group, likely reflecting the extreme toll of depression (e.g., Mann, 2002).

Impaired functioning and consequences of depression

The low mood, reduced energy, pessimism, and lack of motivation associated with moderate and severe depression obviously interfere with a person's ability to go to work, perform chores, and relate to family and friends. At depression's worst, the afflicted person may spend endless hours in bed or staring into space, or aimlessly pacing and brooding—often finding it difficult to manage even minimal tasks such as bathing or getting dressed. The negativism, hopelessness, and lack of motivation are often a source of incredulity or even of frustration and impatience to others, because depression is often erroneously viewed as a lack of willpower or strength of character. It is therefore not difficult to foretell the development of interpersonal conflicts added on to apparent problems in performing typical roles. Because depression is a common, often recurring or chronic problem, its consequences can add up to enormous proportions. In this section both the psychic and tangible "costs" of depression—to the person and to society—are noted.

Global burden of depression. The *Global Burden of Disease* study by the World Health Organization (WHO) computed the costs of different diseases in terms of "disability-adjusted life years" (C. J. Murray & Lopez, 1996) across both developed and less-developed nations. According to its calculations, depression was responsible for more disability than any other condition during the middle years of adulthood. The U.S.-based Medical Outcomes Study identified over 11,000 patients who were being seen for various medical problems or depression in representative health care settings in different U.S. locations (Wells et al., 1989). Patients who had depressive disorders or depressed symptoms were compared on self-reported measures of functioning with medical patients suffering from one of eight chronic medical problems (including diabetes, hypertension, coronary artery disease, back problems, angina pectoris, arthritis, lung problems, or gastrointestinal disorder). Individuals with depression had significantly worse social functioning than patients with each of the eight medical conditions, worse role functioning in major roles than six of the medical conditions, and significantly more days in bed than six medical conditions. Even physical functioning was rated by depressed individuals as worse than that of four groups of chronically medically ill patients. Further, the study indicated that those with depressive symptoms only—not just diagnosed depressive disorders—showed poor functioning. The surprising findings of these two studies have brought attention to the enormous impact of depression, suggesting that it is not an insignificant lapse of emotional strength, but a serious problem with far-reaching consequences. Add to personal debility the mortality associated with suicide and medical consequences, diminished work and family performance, and the impact on loved ones and caregivers, its economic costs have been measured in the billions—for direct treatment, indirect costs arising from mortality, and from burdens due to reductions in productivity (Wang & Kessler, 2005).

Impairing effects of mild depression. In general, the severity of psychosocial impairment varies with the severity of depression, and may disappear entirely when depression remits (e.g., Judd, Akiskal, Zeller, Paulus, Leon, & Maser, 2000). However, it might be somewhat surprising to learn the extent to which even relatively mild depression also interferes with normal functioning (Broadhead, Blazer, George, & Tse, 1990; Gotlib, Lewinsohn, & Seeley, 1995; Wells et al., 1989). As an example, J. Johnson, Weissman, and Klerman (1992) studied the association between depressive symptoms in community residents and use of services and evidence of impairment in a survey of more than 18,000 representative adults in five U.S. cities, comparing those with no depression, mild symptoms, or diagnoses of major depression or dysthymic disorder. There was a significantly higher rate of negative outcome for those with even mild symptoms compared with no symptoms on each of several indicators of impairment: use of emergency services for an emotional problem, use of minor tranquilizers, reported poor physical health, absence from work for more than 1 week due to emotional problems, and suicide attempts. Since mild symptoms of depression are fairly common in the general population, they would appear to account for a sizable portion of the community's costs for provision of services and those due to economic loss and poor health.

Research has documented at least three specific areas in which depression causes significantly impaired functioning: work, family, and marital/interpersonal relationships. A fourth area will also be described separately: the emerging study of the effects of depression on medical conditions. In the following sections the emphasis is on the consequences of depression—how depression has a negative impact on work and family domains. It is important to acknowledge, of course, that the relationship between depression and functioning in important roles is bidirectional, since problems in adjustment may cause or exacerbate depressive conditions. The contribution of stressors, family, and marital difficulties as causes of depression will be covered in later chapters.

Effects of depression on work

Studies clearly indicate that depression is associated with costly absenteeism from work (e.g., Kessler et al., 2003; Ormel, VonKorff, Ustun, & Pini, 1994). Depression also creates what has been called "presenteeism," the reduction in the quality and productivity of work even when the person is present in the workplace. For instance, Stewart, Ricci, Chee, Hahn, and Morganstein (2003) interviewed workers who had been selected because of depression or absence of depression on a survey, and asked them how often they lost concentration, repeated a job, or worked more slowly than usual. An index of "lost productive time" was calculated, indicating 8.4 hours per week for those with major depression compared to 1.5 hours per week for the nondepressed. The authors extrapolated from these figures to calculate that the cost of total lost productive time for those at work but with diminished efficiency is far greater (US$18 billion per year) than the cost of "absenteeism" (US$3.2 billion). Another study collected "moment in time" data by electronically signaling workers at 5 random times per day to write about their work performance (Wang et al., 2004). Those with major depression had decrements in task focus and performance that were calculated to approximate to the equivalent of 2.3 days of absence of work per month attributable to depression.

It might be assumed that those in student roles would suffer similar problems with decreased academic effectiveness. Although no daily performance data have been reported, there is clear evidence that depression is significantly associated with increased rates of failure to complete high school, failure to enter college, and failure to complete college (Kessler, Foster, Saunders, & Stang, 1995).

Effects of depression on parent–child relations

Studies of family relationships have indicated significant impairment of the parental role when a person is depressed (reviewed in Cummings & Davies, 1999; Gelfand & Teti, 1990; Goodman & Gotlib, 1999; Hammen, 1991a). Depressed parents typically want to be good parents, but the depression takes an enormous toll on their energy, interest, patience, and mood—all of which doubtless impair their abilities to sustain positive, supportive, and attentive relationships with their children. In a review and meta-analysis, Lovejoy, Graczyk, O'Hare, and Neuman (2000) found that overall, depressed mothers differed significantly from nondepressed mothers. They displayed more negative and disengaged behaviours, and were also less positive. In Chapter 6, we present more details on parent–child problems occurring in the families of depressed parents—and the risk to the offspring of developing depression and other maladjustment.

Effects of depression on marital relationships

Depression may also take a toll on marital relationships. As with work and parenting, difficulties in marriages may cause or contribute to depression, but often it is the depression that causes marital problems (see Chapter 6). Studies have indicated a strong association between depression and presence of marital distress (reviewed in Whisman, 2001; Zlotnick, Kohn, Keitner, & Della Grotta, 2000). Kessler, Walters, and Forthofer (1998b) examined patterns of psychiatric disorders and divorce in an epidemiological sample. Although causality cannot be established unequivocally, they found that depressive disorders were nearly twice as likely to be followed by divorce compared to those without depression.

The effects of depression are diverse, probably including irritability, withdrawal, dependency, and other symptoms. Also, of course, depressed spouses are often viewed as a great burden, causing worry, reducing the sharing of pleasurable activities, failing to respond to encouragement and support. Indeed, a survey of spouses of depressed individuals found these and numerous other complaints, and also discovered that fully 40% of the spouses were sufficiently distressed by the depressed person to warrant treatment themselves (Coyne, Kahn, & Gotlib, 1987).

Depression, death, and health

Depression and suicide. Depression is one of the few psychological disorders that can be said to be fatal. Of all of the consequences, suicide is, of course, the starkest consequence of the individuals' feelings of hopelessness and debility. While there are many contributors to suicide that may be unrelated to depression, the disorder in general and its symptoms of hopelessness in particular are especially predictive of suicide. Indeed, suicidal thoughts are a symptom of the syndrome of depression. Diagnosable depressive disorders have been implicated in 40% to 60% of instances of suicide (Clark & Fawcett, 1992; Fowler, Rich, & Young, 1986; Henriksson et al., 1993). Records of more than 39,000 unipolar depressed hospital patients in Sweden followed up from time of admission were found to be associated with a 20 times higher rate of suicide death over time than the general population (Osby, Brandt, Correia, Ekbom, & Sparen, 2001).

The decision to commit suicide and the actions taken toward that goal may be consequences of negativistic thinking that is characteristic of depression, such as a sense of futility, a view that the future is bleak and bad conditions are unchangeable, that there is nothing one can do can relieve the pain of depressive feelings, and the belief that one is worthless and that others would be better off without one. Such attitudes, when assessed on a scale measuring "hopelessness," have been found to be associated with a greater likelihood of eventual suicide in outpatients (A. T. Beck, Brown, Berchick, Stewart, & Steer, 1990). Clinicians and researchers have learned that it is extremely difficult to accurately predict who will commit suicide among those who are depressed, who may threaten suicidal action, or who have made prior attempts (Goldstein, Black, Nasrallah, & Winokur, 1991).

However, G. K. Brown, Beck, Steer, and Grisham (2000) found that severity of depression, hopelessness, and suicidal ideation were significant predictors of eventual suicide in a sample of nearly 7000 psychiatric outpatients.

Depression may also be fatal in other ways besides suicide, or it can have implications for medical diseases. Increasingly depression is implicated in the onset and course, as well as reactions to, many medical conditions. A thorough discussion of these issues is beyond the scope of this book; an overview of key issues is presented.

Depression in response to disease. Any long-term medical condition is likely to be associated with increased rates of major depressive disorder, as disability, medical symptoms, and implications for mortality may be severely stressful and upsetting. Unfortunately, the depression in response to disease and disability may contribute to additional impairment and reduced quality of life beyond that caused by the disease itself (reviewed in Katon, 2003). This also translates into increased costs of medical care—more primary care visits, more emergency room, pharmacy, laboratory, and hospitalization costs associated with depression. For example, Katon, Lin, Russo, and Unutzer (2003) found that total costs of medical services were significantly higher in the past 6 months among depressed (subclinical depressive symptoms and major depression) compared to nondepressed older adults, after controlling for chronic medical illness. Many other studies have reached similar conclusions—depression adds greatly to health care costs beyond the effects of medical disorders.

But in addition to possible depressive experiences in reaction to disease, depression may also result from certain disease processes themselves, affecting neuroendocrine, neurological, and immunological processes that may be implicated in the causes of depression. Several medical illnesses are known to be especially associated with depression. These include certain cardiac diseases, diabetes, some neurological disorders such as stroke, Alzheimer's, and Parkinson's disease, and obesity (see reviews in D. L. Evans et al., 2005; Katon, 2003). The following section presents a few of the many diseases in which depression plays a role.

Depression as a risk factor and predictor of the course of disease. Depression is a risk factor for the development of coronary heart disease. Reviews of studies of people who were healthy at baseline and followed up over periods ranging from 4 to 15 years, found that depression increased the risk of death by heart disease or of having a heart attack (myocardial infarction) by a factor of 1.64 (Rugulies, 2002). There is also considerable evidence that depression increases the risk of death or further heart disease progression among those who have already been diagnosed with heart disease (e.g., Suls & Bunde, 2005). For example, a study of individuals who were followed after experiencing a heart attack found that those who were depressed after their heart attacks were more likely to die during the follow-up period (Frasure-Smith, Lesperance, & Talajic, 1993; see also Frasure-Smith & Lesperance, 2003). It is hypothesized that depression affects coronary heart disease medically through processes affecting vascular pathology, heart-functioning changes, immunologic, and platelet functioning (reviewed in Evans et al., 2005). Moreover, depression is associated with a number of behavioural risk factors that contribute to cardiac-disease onset and progression, including smoking, being overweight, poor nutrition, and insufficient exercise, and failure to follow treatment recommendations.

Diabetes is another disease in which depression has been shown to be a risk factor (type 2 diabetes mellitus; e.g., Eaton, Armenian, Gallo, Pratt, & Ford, 1996). Depression is associated with biological abnormalities such as insulin resistance and secretion of inflammatory cytokines that might contribute to diabetes onset (Musselman, Betan, Larsen, & Phillips, 2003). Evans et al. (2005) note that depression also contributes to severity and complications of the course of diabetes by reducing compliance to medication and healthy lifestyle changes.

Similarly, certain neurodegenerative disorders such as Parkinson's and Alzheimer's disease—as well as stroke and epilepsy—also show a bidirectional association with depression. Depression may contribute to the onset or course of these disorders, and these disorders are also associated with increased risk of depression (Evans et al., 2005). Obesity is a disorder that has received increased scrutiny in recent years, and not surprisingly, there appears to be a bidirectional association as well, operating through a number of biological as well as behavioural factors (e.g., reviewed in Chapman, Perry, & Strine, 2005).

Implications. Taken together, the picture that emerges of depression is one of a disorder that may have such negative consequences for family relationships, work, and health that it might actually contribute to adverse conditions that prolong depression or increase the likelihood that it will recur. As we will see in later chapters, many psychological factors are thought to cause depression, such as stressful life events, interpersonal difficulties, and negative attitudes about the self and others. It is possible that some of these same factors actually worsen as a function of the debilitating nature of depression.

Summary

- Depressive disorders typically start in adolescence or young adulthood, with major depression usually lasting 4 to 6 months even if untreated. Depressions are commonly but not inevitably recurrent, and some individuals have a fairly chronic course.
- Earlier onset of depressive disorder generally portends more severe and recurrent depression with greater impairment.
- Depressions may differ in their etiological, course, and treatment implications depending on whether they first begin in childhood, adolescence, adulthood, or older adulthood.
- The consequences of depression—even at fairly mild levels—on work, marriage, parenting, and health may be considerably negative not just for the individuals involved but also for society.
- Health, marital, parental, and work impairments due to depression may contribute to further depression in a vicious cycle if untreated.

Who is affected by depression? 3

In this chapter we explore three issues. First, how common is depression and how many people are affected? Second, are some segments of the population more prone to depression than others? The third issue is *why* some groups are more depression-prone than others, and what might be the implications for understanding depression.

Prevalence of depression

One of the greatest challenges of depression is that it is common, afflicting large segments of the population. Indeed, its frequency is the reason that it has been termed the "common cold" of psychological disorders. When considering how frequent depressive disorders may be, it is helpful to consider two measures, one concerning how many depressed people there are in a given period, and the other indicating how many people experience significant depression in their lifetimes.

The most valid method of estimating the frequency of depression, either in a given period or over a lifetime, is a survey of representative adult community members who are systematically interviewed using standard criteria for diagnosing depressive disorders. The achievement of such standardized procedures is a relatively recent development, drawing on interview methods and diagnostic criteria first established in the 1970s. Despite advances, methodological considerations have affected rates of reported depression: ages of the population sampled, changes in the diagnostic criteria for disorders over time, as well as alterations in interview methods (Kessler et al., 2003). In recent years there has been increasing standardization of methods across nations, using the WHO-CIDI, which itself has gone through several revisions. The use of the WHO-CIDI in randomly selected adult samples permits calculation of population rates of disorders, facilitates cross-national comparisons, and helps to identify mental health needs within diverse communities. The studies below all have used WHO-CIDI methods.

Twelve-month prevalence of depression

Major depressive disorder is a universal phenomenon, occurring with some frequency in every country sampled. A *recent* U.S. survey, the NCS-R (National Comorbidity Study–Replication), assessed a variety of psychological disorders and their co-occurrence. According to this survey, the rate of major depression in the past 12 months was 6.6% (Kessler et al., 2003). The European Study of the Epidemiology of Mental Disorders based on six nations (ESEMeD/MHEDEA 2000 Investigators, 2004) reported 3.9% major depression overall.

A 14-country study, including the ESEMeD samples plus the USA, Japan, and six developing nations in the Middle East and Africa, Asia, and the Americas, reported on "mood disorders" including major depression, dysthymia, and bipolar disorder. They found a wide range of 12-month rates across different nations, as illustrated in Table 3.1 (WHO World Mental Health Survey Consortium, 2004).

Lifetime diagnoses of depression

Not only is depression fairly common at any given moment or within the past year, but its lifetime prevalence is notably high. The European ESEMeD study (ESEMeD/MHEDEA 2000 Investigators, 2004) reported a lifetime rate of 12.8% major depression, and 4.1% dysthymia. The U.S. NCS-R reported 16.2% lifetime major depression. A WHO-CIDI-based study of 10 countries in North America, Latin America, Europe, and Asia reported a range of lifetime major depression from 3% in Japan to 16% in the USA (Andrade et al., 2003). Surveys commonly report higher rates of major depression in industrialized countries than developing nations, but urge caution in interpretation since cultural differences in the meaning, experience, and willingness to acknowledge depressive symptoms may all affect rates (WHO World Mental Health Survey Consortium, 2004).

Two additional points about the epidemiology of depression warrant mention. One is that whether current or lifetime, depressive disorders are highly likely to co-occur with other psychological disorders (more than 70% have comorbidity; Kessler et al., 2003). Such disorders, as noted in Chapter 1, occur either concurrently, or most commonly, other disorders occur historically prior to depressive

TABLE 3.1

Proportion of adults with diagnosis of mood disorder

Country	Percentage with mood disorder in 12 months
Americas	
Colombia	6.8
Mexico	4.8
United States	9.6
Europe	
Belgium	6.2
France	8.5
Germany	3.6
Italy	3.8
Netherlands	6.9
Spain	4.9
Ukraine	9.1
Middle East and Africa	
Lebanon	6.6
Nigeria	0.8
Asia	
Japan	3.1
People's Republic of China	
Beijing	2.5
Shanghai	1.7

disorders. The other point is that in addition to diagnoses of major depression or dysthymia, rates of elevated depressive symptoms at the subclinical level are notably high and potentially impairing. For example, Kessler and colleagues (1997c) reported that in addition to the lifetime rate of major depression, another 10% of the U.S. population had experienced minor depressive disorder at some point.

Age and depression

For many years, depression was considered a disorder of middle age or older. However, as we explored in Chapter 2 on the age of onset of depression, it is now apparent that the common age of onset of depression is in youth or early adulthood. Thus, it is not surprising to observe that the proportions of people with major depression are higher among younger individuals. U.S. data on major depression by decade of age based on epidemiological data indicate the highest rate of current depression (6.1%) in the younger groups, whereas the lowest rate (3.6%) was in the oldest group (K. C. Burke et al., 1990).

Increasing rates of depression among the young

Not only are the rates of onset and current depression highest among those in their late teens and early 20s, but several studies have now suggested an intriguing possibility: depression has increased among the young. Klerman and colleagues (e.g., Klerman & Weissman, 1989) were among the first to note that rates of depressive disorder were relatively higher in those born more recently, based on retrospective reports from U.S. populations born in different eras. That is, when individuals of all ages are interviewed concerning the experience of major depression in their lifetimes, more of the younger people were reporting depression. This "birth cohort effect" has now been substantiated in an international study. The Cross-National Collaborative Group (1992) employed standardized methods of assessing retrospective reports of depression in various U.S. cities, Paris, Beirut, Alberta (Canada), Puerto Rico, Munich, New Zealand, Taiwan, and Florence, Italy. Respondents were classified by decade of birth, and in all but the Florence sample, rates of major depression were highest by age 25 among those born since 1955. The most recent U.S. NCS-R study has also documented significantly increased rates of depression among those in younger birth cohorts, and higher rates by age 20 among those born more recently (Kessler et al., 2003). A large adolescent community study in Oregon also found a significant age-cohort effect, at least for the young women, even among those between the restricted ages of 14 and 19 (Lewinsohn, Rohde, Seeley, & Fischer, 1993). Those born between 1972 and 1975 were significantly more likely to show major depression than those born between 1968 and 1971.

The trend toward more depression in younger people has raised concerns about alarming rates of adolescent depression. Indeed, the high rates of major depression among adolescents in the Lewinsohn study appeared to be higher than those in the general U.S. population; based on lifetime and new incidence rates during their follow-up period, the investigators estimated that 28% of the youth would develop major depression by age 19 (Lewinsohn et al., 1998).

Oldehinkel, Wittchen, and Schuster (1999) followed a large representative sample of 14- to 17-year-olds for nearly 2 years, and found a lifetime cumulative rate of major depressive disorder of 12.2% (overall 20% including dysthymia and subclinical major depression). Interestingly, those with subclinical major depression had significant impairment, similar to those with full diagnostic major depression. Numerous studies confirm high rates of both diagnoses and depressive symptoms in youth—typically higher than in general adult population surveys.

What could account for this alarming trend toward more depression among the young? Various explanations have been considered, including both methodological artifacts and psychosocial causes. For instance, it might be argued that younger people are over-reporting depression because they are more knowledgeable about depression, and more willing to acknowledge it. Thus, perhaps the increased rates are simply reflecting a lower threshold for counting depressive experiences. Arguing against such an artifact, however, Klerman and Weissman (1989) observed that objective measures of distress such as suicides and hospitalization have also increased for young people.

Another argument is that older people have forgotten their previous depressions, and that the apparent increase in depression is really a memory artifact. Paykel, Brugha, and Fryers (2005) reviewed several studies suggesting that individuals commonly forget key symptoms over time, possibly not recalling enough to qualify for a diagnosis. Thus, lifetime rates based on recall might be underestimates in general, and possibly especially for older adults. Clearly, resolving the question of the validity of increasing rates of depression requires long-term longitudinal studies using the same, well-developed methods at each assessment. Recently two different methodological alternatives to retrospective reporting of lifetime depression have addressed the issue. Murphy and colleagues (Murphy, Laird, Monson, Sobol, & Leighton, 2000) collected information on depression symptoms using similar assessment methods in 1952, 1970, and 1992. Their results over the 40 years indicated a stable rate of current depression approximating the DSM criteria for depressive disorders. Despite stability, however, they also observed increased rates of depression in younger women appearing in the 1992 data. Other investigators employed a longitudinal analysis in which women of different ages were assessed for depressive symptoms 3 times in a 10-year period (Kasen, Cohen, Chen, & Castille, 2003), a procedure that permitted separating age and birth cohort (divided into pre-1945 and post-1945 birth dates). The investigators found more depression among the younger women in the post-1945 cohort, but a flat distribution by age in the earlier-born cohort. Taken together, the two studies suggest some support—at least for women—of increasing rates of depression in more recently born samples. However, further research is needed to establish the generality of these results to major depressive disorder in both males and females, in those born in the past 20 or 30 years.

In addition to the contribution of possible method artifacts accounting for some of the dramatic birth cohort differences in depression, investigators also sought psychological explanations. It has been suggested that changing cultural trends, such as breakdown in the family and increasing social mobility, are not only potential sources of depression but might also reduce the available resources for helping individuals cope with stressful situations that cause depression. Some have argued that cultural shifts emphasizing materialism and personal attainment, to the relative de-emphasis on serving God, community, and broader social goals, have left young people with greater pressure for success and less opportunity for fulfillment and sense of meaning (e.g., Seligman, Reivich, Jaycox, & Gillham, 1995). In later chapters we review various theories of the causes of depression that explore the role of stress, family and inter-personal relations, social support, and beliefs about the self and the future as they pertain to depression. Clearly, for any theory of depression to be credible, it must be capable of helping to account for the increasing rates of depression in young people.

In addition to the search for the origins of depression among the young, it will also be important for researchers to consider the impli-cations of youthful depression. As we indicated in previous chapters, the consequences of depression may include considerable impair-ment and the chance of recurrent or even chronic disorder. When depression interferes with normal development in children and ado-lescents, and when it impedes achievement of stable family and occupational adjustment, it can certainly set the stage for continuing depression. Thus, as noted in Chapter 2, youth depression may be particularly disabling and pernicious in terms of its future course and its potential influence on the lives of the affected person and those around him or her.

Epidemiology of depression in children and adolescents

Most epidemiological surveys have included only adults and excluded children and youth. Estimates of their depression, therefore, have been based on limited surveys such as those noted for adolescents. Angold and Costello (1993) summarized surveys of children and adolescents, and despite considerable variability due to different samples and methods, major depression in youngsters generally fell in the 6% to 8% range (in a 6- to 12-month period). However, the overall finding obscures important differences between preadolescent and adolescent age groups. The great majority of major depressive episodes in youngsters occur around age 13 and after (e.g., Oldehinkel et al., 1999). Younger than about age 12, depression is fairly rare—affecting 2% to 3% of the population (e.g., Angold & Rutter, 1992; Costello, Mustillo, Erkanli, Keeler, & Angold, 2003; Egger & Angold, 2006). Depression in preschool age children apparently occurs in less than 1% (Kashani & Carlson, 1987), but data on young children are sparse.

Depression in older adults

Depression is less common in older years than younger, for the most part. Indeed, Kasen and her colleagues (2003) found that women's rates of depressive symptoms declined over repeated testings in a 10-year period. The European Study of the Epidemiology of Mental Disorders also found lowest rates of depression in the oldest groups (ESEMeD/MHEDEA 2000 Investigators, 2004). However, depression among the elderly, while apparently not as common as among younger groups, raises its own unique issues. For one thing, demographic trends clearly indicate that the numbers of older adults are increasing due both to the aging of the post-WWII baby boom and to the greater longevity of elders due to improved health care in most nations. Recently it has been noted that after periods of relatively low rates in adulthood and middle age, there is some indication that rates increase in old age (Blazer, 2003; Burke et al., 1990; Steffens et al., 2000). Wallace and O'Hara (1992) studied changes in depressive symptoms in a rural sample of people age 65 and over, retesting them 3 and 6 years later. They found significant increases over time in depressive symptoms—especially among the very old, age 85 and above— suggesting that late life may be a time of increased depression risk.

Depression among the older segments of the population has often been misunderstood. Sometimes its manifestations as problems of memory and loss of energy and other bodily symptoms are misinterpreted as senescence, an irreversible decline in mental and physical capabilities. Thus, depression that can be treated might be misdiagnosed as a largely untreatable problem.

Another important aspect of elderly depression is that it can be quite literally life-threatening. Rates of suicide are highest among older white males and among some cultures such as the Chinese, among older females (e.g., Group for the Advancement of Psychiatry, 1989; Rockett & Smith, 1989). Particularly if depression is caused by or accompanied by social isolation and poor health, it readily leads to hopelessness and suicidality (Clark & Fawcett, 1992; McIntosh, 1992). Moreover, as noted in Chapter 2, because depression appears to compromise the functioning of the immune system, it might impair the body's resistance to disease. Among older people who become increasingly afflicted with ailments, reduced immune functioning due to depression might predict a more severe or fatal course of illness.

Gender differences in depression

In addition to age differences in who is affected by depression, one of the most striking characteristics of depression is that it is far more common among women than men. Across different methods of study and different countries of the world, with few exceptions studies report roughly a 2:1 rate of depression for women compared to men (Andrade et al., 2003; ESEMeD/MHEDEA 2000 Investigators, 2004; Kessler, 2003; Kessler et al., 2003; Oldehinkel et al., 1999; Paykel et al., 2005). The most valid studies for examining sex differences are community surveys, since rates based on those who seek treatment might be biased by women's known tendency to admit to and seek help for emotional problems. The epidemiological surveys of communities are clear: whether in the USA, New Zealand, Taiwan, or Seoul, or any other location that has been surveyed, the excess of women meeting criteria for depressive disorders is readily apparent and has remained fairly stable for years (e.g., Weissman & Olfson, 1995). For example, among U.S. adults aged 15 to 54, lifetime rates were reported as 12.7% for men and 21.3% for women (Blazer et al., 1994). In a sample of 14- to 17-year-olds in Europe, 1-year prevalence rates of major depression were 8.9% for girls and 4.7% for boys (Oldehinkel et al., 1999).

Gender differences in children and adolescents. Interestingly, among children, boys and girls do not differ in rates of depression (or in some studies, boys actually have higher rates than girls of depression as well as most other disorders—e.g., Angold & Rutter, 1992; Costello et al., 1988; Fleming, Offord, & Boyle, 1989). However, by adolescence the gender gap is quite apparent in both symptoms and diagnoses, and major depressive disorder reaches adult rates by early adolescence (e.g., reviewed in Hankin & Abramson, 2001). For instance, a prevalence of 7.6% for girls aged 14 to 16 compared with 1.6% for boys of the same age was reported by P. Cohen, Cohen, Kasen, and Velez (1993). While there is some disagreement about when the gender differences emerge, most studies agree that it is in early-to-middle adolescence (approximately 11 to 14 years; Angold & Rutter, 1992; Hankin & Abramson, 2001; Silberg et al., 1999).

Why do more women show depression than men? And why do the differences emerge in early adolescence?

Why more depression in women?

Numerous efforts have been devoted to explaining sex differences in depression (e.g., Hankin & Abramson, 2001; Kessler, 2003; Nolen-Hoeksema, 1990, 2002), hypothesizing multiple contributing factors. The gender differences appear in virtually every culture studied, and in nearly every age group except preadolescent children. Some have argued that the gender effects may be partly due to "artifacts" of sex role differences that affect perceptions, symptom expressions, and reports rather than "actual" differences. To some extent it is likely that the excess of depression in women may stem partly from perceptions that depression represents emotional "weakness" and is therefore shunned by males as unacceptable behaviour. Males may experience depression but express their symptoms differently (e.g., by emphasizing physical complaints or work difficulties rather than subjective distress, possibly leading to different diagnostic outcomes—or, by excessive use of alcohol and drugs to obscure depressive feelings). While differences in male and female role socialization may contribute somewhat to gender differences in the experience and expression of diagnosable depression, the major explanations have focused on biological and psychosocial differences between women and women.

Biological differences. Hormonal changes associated with pregnancy and the postpartum period, menstrual cycles, and menopause may seem like strong candidates as explanations for gender differences in depression. However, as we review in Chapter 4, studies of hormone–depression associations are complex, have small effects even when major hormonal shifts occur, and appear to depend on various psychological and contextual factors. Another biological "suspect" concerns effects of stress. As discussed in later sections of the book, recent emphasis on abnormalities of the stress response system in depression may have implications for women to the extent that such processes are affected by hormones—and because of women's apparently greater exposure and reactivity to stressors. Moreover, complex associations among stress, hormonal activity, and depression may also be affected by genetic contributions (e.g., Silberg et al., 1999).

Stress exposure. There are several variants of the idea that women experience greater stress than men do, and that it is the stress (or stress interacting with some predisposing vulnerability) that causes depression. One version is that in general, women's lives are more stressful due to diminished opportunity and lower status than males—that women are poorer, have less power to control their own destinies, have lower status jobs or roles, have less access to sources of acclaim and reward than men do. It has also been hypothesized, that women also may be at risk for depression to the extent that their lives include "dual roles" such as worker and parent that might be in conflict, or hold dual roles that may be more demanding than those of men (e.g., spouse and worker). Support for the negative effects of dual roles for women was reported by Aneshensel, Frerichs, and Clark (1981) based on a large epidemiological survey. They found that among people who were both married and employed, women were more depressed than men—but among unmarried respondents, working men and women did not differ.

A second approach to stress has focused on occurrence of stressful life events, suggesting that women are exposed to greater levels of stress than are men. In a large survey of adult twin pairs, female subjects reported significantly more events overall than did men (Kendler, Neale, Kessler, Heath, & Eaves, 1993b). Their frequencies of negative events in the past year exceeded those of men in all content categories, with statistically significant differences in 6 of the 9 categories: interpersonal difficulties, financial, marital, and work problems, as well as events happening to others in their networks (illness/accidents and crises happening to family members and close friends). Women may be more affected by the stressors that happen to others than are men, to the extent that women tend to be more embedded in family and social networks than are men. Other studies have also reported higher rates of stressful life events among women than men, including adolescent samples and especially interpersonal life events (e.g., Ge, Lorenz, Conger, Elder, & Simons, 1994; McGonagle & Kessler, 1990; Rudolph & Hammen, 1999; Shih, Eberhart, Hammen, & Brennan, 2006). However, some studies have not found significant gender differences in stressors (Kendler, Thornton, & Prescott, 2001b; Maciejewski, Prigerson, & Mazure, 2001).

A third type of stress concerns chronic strain and ongoing negative life circumstances. If measured as poverty and single-parenting, women's rates of chronic stressful conditions exceed those of men, and these circumstances are often associated with depression (e.g., G. W. Brown & Moran, 1997; Bruce, Takeuchi, & Leaf, 1991). Experiencing chronic illness and serving as primary caretakers for ill relatives also appear to be circumstances experienced by more women than men, and such conditions are also associated with depression (e.g., Maciejewski et al., 2001).

A fourth type of stress concerns trauma exposure. Analyses of women's potentially greater stress exposure and consequent depression must also consider the experience of sexual victimization (both childhood molestation and adult sexual assault), which is much higher in women than men, and is well-known to be associated with later depressive experiences (e.g., G. R. Brown & Anderson, 1991; Weiss, Longhurst, & Mazure, 1999). Fergusson, Swain-Campbell, and Horwood (2002), for example, found in their longitudinal sample that young women up to age 21 reported significantly higher rates of exposure to sexual violence than did young men, and that their experiences were associated with occurrence of major depression.

Across various realms of stressful experiences, therefore, there is evidence of women's greater stress exposure and association between the exposure and later depression. However, it must be emphasized that the link between stress and depression varies considerably by numerous factors such as the person's coping skills and resources, interpretations of the meaning of the stressor, and likely biological processes—all of which are discussed in greater detail in later chapters.

Coping factors. Some investigators have suggested that instead of, or in addition to, stress factors that promote depression, women might experience fewer of the coping resources necessary to combat stress and depression, than men do. Certainly, disadvantaged women exposed to chronic adversities simultaneously experience the reduction of coping resources, such as financial and material help, stable marital relationships, and although they may have family and social networks, emotional support might itself be reduced if the others are taxed by their own adversities associated with disadvantaged status (e.g., Belle, 1990).

Women may also have characteristic ways of coping with depression that might actually intensify the dysphoria. Nolen-Hoeksema (1991) has proposed that when experiencing emotional distress, women display a response style that emphasizes rumination, self-focus, and overanalysis of the problems and of their own emotions. In contrast, men use more distraction and direct problem solving. When ruminative responses are employed, they tend to intensify negative, self-focused thinking and to interfere with active problem solving—hence deepening or prolonging the symptoms of depression. Taking problem-solving steps or distracting oneself by activity, by contrast, might help to reduce and shorten the depressive experiences. Nolen-Hoeksema argues that sex role socialization sets the stage for gender differences in coping styles, with boys being discouraged from showing emotionality and being encouraged to learn to take action, while girls are given license to express emotions and even encouraged to analyse them and discuss them with others. A series of studies has demonstrated support for these hypotheses, including gender differences in coping style and the association of ruminative coping with depression (e.g., Nolen-Hoeksema, Morrow, & Fredrickson, 1993; reviewed in Nolen-Hoeksema & Girgus, 1994; Nolen-Hoeksema, 2002; see Chapter 5).

Why do gender differences emerge in early adolescence?

As with adult gender differences, there have been numerous approaches to explaining the emergence of sex differences in adolescence. Nolen-Hoeksema and Girgus (1994) proposed three separate models to explain the effect: (1) boys and girls have the same causal factors but such factors become more prevalent for girls in adolescence; (2) factors leading to depression are different for boys and girls, and girls' factors become prevalent in adolescence; (3) gender differences in personality characteristics that serve as diatheses for depression are present before adolescence, and *interact* with adolescent challenges which may be greater for girls, to cause greater depression in young women.

In analysing the validity of each of the models, a number of topics have been examined. For instance, one popular argument is that pubertal hormones set the stage for development of depression. Several studies have investigated the role of pubertal status on depression in adolescents. Earlier studies generally concluded that depression emerges in young women independent of whether or not they have achieved puberty (e.g., Angold & Rutter, 1992). Other research has suggested that it is not hormonal pubertal status as such, but rather the meaning of pubertal changes in the context in which they occur such as school situations in which early pubertal changes in girls may attract unwanted attention or involved undesirable bodily changes (Petersen, Sarigiani, & Kennedy, 1991). This line of reasoning is also supported by research that indicates that negative body image is associated with girls' depression (e.g., Allgood-Merten, Lewinsohn, & Hops, 1990). As explored in Chapter 4, more recent research using improved measures of gonadal hormones found that actual changes in androgen and estrogen levels were more associated with depression in young women than were bodily (morphological) changes (Angold, Costello, Erkanli, & Worthman, 1999). These results suggested that psychosocial changes associated with body image and environmental context may be less important than actual hormonal shifts. However, since all girls experience the hormonal changes but only some become depressed, further study of the mediators between hormone levels and depression is needed.

The role of stressors may also be important in the development in adolescence of gender differences in stressors. As noted in a previous section, adolescent girls appear to have higher rates of stressors than do boys (e.g., Shih et al., 2006). These may include heightened exposure to sexual violence and abuse especially during adolescence (e.g., Fergusson et al., 2002). Several investigators have hypothesized that adolescence is also a time of increasing sensitivity to social status and peer acceptance including romantic success. Cyranowski, Frank, Young, and Shear (2000) note that gender-based differences in affiliative needs (females' preference, compared with males', for intimacy and communication in relationships) intensify in adolescence, as girls face increased pressure to conform to feminine gender roles and show increased interest in romantic relationships. Increased focus on attractiveness and body image may accompany increased affiliative needs, but subject female adolescents to additional sources of low self-esteem (e.g., reviewed in Hankin & Abramson, 2001). Factors that reduce self-esteem set the stage for depression—especially if they occur in the context of additional risk factors, such as insecure parent–child bonds and low coping skills, that interact with stressful life events to increase likelihood of depression (Cyranowski et al.,

2000). Several studies have indeed suggested that adolescent girls are more sensitive (become depressed) to the effects of stress—especially interpersonal stress—than boys (e.g., Rudolph, 2002; Rudolph & Hammen, 1999; Shih et al., 2006). Through their relatively greater investment and involvement in peer relationships, girls may also play a role in creating more stressors as friendship and peer loyalties and alliances shift. Such increased exposure to stressful events may contribute to depression.

In addition to girls' increased exposure to major stressful experiences in early adolescence, Nolen-Hoeksema and Girgus (1994) review research suggesting that girls are also exposed during this time to various defeating and demoralizing expectations about their roles. Emphasis on "feminine" pursuits and behaviours may place considerable demands on the young women to conform to expectations and restrict their ambitions and independence, compared to expectations for boys. Girls, for example, may be "punished" for competence and assertiveness, and rewarded for conforming to roles that might be stereotypically feminine but potentially less satisfying or more stressful. However, Nolen-Hoeksema and Girgus (1994) argue that a resulting sense of defeat and distress may not necessarily produce depression, unless it interacts with passive, less instrumental coping styles, such as rumination—as noted earlier.

In evaluating all the possible sources of the emergence of gender differences in adolescence, Nolen-Hoeksema and Girgus (1994) conclude that the interactive model best fits the data. That is, before adolescence, girls develop more risk factors than do boys, and in adolescence they experience more social and biological challenges that lead to the experience of depression. Thus, the interaction of girls' prior vulnerabilities and heightened adolescent stresses/challenges promotes more depression in girls.

Depression and other social-demographic factors

Although depression is a universal disorder with substantial current and lifetime rates in most cultures, variability by social, ethnic, and cultural factors may provide additional clues about contributors to the risk for depression.

Ethnicity and cultural differences.   Cross-cultural differences, where they do exist, are most pronounced between Western and non-Western cultures. As noted earlier in this chapter, Westernized industrial nations tend to have significantly higher rates of major depression than do developing countries (Andrade et al., 2003; WHO World Mental Health Survey Consortium, 2004). However, caution is needed in drawing firm conclusions that Western rates are actually higher, because the methods for defining depression in different cultures may not be fully comparable despite use of standardized assessment instruments. The expression of depressive symptoms, for example, may vary by culture, so that the same measurement instruments may not be equally appropriate. One important cultural difference is the extent to which individuals distinguish between emotional and somatic experiences. The Western mind makes a distinction between mind and body that most of the non-Western world would find strange (Kleinman, 1991; Manson, 1991). Accordingly, depressive symptoms are more likely to be expressed as bodily complaints than subjective, self-oriented distress ("I'm a loser," "no one cares about me") in many cultures. This pattern might be misinterpreted if only Western-based diagnostic tools were used. Similarly, cultures differ in the extent to which it is desirable and acceptable to admit certain experiences, such as suicidal thoughts, that might affect the diagnosis of depressive conditions. Thus, the meaning of different rates of depression in different cultures requires cautious interpretation.

Within the USA, extensive studies have been conducted on ethnic subgroups, permitting evaluation of possible cultural differences separate from socioeconomic status. The National Comorbidity Study-Replication, sampling English-speaking households, found that Hispanics and Blacks both had lower rates of lifetime major depression than did Whites (J. Breslau, Aguilar-Gaxiola, Kendler, Su, Williams, & Kessler, 2005a). However, analysis by age indicated that, among Hispanics, these patterns were accounted for by younger people, as few differences occurred between groups of Whites and Hispanics older than age 43. Blacks showed lower rates of depression compared to Whites at all ages. These authors suggested that factors in childhood such as religious and family values may protect those in disadvantaged groups when young. On the other hand, J. Breslau, Kendler, Su, Gaxiola-Aguilar, & Kessler, (2005b) found that in contrast to patterns of lower major depression occurrence in Blacks and Hispanics, rates of persisting depression including dysthymia were higher among Hispanics and Blacks (see also Riolo, Nguyen, Greden, & King, 2005).

Immigrant status has also been examined for its effects on psychological disorders. A study comparing U.S. and foreign-born Mexican Americans and Whites found that foreign-born groups were at significantly lower risk for mood disorders compared to U.S.-born groups (Grant, Stinson, Hasin, Dawson, Chou, & Anderson, 2004). However, U.S.-born Mexican Americans had higher rates of depression than foreign-born Mexican Americans, suggesting a negative effect of acculturation on mental health, although their rates of depression were lower than those of U.S.-born Whites. Overall, studies of differences in patterns of depression among subgroups within a population can be explored to clarify the cultural beliefs and customs, socioeconomic, and stress factors that affect rates of depression.

Additional social determinants of depression. In earlier studies that examined differences in depression between rural and urban community residents, urban areas generally had higher rates of depression (e.g., Smith & Weissman, 1992), but recent studies in the USA have failed to find such differences (Kessler et al., 2003). On the other hand, the European Epidemiology Study did report higher rates of depressive disorders in large and medium-sized cities compared with rural areas (ESEMeD/MHEDEA 2000 Investigators, 2004).

In general, depression increases with lower social status. Lower income level is generally associated with more depression (e.g., Kessler et al., 2003). Numerous studies have shown that poverty is associated with increased risk for virtually all forms of psychological disorder. Often the correlation is bidirectional: people with disorders are too impaired to sustain work and income, and also poverty is a stress that may overwhelm healthy coping. In order to more closely characterize the causal direction of effect, Bruce et al. (1991) examined the development of new onsets of disorders in previously well people 6 months later among people who were below the poverty line in income. They found that the poor were more than twice as likely to develop major depression as people who were not poor. Of course poverty itself is not the major mechanism causing disorder; it is likely the associated stress, strain, exposure to adversity, and lack of resources to cope with difficulty that contribute to disorder. Such processes are reviewed more extensively in later chapters.

Also, unemployment or employment in lower status occupations are typically more likely associated with depression. Several studies have additionally found that being a homemaker (that is, not employed outside the home) is associated with higher levels of depressive disorder (e.g., G. W. Brown & Harris, 1978; Kessler et al., 2003), as is unemployment (e.g., ESEMeD/MHEDEA 2000 Investigators, 2004). Finally, depression is usually found to be more common among those with lower levels of educational attainment (e.g., ESEMeD/MHEDEA 2000 Investigators, 2004; Kessler et al., 2003).

Finally, marital status is also related to depression. Those who were never married or previously but not currently married report higher rates of depression than the continuously married (ESEMeD/MHEDEA 2000 Investigators, 2004; Kessler et al., 2003). However, it is also apparent that married individuals in unhappy relationships have a high risk for depression. For instance, G. W. Brown and Harris (1978) found that married women who lacked a close, confiding relationship with their partners were 4 times more likely to develop major depression when faced with a major stressor than stressed women who had such a relationship. Associations between depression and marital relationships are discussed in more detail in Chapter 6.

Overall, the demographic correlates of depression–such as gender, age, and social status—help point in the direction of causal factors. Clearly, any biological model of depression must acknowledge the tremendously important social factors that shape distributions of depressive disorders. On the other hand, any psychological models of depression must be able to account for the concentration of depressions among women, the young, and the disadvantaged. In the next chapters, we turn to an exploration of etiological models of depression.

Summary

- Major depression is highly prevalent especially in Westernized cultures, and affects an average of one person in eight during their lifetimes; substantial numbers of people also experience dysthymic disorder or subclinical major depression.
- Depression mainly affects adolescents and young adults, with evidence of increasing rates among young people born in more recent decades compared to older generations. There is some evidence that rates are also elevated in elderly populations.
- Women are twice as likely to experience major depression as men, and gender differences occur across cultures.
- Women's elevated rates of depression emerge in adolescence, and explanations focus on biological factors such as female hormones, women's apparent greater exposure to stressors, and to gender differences in coping styles and resources.
- Besides age and gender, additional sociodemographic factors are associated with elevated rates of depression, including social

disadvantage, cultural differences, and marital status. Thus, theories of the origins of depression must be able to account for diverse social factors that determine who is affected.

Biological aspects of depression 4

Many elements of depression suggest that biological features may be important to understanding its origins. First, the symptoms themselves include physical changes: disruption of sleep schedules (insomnia or too much sleep), appetite changes leading to weight loss or gain, psychomotor changes, and the experience of fatigue, heaviness, and lack of energy. Second, it is well known that depression runs in families—although of course such patterns lend themselves to psychological as well as biological explanations. Third, the apparent success of antidepressant medications is consistent with a biological process in depression—although it would be fallacious to assume that an effective biological treatment implies a fundamental biological cause, since medications might have their effects by stabilizing a process disrupted by psychological factors. Finally, it is also known that certain drugs used to treat medical illnesses may cause depression, and that particular kinds of head injuries and illnesses may also cause depression through biological pathways. These considerations all support the importance of viewing the possible biological origins of depression, and considerable research has been devoted to such issues. This chapter reviews key developments.

Conceptual issues in the biology of depressive disorders

The task of identifying biological factors in depression is enormously complicated by the complexity of the interactions among various processes (e.g., circadian rhythms, neurotransmitters, brain regions, endocrine systems) as well as by the limited understanding of and tools for studying such intricate processes. Compounding the difficulty of drawing useful conclusions, conceptual issues are often ignored. Two such difficulties are briefly discussed here.

Causality vs. correlation.   When depressed and nondepressed groups are compared and yield differences on a biological factor, what is the appropriate conclusion? Frequently, the conclusion or implication drawn is that the factor is of etiological significance—that is, it is the underlying cause of the depression. It is conceivable, even likely, that many biological "differences" simply reflect *consequences* of depression due to changes in sleep, appetite, or activity, or emotional distress. Or, they may be *correlates* of some other unknown process but in themselves have little etiological significance. The increasing use of longitudinal studies that examine depressed people during and after depressive episodes will help to determine which biological parameters are "state-dependent" and simply reflect depression-related changes, and which are more stable. However, even if stable, it may still be difficult to conclude that the biological parameter has causal significance, because it may reflect a residual of the depressive episode itself (a "scar"). Therefore, designs that are not only longitudinal but identify potential subjects at risk for depression before they actually experience episodes may be needed to help clarify the status of the biological factor. It is further necessary to keep in mind that a putative "marker" or indicator of potential vulnerability may itself not have causal significance but may simply be a correlate or indicator of some other process that has etiological features.

This is not to say that "markers" or "correlates" may not be important to study. They may indeed help to clarify the pathophysiological process that occurs when depression is instigated for whatever reason. As such, they may play some important role in understanding the course or indicating a treatment mechanism. Unfortunately, however, they are often assigned causal significance not warranted by the design or data.

Static vs. transactional models.   Another conceptual challenge concerns the nature of the model of biological effects in depression. Some investigators appear to subscribe to simple "main effects" models, such as genetic defects or neuroendocrine dysregulation, implying that such factors are necessary and sufficient causes of depression. However, existing evidence best supports a diathesis-stress model, requiring a pathophysiological diathesis which must be triggered by some environmental or physical stressor. There are two difficulties with this approach, however. One is that there has simply been insufficient attention to an integration of biological and stress or psychosocial factors. Hopefully, this will change with increasing appreciation of the advantages of such models—and a few examples have been presented (or will be discussed in later chapters).

A second difficulty is that diathesis-stress models may tend to be static, focused on the interaction of the two factors but disregarding the potential dynamic mechanisms that might involve the influence of the diathesis and stress on each other. Several recent models, in contrast, suggest a highly transactional influence of the stress, episode, and diatheses on each other over time. For instance, Post (1992) has suggested that repeated episodes of both recurrent uni-polar and bipolar disorder might alter the brain at the cellular level to changes its sensitivity to stress—thus in time producing an organism reacting at such low levels of stress as to have virtually "auto-nomous" episodes. Similarly, Gold, Goodwin, and Chrousos (1988) proposed a model of depression that implicates defective stress regulation. Stemming from a possibly genetically transmitted vulner-ability in stress-homeostatic processes, a child exposed to chronic stress early in life would experience unusually intense and prolonged reactions that lead to the sensitization of critical limbic sites and may damage the homeostatic neuroendocrine processes, predisposing the person to major depression when real or symbolic stressors occur. There is some emergent research indicating a transaction between genetic vulnerabilities and stressful events (e.g., Caspi et al., 2003, Kendler et al., 1995 discussed in more detail later in the chapter), showing that such transactional research is a productive direction for future investigation.

Genetic research in depression

Traditionally, the methods of genetic research have included family studies, twin studies, and, more rarely, adoption designs. Recently, advances in molecular genetics and statistical models have added to the array of methods in a rapidly changing explosion of interest in the genetics of psychopathology.

Family studies

Family studies identify a *proband*, the target participant, and then interview or otherwise obtain information regarding the psychiatric status of each of the proband's primary relatives. The advantage of such studies is that they are reasonably easy to conduct, and therefore a considerable amount of information has been obtained regarding the patterns of familial transmission of unipolar depression. The disadvantage, however, is that results of such methods cannot be attributed entirely to genetic factors, since psychological variables such as being reared with ill relatives or exposed to common depressogenic processes cannot be ruled out as important determinants.

A meta-analysis of the most rigorously controlled family studies (e.g., strict diagnosis procedures and recruitment methods) indicated that major depression is significantly more likely to run in close relatives of a participant with major depressive disorder than in families of probands without depression (Sullivan, Neale, & Kendler, 2000). It is estimated that the rate of major depression in family members is 10% to 25%, which is 2 to 4 times higher than that of controls (Levinson, Zubenko, Crowe, DePaulo, Scheftner, & Weissman, 2003). Several reviews have suggested that heritability is most apparent in depressions that have both early age of onset (variously defined but generally by young adulthood) and a recurrent course (Levinson et al., 2003; Sullivan et al., 2000; Zubenko, Hughes, Stiffler, Zubenko, & Kaplan, 2002). There is also emerging evidence that depressions that are chronic (including dysthymic disorder), or more severe and impairing, are particularly likely to suggest heritable patterns in families (Hayden & Klein, 2001; Levinson, 2006; Mondimore et al., 2006; Sullivan et al., 2000).

Research on the children of depressed parents represents an often-studied version of family patterns of depression. Such research indicates that children of a depressed parent have approximately a 50% chance of developing a disorder of some kind, with possibly 20% to 40% becoming depressed (e.g., Beardslee et al., 1998; see Hammen & Brennan, 2001; Pilowsky et al., 2006). Such research highlights the difficulty of inferring genetic sources of risk for depression based on family studies, since the influence of quality of family life, parent–child relations, and other environmental factors may be nongenetic contributors to disorders in the offspring. The influence of such psychological and social factors is explored in Chapter 6.

Twin studies

Owing to the overlap of environmental and genetic factors operating in families with major depressive disorder, twin and adoption studies offer methods of assessing genetic factors separate from environmental influences. Adoption studies, in which individuals of known genetic lineage are raised in nonparental environments, are quite rare and subject to methodological shortcomings. Sullivan et al. (2000) summarized the limited data from adoption samples and concluded that they were consistent with genetic contributions to major depression.

Many investigators have turned to *twin-study* methods. Since identical (monozygotic) twins share 100% of their genes, they should be more similar to each other in the expression of a disorder (concordance) than would twins who are not identical (dizygotic) and who share an average of 50% of their genes. Twin studies can assess concordance, and, also, through the use of complex statistical analyses, can provide estimates of genetic and environmental contributions to depression. Several large community samples of twins from the USA, Australia, and Sweden, as well as samples based on patients in treatment, have been conducted with modern methods of assessment of depression and zygosity. For instance, Kendler and Prescott (1999) studied 3790 monozygotic and dizygotic male and female twins, and found significantly greater concordance in monozygotic than dizygotic twins, affirming a genetic contribution to depression. In a meta-analysis of well-designed twin studies, Sullivan and colleagues (2000) estimated that the heritability of major depression is in the range of 31% to 42%, which may be characterized as a moderate effect of genetic factors. The results also suggested that the influence of individual environmental factors, such as personal stressful events, is an additional important contributor to depression.

Specific genes and gene–environment associations

Although evidence strongly suggests a moderate genetic component to depression, two issues limit the meaning of such findings. One is that the nature of the genetic mechanisms is unknown. The other is that the genetic effects in depression are relatively modest compared to other major forms of disorder such as schizophrenia or bipolar disorder, while the environmental component of depression is substantial. Fortunately, recent developments in research have provided exciting directions for expanding our understanding of genetic issues in depression.

Search for specific depression-related genes. Recent years have seen rapid development of methods of genetic analysis and increased understanding of the human genome. Nevertheless, there are many methodological and practical barriers to the identification of the specific genetic bases of depression. One such difficulty is the likelihood that there are multiple genes with small effects contributing to complex human behaviours such as depression, making it very difficult to detect and replicate patterns in different samples (e.g., Plomin, DeFries, Craig, & McGuffin, 2003). Different gene-finding strategies include linkage, association, and candidate-gene studies. Linkage analysis is conducted in samples of families with multiple affected members, including sibling pairs or large extended families, seeking patterns in which a known DNA marker is co-inherited with the depression phenotype, suggesting that suscept-ibility for depression is located (and genetically transmitted) near the chromosomal location of the known marker. To date, several chromosomal locations have been noted and await replication and explication (e.g., Camp et al., 2005; Levinson, 2006). Association studies typically involve comparing "cases" and controls to detect differences in genotypes, particularly focused on suspected gene candidates or regions of interest. Candidate-gene studies focus on genes with known function bearing a plausible relationship to mech-anisms of depression. For instance, as reviewed elsewhere in this chapter, neurotransmitter systems, especially the serotonergic system, or hypothalamic-pituitary-adrenal axis and stress reactivity systems have been implicated in depression, and their genetic char-acteristics have recently been the focus of gene-finding research.

Meta-analyses of association studies focused on candidate genes have indicated modest evidence of a serotonin transporter gene polymorphism (5-HTTLPR; Levinson, 2006), but somewhat incon-sistent results for other suspect genes such as brain-derived neuro-trophic factor (BDNF) and others (e.g., Garriock et al., 2006) that may nonetheless eventually prove to be informative as new large-scale studies emerge or as samples are combined in meta-analyses. Inter-estingly, several studies have reported associations of the serotonin transporter polymorphism with neuroticism and related personality traits (reviewed in Levinson, 2006), consistent with twin studies showing not only that neuroticism is genetically transmitted but also that neuroticism predicts susceptibility to depression (e.g., Fanous, Gardner, Prescott, Cancro, & Kendler, 2002; Kendler, Gatz, Gardner, & Pedersen, 2006b). It is intriguing to speculate that one genetic pathway to depression is described in part by serotonergic processes that are expressed as trait neuroticism or something akin to it, which is characterized as negative emotionality and stress reactivity.

Studies of gene–environment interactions. In view of clear evidence of environmental contributions to depression and modest-to-moderate genetic effects, it is unsurprising that the combination of the two may be the strongest predictor of depression rather than either alone. While gene–environment interactions (diathesis-stress models) have long been hypothesized, recent evidence has specifically indicated that depression is substantially more likely to occur when genetically susceptible individuals experience stressful life events. Kendler and colleagues (1995) demonstrated in twin samples that women at greatest genetic risk (they were identical co-twins of depressed women) and who experienced recent stressful life events were more likely to become depressed. In contrast, women at lowest risk for depression (they were identical co-twins of nondepressed women) who experienced a severe life event were significantly less likely to become depressed. The authors suggested that genetic factors influence the risk of depression in part by lowering the sensitivity of individuals to the impact of stressful events. Caspi et al. (2003) were the first to demonstrate that a specific functional polymorphism in the serotonin system, 5-HTTLPR, was predictive of depressive symptoms, diagnoses, and suicidality only in combination with stressful life events. Individuals with two copies of the short allele were significantly more likely than those with one short and one long, or two long alleles, to experience depression if they experienced recent major stressors. The associations between genetic variation and outcomes as a function of stressful life events are illustrated in Figure 4.1. Other groups have now refined and replicated these 5-HTTLPR gene–environment interactions (e.g., Eley et al., 2004; Jacobs, Kenis, Peeters, Derom, Vlietinck, & van Os, 2006; Kendler, Kuhn, Vittum, Prescott, & Riley, 2005b; Wilhelm et al., 2006).

In addition to further replications of existing findings and exploration of additional genetic loci, research is needed to clarify the mechanisms by which genetic factors have their influence on depression outcomes. The serotonin transporter polymorphism implicated in depression in response to stressful life events, for example, may be manifest behaviourally as dysfunctional emotionality in response to stress (neuroticism). Hariri et al. (2005) used neuroimaging techniques to explore how individuals with different polymorphisms of the 5-HTTLPR gene responded to an amygdala activation task involving perception of fearful and angry faces. They found that normal, never-depressed individuals who had the short allele form of the 5-HTTLPR gene showed amygdala hyperreactivity in response to the emotion-arousing stimuli compared to other groups. The results suggest that the serotonin transporter polymorphism is linked to the brain's processing of emotional threat information,

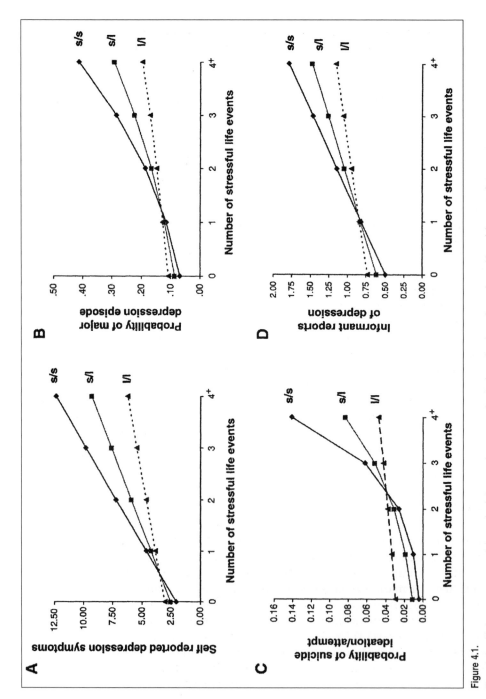

Figure 4.1.

The relationship between stress and depression is increased among people who have the short–short polymorphism of the serotonin transporter gene.

From Caspi, A., Sugden, K., Moffitt, T. E., Taylor, A., Craig, I. W., Harrington, H., McClay, J., Mill, J., Martin, J., Braithwaite, A., and Poulton, R. (2003). Influence of life stress on depression: Moderation by a polymorphism in the 5-HTT gene. *Science, 301*, 386–389. Reprinted with permission from the American Association for the Advancement of Science.

possibly helping to shed further light on neurobiological mechanisms by which stressful environmental experiences eventuate in depression in some people but not in others.

Gene–environment correlations.   Genetic factors may be involved not only in how individuals react to environments but also in gene–environment "correlations" (Rende & Plomin, 1992), including things individuals do to affect the environment or select themselves into certain environments. For example, genetic studies have shown a compelling heritable component in the occurrence of stressful life events (e.g., Kendler et al., 1993b; McGuffin, Katz, & Bebbington, 1988; Plomin, Lichtenstein, Pedersen, McClearn, & Nesselroade, 1990). As we explore in Chapter 5, depressed individuals contribute to the occurrence of stressful life events (e.g., Hammen, 1991b). The characteristics of the person that generate stressors may include behaviours that evoke negative responses from others, or involve dysfunctional problem-solving skills and limited ability to resolve issues before they become acute stressors. For example, Saudino, Pedersen, Lichtenstein, McClearn, and Plomin (1997) found several genetically linked personality variables that predicted controllable and undesirable life events. A number of studies have shown associations between genetically mediated neuroticism and occurrence of stressful life events (e.g., Kendler, Karkowski, & Prescott, 1999; Kendler & Karkowski-Shuman, 1997). Thus, predictors of depression that are often attributed to environmental circumstances may actually include genetic components. Clearly, advances in genetic research will increasingly inform our understanding of risk and its mechanisms.

Neurotransmitters and depression

Historically, there has been considerable interest in the potential role of monoamine neurotransmitters (especially serotonin, norepinephrine, and dopamine) in mood disorders. Neurotransmitters are, of course, the "chemical messengers" by which neurons communicate and link the regions and functions of various parts of the brain. The monoamine neurotransmitters were known to be especially important in the functioning of the limbic system of the brain (amygdala, hippocampus, hypothalamus, and related structures of the "old" brain), areas that play a major role in the regulation of drives (e.g., appetite) and emotion. Limbic system neurotransmitter pathways link this region with other parts of the brain, and also, through the hypothalamus, exert control over the endocrine and autonomic nervous systems (Shelton, 2000; Shelton, Hollon, Purdon, & Loosen, 1991).

In the 1950s, several medications were observed either to cause or decrease depression, and it became known that they had their effects on the central monoamine neurotransmitters. For example, tricyclic antidepressants such as imipramine were found to block the synaptic reuptake of amines into the presynaptic neurons, thus increasing their availability (reviewed in McNeal & Cimbolic, 1986). Based on the apparent monoaminergic effects of drugs, Schildkraut (1965) articulated a catecholamine model of affective disorders that claimed depression results from insufficiencies of the monoamine neurotransmitters (primarily emphasizing norepinephrine and serotonin), while mania resulted from too much. For about two decades, numerous studies of effects of various antidepressant medications focused on the immediate, acute, effects of antidepressant medications on various neurotransmitters.

However, difficulties with the simple catecholamine model became readily apparent. New generations of effective antidepressant medications appeared that did not have the same tricyclic neurotransmitter-increasing effects. Also it became clear that simple theories of excess or deficit were inadequate since antidepressant drugs have immediate effects on increasing neurotransmitters but did not as immediately alter mood. It typically takes several weeks for the depression to diminish. This delayed effect appeared to be more in keeping with a longer-term mechanism, such as changes in the density or sensitivity of receptors in the neurons. Consistent with such a hypothesis, there is now robust evidence from brain imaging and PET (positron emission tomography) studies in living patients that brain serotonin receptors are reduced in patients with major depression (P. A. Sargent et al., 2000; Yatham et al., 2000). Moreover, the serotonin transporter, the protein which is involved in removing serotonin from extracellular regions in the brain sites, is elevated in depressed patients with extreme dysfunctional attitudes (J. H. Meyer et al., 2004). Moreover, as noted earlier, genetic studies have indicated that polymorphisms in the serotonin transporter gene moderate the impact of stressful life events on depressive symptoms and major depression (Caspi et al., 2003; Hariri et al., 2005; Jacobs et al., 2006; Kendler et al., 2005b).

Particular attention has also focused on the expression of neurotrophic factors (e.g., BDNF) necessary for the survival, differentiation, growth, and function of particular neurons (Duman & Monteggia, 2006; Hashimoto, Shimizu, & Iyo, 2004). Such factors are important in neuronal plasticity; that is, the growth and formation of new synaptic connections, underlying learning and memory. It has been hypothesized that decreased expression of neurotrophic factors contributes to the development of depression. First, depression is associated with reduced BDNF, whether assessed through the analysis of postmortem hippocampus or through blood serum levels in patients who have never had antidepressants (Duman & Monteggia, 2006; Shimizu et al., 2003). Second, the expression of neurotrophic factors in limbic structures is reduced by physical and psychological stress, which could in turn contribute to the atrophy of brain structures such as the hippocampus and prefrontal cortex that has been observed in depressed patients (Duman & Monteggia, 2006). Third, antidepressant medications upregulate neurotrophic factors, with this effect occurring at a timescale consistent with the therapeutic effects of pharmacotherapy, and potentially accounting for the reversal of atrophy produced by continued pharmacotherapy (Sheline, 2003).

Neuroendocrine functioning in depression

Humans' responses to stressful situations, mediated by complex biological systems, serve the goal of sustaining existence in the face of threat through a combination of activating survival-related functions and inhibiting less central functions, leading to essential changes in focus of attention, physiological activation, execution of behaviours, and sustained energy necessary to serve actions and protect the body. When stressor threat is no longer salient, the body resumes its normal levels and processes of functioning. However, it has long been known that sustained biological responses to stress may have negative consequences, leading to physiological changes that result in illnesses and psychological disorders.

Considerable attention in depression research has focused on the dysregulation of the stress response. Key components are the hypothalamic-pituitary-adrenal (HPA) axis and the related corticotrophin-releasing hormone (CRH) and locus coeruleus-norepinephrine (LC-NE) systems, that include limbic and cortical pathways bidirectionally interconnected through various neurotransmitter and hormonal circuits (Boyce & Ellis, 2005; S. E. Meyer, Chrousos, & Gold, 2001). In response to perceptions of stress and threat, the neuropeptide CRH is released in the hypothalamus, triggering release of adrenocorticotropic hormone (ACTH) in the anterior pituitary gland. ACTH in turn stimulates release of glucocorticoid hormones that are synthesized in the cortex of the adrenal glands. The primary glucocorticoid hormone is cortisol, which triggers a cascade of functions that are adaptive in the acute phases of response to stress, and which normally resolves quickly through inhibitory feedback processes in the HPA axis. However, failure to normalize, resulting in sustained high cortisol, has deleterious effects giving rise to physiological changes thought to promote a variety of illnesses including hypertension, obesity, heart disease, and various immunologic diseases (e.g., S. E. Meyer et al., 2001; Thase, Jindal, & Howland, 2002a).

Depression has been linked with elevated cortisol and related neurohormones. Numerous studies have indicated higher levels of cortisol and abnormalities in cortisol regulation among depressed compared to nondepressed individuals (e.g., reviewed in Plotsky, Owens, & Nemeroff, 1998; Ribeiro, Tandon, Grunhaus, & Greden, 1993). Furthermore, depressed patients show slower recovery of cortisol levels in response to psychological stress than controls (see meta-analysis by H. M. Burke, Davis, Otte, & Mohr, 2005). Individuals who display evidence of abnormal cortisol regulation even after treatment are more likely to relapse and generally have a poorer clinical prognosis than patients whose cortisol functions returned to normal after treatment (e.g., Ribeiro et al., 1993). Investigators have used biological challenge tests with depressed patients, including administration of synthetic cortisol, dexamethasone (DEX), to observe whether patients display normal or abnormal patterns of return to baseline. Recently, to improve the DEX test, it has been combined with a CRH challenge test, the DEX/CRH test, with studies indicating that abnormalities in test results predict higher risk of relapse in remitted patients (e.g., Aubrey et al., 2007) and worse response to treatment (Brouwer et al., 2006). It appears that sustained hypercortisolism damages the stress system, including death of cells in the hippocampus (Sapolsky, 1996) with generalized effects on the circuits underlying emotion regulation.

It is hypothesized that both genetic and environmental factors account for individual differences in how individuals respond to (and recover from) HPA system activation. Genetic differences in species of animals and nonhuman primates have been shown to be associated with differences in emotional behaviour and glucocorticoid responses to stress (e.g., Boyce & Ellis, 2005; S. E. Meyer et al., 2001). Human genetic polymorphisms in the glucocorticoid receptor (GR) have been hypothesized as a source of impaired negative feedback regulation contributing to hyperactivity of the HPA axis in depression (e.g., Holsboer, 2000). Evidence is emerging of GR polymorphisms associated with increased risk of developing major depression (van Rossum et al., 2006), and differences in response to treatment for depression (e.g., Brouwer et al., 2006; van Rossum et al., 2006).

Adverse environmental factors, especially those associated with early childhood development (or even prenatal exposure), have attracted considerable interest as possible contributors to abnormal biological stress regulation. Gold et al. (1988) speculated that brain circuits associated with stress reactions may have been sensitized as a result of early, acute exposure to stressors such that in adulthood, depressive reactions to stress may be readily activated even by mild or symbolic representations of early stress precipitants. Evidence supports the impact of prenatal and postnatal stress, as well as disruptions of the parent–child bond, on abnormalities of HPA functioning in animal and human subjects (reviewed in Heim & Nemeroff, 2001; Kaufman, Plotsky, Nemeroff, & Charney, 2000; S. E. Meyer et al., 2001; Plotsky et al., 1998). Moreover, considerable research such as that reviewed in Chapter 6 on social relations and depression indicates an association between early childhood adversities and later depression. Limited but increasing evidence draws links between all three: early adversity, abnormalities of the HPA, CRH, and LC-NE systems, and depression. For instance, Essex, Klein, Cho, and Kalin (2002) assessed cortisol levels in 4.5-year-olds, and found that children who had been exposed to maternal stress both in infancy and concurrently had significantly higher levels of cortisol than nonstressed children or those exposed only to either but not both periods of maternal stress. Moreover, the children with elevated cortisol had higher rates of behavioural and emotional symptoms (especially internalizing symptoms) approximately 2 years later. Although not specifically about depression, the results are consistent with the idea that early stress exposure predicts elevated cortisol when stress occurs later in life, and the pattern is predictive of later symptomatology. Heim and colleagues (2000) compared groups of women who had been sexually or physically abused in childhood and who were currently depressed or not depressed with those who were depressed without abuse, and controls with no abuse and no depression. Compared on various measures of HPA axis functioning, the results were consistent with the hypothesis that early abuse experience is associated with cortisol hyperreactivity among the depressed women compared with other groups.

Overall, given the critical role of stressful events and circumstances as precipitants of depression, research on neuroendocrine processes of stress reactivity holds considerable promise as an illustration of the importance of integrative biopsychosocial models of depression. Emerging theories and data help to shed light on why some individuals develop depression in the face of stress while others do not, and remind us of the need for models in which bidirectional transactions among biological and environmental processes mould the person over the course of development. Such models also remind us of the complexity of multiple interacting biological systems with many questions about both normal and dysfunctional development remaining to be resolved.

Circadian rhythm dysregulation

For some depressed persons, a pattern of recurrent episodes of depression, and the symptoms such as worse mood in the morning (diurnal variation) and early morning awakening have, along with other biological findings, led to the speculation that some depressions (including bipolar affective disorders) may stem in part from some disruption of the circadian rhythms. Circadian rhythms are normal cycles of physical and behavioural processes, such as those that follow a 24-hour course linked with day–night changes. Sleep patterns, body temperature, and certain hormonal fluctuations (e.g., melatonin and cortisol) are among the processes that follow a circadian rhythm pattern. For instance, as noted earlier, depressed patients show HPA-axis dysregulation, including more erratic patterns of everyday cortisol secretion (Peeters, Nicolson, & Berkhof, 2004; Yehuda, Teicher, Trestman, Levengood, & Siever, 1996) and reduced 24-hour cortisol amplitude (Posener, DeBattista, Williams, Kraemer, Kalehzan, & Schatzberg, 2000).

Sleep disturbance patterns. A number of studies have found disruption in sleep patterns, both behavioural and as measured by EEG recordings. For example, over the past 35 years, three sleep pattern abnormalities have been well documented in depressed patients (Riemann, Berger, & Voderholzer, 2001; Tsuno, Besset, & Ritchie, 2005). One is sleep continuity problems, including difficulty falling asleep or staying asleep, and waking up early. These abnormalities are present in about 80% of people in a major depression, although they are not limited to depressive conditions (Ford & Kamerow, 1989). A second abnormality is decreased slow-wave (delta) sleep, as recorded by brainwave activity during sleep. The third abnormality is alterations in the nature and timing of Rapid Eye Movement (REM) sleep. In 50% of depressed patients, the interval between sleep onset and the occurrence of the first period of REM sleep is shortened, less than 60 minutes, compared to 1–2 hours for nondepressed people. There is also increased REM sleep; a prolongation of the first REM period and increased number of eye movements during REM periods (REM density). These patterns are most apparent in patients with more severe symptoms and with a history of recurrent major depression (Jindal et al., 2002; Thase et al., 1995; Thase, Kupfer, Fasiczka, Buysse, Simons, & Frank, 1997). Moreover, sleep disturbance is a prospective predictor of the onset of an episode of major depression (Breslau et al., 1996; Chang, Ford, Mead, Cooper-Patrick, & Klag, 1997; Riemann & Voderholzer, 2003) and acts as a prodromal symptom in the 5 weeks prior to the recurrence of a depressive disorder (Perlis, Giles, Buysse, Tu, & Kupfer, 1997), suggesting that disturbed sleep may be a vulnerability factor for depression.

There has been some debate as to the extent to which abnormal sleep EEG patterns normalize during remission from the depressed episode, with a number of studies showing that certain sleep abnormalities including reduced REM latency and reduced slow-wave sleep were maintained during remission of symptoms, whereas sleep disturbance and REM density reversed on symptomatic improvement (Jindal et al., 2002; Thase, Fasiczka, Berman, Simons, & Reynolds, 1998). These results suggest either that the former are stable traits—possibly serving as markers for future risk of relapse—or possibly they do return to normal levels with the passage of time (Riemann et al., 2001).

Antidepressant medication treatment invariably suppresses REM sleep, and some have even argued that this effect may be a critical process in reducing depression (Duncan, 1996; Riemann et al., 2001; Winokur, Gary, Rodner, Rae-Red, Fernando, & Szuba, 2001). There is some evidence that in drug-free depressed patients, more abnormal sleep profiles predicted worse treatment response to psychotherapies, suggesting that sleep abnormalities indicate more severe neurophysiological substrates for depression that warrant pharmacotherapy (Thase et al., 1997).

Studies of depressed children and adolescents have found mixed results, with some studies replicating the findings in adults, but other studies failing to demonstrate clear sleep abnormalities. Six out of 10 adolescent studies have found shortened REM latency and 5 out of 10 reported sleep disturbance (see summary in Rao et al., 2002). Maturational factors are one potential source of the variable and inconsistent results. Because of the brain's continuing development during adolescence, "adult" sleep patterns may not always have yet occurred. Another source of inconsistencies may be methodological issues, in that early-onset (adolescent) depressives may contain a heterogeneous sample that includes undiagnosed bipolars while the control samples may include persons who are at risk for depression but have not yet shown it. Rao et al. (1996) followed adolescent depressives for an average of 7 years, and were able to differentiate those with recurrent unipolar depression and those who never developed depression. When the depressed and control groups were compared on their initial sleep data collected during adolescence, they differed in the predicted fashion on REM density and REM latency (Rao et al., 1996). Interestingly, these "depressive" patterns were also observed among the initially normal controls who went on to develop depression over the course of the follow-up. Furthermore, in a re-analysis of this sample, separating those who had a unipolar depression course from those patients who had a bipolar course, the expected pattern of shortened REM latency was found in unipolar depression but not in bipolar depression (Rao et al., 2002).

Taken together, the abnormal patterns of circadian rhythm functions such as cortisol secretion and sleep disturbances have suggested a dysfunction of some type. One hypothesis is that there is a disorganization or desynchronization of different cycles in relation to each other. Normally, REM patterns and cortisol fluctuate in synchrony with the sleep–wake cycle. Early morning awakening, diurnal variation, and the abnormalities noted have suggested a "phase advance" of the REM and cortisol secretion circadian rhythms in relation to the sleep–wake cycle. The desynchrony results in biological disturbances causing the symptoms of depression. Interestingly, sleep deprivation has been shown to reduce depression, at least temporarily, possibly by bringing the circadian rhythms back into alignment with each other (Giedke & Schwarzler, 2002).

Circadian rhythms are related to day–night patterns, which of course are affected by season of the year. As noted in Chapter 1, a subgroup of depressed patients (including both unipolar and bipolar disorders) experience SAD marked by depression at certain times of the year (usually winter months in the Northern Hemisphere). We know that animal behaviours are highly affected by changes in light and temperature, with hibernation in winter months associated with decreased activity and increased sleep. It has also been speculated that mood disorders might represent exaggerated seasonal variations. In general, it appears that more depressions occur in the Autumn and Winter (F. K. Goodwin & Jamison, 1990). Thus, one mechanism of depression (or at least SAD) might be abnormalities in light sensitivity or circadian rhythm functioning in response to detection of light. Consistent with this hypothesis, patients with SAD demonstrate prolonged nocturnal melatonin secretion in Winter relative to Summer that is absent in healthy controls, indicating a greater biological sensitivity to these seasonal changes and their effect on circadian rhythms in SAD (Wehr et al., 2001). There is also evidence that patients with SAD have circadian rest–activity rhythms that are significantly phase delayed and less well entrained to the 24-hour day, and that these circadian rhythms can be phase advanced by phototherapy (Teicher et al., 1997; Winkler et al., 2005).

Moreover, it should be noted that HPA-axis functioning and circadian rhythms are not independent of neurotransmitter functioning. Indeed, complex relationships between these systems and acetylcholine, serotonin, norepinephrine, and dopamine have been noted (Riemann et al., 2001). Thus, while investigators are gaining increased knowledge about various abnormalities associated with depression, their role as causal factors remains unclear, and their mechanisms of operation remain to be described.

Brain structure and functioning in depression

Individuals who sustain injuries or strokes in the frontal part of the brain have often been observed to display depression. Higher rates of depression are found in neurologic illnesses associated with cortical and subcortical atrophy including stroke, Huntington's disease, epilepsy, Parkinson's disease, and Alzheimer's dementia (Sheline, 2003). Similarly, mild traumatic brain injury is a prospective predictor of onset of major depression in long-term follow-up studies (Holsinger et al., 2002; Koponen et al., 2002). One condition, *poststroke depression*, has been estimated to affect 30% to 50% of individuals after acute stroke. The quality of the depression is indistinguishable from major depressive episodes not caused by medical problems. These illnesses involve damage to limbic brain structures critical in emotional arousal and control (hippocampus, thalamus, amygdala, and basal ganglia), as well as damage to the prefrontal cortex which modulates and regulates activity in the limbic system, in addition to serving higher intellectual functions such as planning. It has therefore been hypothesized that abnormalities and dysfunctions within this neuroanatomic circuit may account for the symptomatology of depression (Sheline, 2003).

Building on such observations and hypotheses, investigators have investigated the possibility of brain abnormalities in depressed patients. Magnetic resonance imaging (MRI) scanning studies, for example, have provided evidence of structural abnormalities in the frontal regions of unipolar depressed patients, including volume reductions in prefrontal cortex relative to controls (Drevets, 1998, 2001; Drevets et al., 1997). There is also extensive evidence for reduced hippocampus volumes in depression, with greater hippo-campal loss associated with longer durations of depressive illness (Sheline, Sanghavi, Mintun, & Gado, 1999) and with greater memory dysfunction (MacQueen et al., 2003). These structural changes are consistent with the neuroendocrine and neurotransmitter processes reviewed above: both the neurotoxicity associated with elevated cortisol levels resulting from HPA-axis dysfunction, and the down-regulation of neurotrophic factors necessary for neuronal growth could cause reduction in prefrontal and hippocampal volumes.

Functional brain imaging (e.g., fMRI and PET scanning) has further investigated the activity of different brain areas by assessing cerebral blood flow and glucose metabolism in depressed patients. These studies have indicated that during the resting state without any mental or emotional task, patients with depression show reduced activity in the dorsolateral prefrontal cortex and anterior cingulate cortex (R. J. Davidson et al., 2002; Drevets, 1998; Drevets et al., 1997), with this functional activity normalized following successful treatment (e.g., Brody et al., 2001). These regional changes in brain activation in major depression partially mirror those found during functional brain imaging of healthy controls following the induction of sad mood (Mayberg et al., 1999). In addition, mood provocation produced different patterns of brain activation in currently depressed and remitted depressed patients compared to normal controls during PET: both sets of patients showed decreases in cerebral blood flow in orbitofrontal cortex, and remitted depressed patients also showed decreases in cerebral blood flow in anterior cingulate cortex (Liotti, Mayberg, McGinnis, Brannan, & Jerabek, 2002). Interestingly, this differential brain activation response to mood challenge in remitted depressed patients compared to nondepressed controls parallels the differential activation of dysfunctional (depressive) attitudes in response to mood challenge, which is discussed in Chapter 5.

A further method for assessing cortical functioning is electro-physiological (EEG) recording. Davidson and his colleagues (R. J. Davidson et al., 2002; R. J. Davidson & Irwin, 1999) reviewed evidence from various sources, concluding that depression is associated with reduced left prefrontal cortex activation relative to right prefrontal cortex activation, consistent with experimental studies showing a role for right prefrontal cortex activation in negative affect. This pattern of activation is also found in formerly depressed patients. Interestingly, repeated transcranial magnetic stimulation (rTMS) at high frequency (which is presumed to have an excitatory effect on cortical activity) to the left dorsolateral prefrontal cortex (DLPFC) significantly reduces depressive symptoms, whereas low-frequency rTMS (which is pre-sumed to have an inhibitory effect on cortical activity) to the right DLPFC significantly reduces depressive symptoms (for further details see Chapter 7). This pattern suggests a potential causal relationship between brain activation and symptoms.

Thus, together these findings from structural and functional imaging, EEG recordings and rTMS indicate that dysfunctions in the neuroanatomical circuit between prefrontal cortex and limbic regions may play a role in the development of depression. Of course, it is still difficult to interpret the relationship between brain functioning and depression, particularly given the complex dynamic relationships between neurotransmitters, neuroendocrine response, stress, brain activity, and functional neuroanatomy. Furthermore, it is difficult to disentangle whether changes in brain structure and functioning are causes of depression, consequences of depression or, as is most probable, both cause and consequence.

The role of female hormones in depression

In view of the robust gender differences in depression as noted in Chapter 3, it has been common to speculate that female hormones likely play an important role in women's greater incidence of depres-sive disorders. There are four hormonally relevant phases of women's reproductive life that have been linked to depression: the emergence of the gender difference around the time of puberty; PMDD and mood shifts during the premenstrual phase; postpartum depression; and depression during menopause and perimenopause.

Attributing depression in women to hormonal causes has been fraught with controversy over the years, and the research examining the linkages has been marred by imprecise methods of assessing hormones, overly simplistic models, small sample sizes, or generally questionable methods of measuring moods. However, new discoveries about brain–hormone relationships, methods of measuring hormones, and improved research designs have contributed promising leads. Unfortunately, we have learned that the extremely complex associations among neurotransmitter and neuroendocrine systems and fluctuating levels of gonadal hormones do not yield clear understanding of their link to depression in women. Moreover, a host of potential genetic and environmental factors appear to modify the associations among hormones, neurobiological variables, and depression. Thus, while increasing evidence points to a role for gonadal hormones in depression, the effects are generally small and work in complex ways with neuroregulatory circuits in currently uncharted processes that may be modified by psychosocial variables.

Pubertal changes and depression. Given the dramatic divergence of rates of depression in males and females beginning in early adolescence, many investigators have suspected that hormonal changes occurring during pubertal development are causally related to depression. In contrast, others have pointed to pubertal timing, rather than pubertal status, arguing that the social and psychological changes accompanying puberty, rather than puberty as such, are challenging and stressful, and may lead to depression. Thus, according to this latter model, girls who mature early compared to other girls may experience unwelcome weight gain, and may attract unwanted attention from males—whereas early maturing boys would welcome their bodily changes and increased masculine features and possibly enjoy protection from depression. Angold, Costello, and Worthman (1998) conducted a large-scale longitudinal study of 9, 11, and 13-year olds, which included assessment of depression and physical changes associated with pubertal development. They found that pubertal status predicted depression better than did age, and that pubertal timing was unrelated to depression. Only after mid-puberty did girls' rates of depression exceed those of boys. This particular study was not able to clarify the mechanisms accounting for depression, whether hormonal or psychosocial. However, in a later analysis, Angold and colleagues (1999) evaluated the contributions of several specific hormones to depression in the same sample. They found that levels of estrogen and testosterone significantly predicted probability of depressive disorder in girls, and that physical bodily changes associated with pubertal development were not related to depression when hormone levels were included in a predictive model. Thus, the results support a direct effect of hormones on negative emotional states. However, the authors caution that the hormones have their effects in concert with psychosocial factors such as personality vulnerabilities and stressors, accounting for patterns in which girls with similar hormonal levels may differ in depressive reactions to stressful events.

The complete picture of how hormones work to increase adolescent girls' likelihood of depression is far from clear. Fluctuating levels of gonadal hormones introduce changes in other systems such as the HPA axis, requiring adjustments and maturation of the feedback mechanisms that might alter responsiveness to stress (Steiner, Dunn, & Born, 2003). Such complex stress-regulatory systems may play an important role in girls' increased depression given the solid evidence that adolescent girls' rates of exposure to stressors, especially interpersonal, are higher than those of boys (e.g., Cyranowski et al., 2000; Shih et al., 2006). Therefore, further research is clearly needed to develop complete models linking hormonal, neuroendocrine, and psychological processes in susceptibility to onset of depression in adolescence.

Premenstrual dysphoric disorder. PMDD, noted in Chapter 1, describes a severe, recurring, and impairing form of the milder and more common premenstrual syndrome, or PMS. Both are defined by negative affect, moodiness, irritability, and physical symptoms whose occurrence are limited to the luteal (postovulatory) phase of the menstrual cycle, remitting soon after the menstrual cycle begins. Recent research findings are consistent with understanding these conditions as biological in nature, rather than as sociopolitical labels demeaning of women or mood instability due mainly to personality or psychological vulnerability. For instance, there appears to be a heritable component to premenstrual disorders (Kendler, Karkowski, Corey, & Neale, 1998), and symptoms are eliminated with medical or surgical interventions (e.g., Steiner et al., 2003). Research has not yet clarified the mechanisms involved, but recent studies suggest that there are normal hormonal levels and activities, but possibly abnormal sensitivity to the serotonergic system which operates in a close reciprocal relationship with gonadal hormones (Steiner et al., 2003). Consistent with a possible role of the serotonergic neurotransmitter system, SSRI antidepressants appear to be effective treatments for the symptoms of PMS or PMDD (Steiner & Born, 2000). Moreover, SSRI antidepressant medications work substantially faster and are still effective when administered intermittently only during the premenstrual phase in PMDD but not in major depression (Steiner, 2000).

Postpartum depression. Postpartum depression may refer to three distinct phenomena: "baby blues", major depression, and postpartum psychosis. Postpartum blues occur in a substantial percentage of women in the first few days after birth. Symptoms of crying, sadness, and upset are short-lived and rarely treated. They are thought to be consequences of the dramatic drops in estrogen and progesterone levels that normally occur at birth. "Baby blues" are normal, resolve quickly, and do not resemble the clinical condition of depression. Postpartum major depression, on the other hand, meets criteria for major depression and may occur in 10% to 15% of women after birth. Since only a minority of women experience such depression, they are clearly not an inevitable response to hormonal changes. Women who do develop postpartum depression appear to be at increased risk for developing future depressive episodes, as indicated in a 4½-year follow-up (Philipps & O'Hara, 1991). As noted in Chapter 1, premenstrual dysphoric disorder, low mood in the first 2 to 4 days postpartum, experiencing stressful events during pregnancy, low social support and a previous history of depression all predict increased risk for postpartum depression (Bloch et al., 2005; O' Hara & Swain, 1996; Robertson et al., 2004).

Postpartum major depressions may also be related to large changes in hormones and cortisol (Weissman & Olfson, 1995). Recent research has also suggested that since pregnancy is associated with hyperactivity of the HPA axis, major hormonal and CRH changes after birth may lead to a prolonged state of HPA-axis hypoactivity (Steiner et al., 2003), triggering depressive symptoms.

About one woman in 1000 has a psychotic postpartum depression with delusions (postpartum psychosis) with rapid onset after childbirth. Women who have had one such postpartum psychosis have an elevated risk for subsequent such episodes. It is believed that most such cases occur among women with bipolar disorder. Extreme forms of such psychotic depressions may include the risk of suicide or infanticide. As Weissman and Olfson (1995) point out, it may be speculated that postpartum psychotic depressions could be linked to low estrogen levels through a sensitization of the central dopamine receptors. However, the rarity of the disorder has contributed to limited research on its mechanisms.

Depression associated with menopausal changes. Clinical lore has long promoted the idea that women's chances of depression increase when she is going through menopausal changes in mid-life. Research on the topic often presented mixed results about whether depression was related to menopausal status as such or to pre-existing depression histories and vulnerabilities and increased stressful life events during middle age. Increasingly consistently, epidemiological studies have indicated higher levels of depressive symptoms in perimenopausal women compared to those not yet entering menopause (e.g., Bromberger, Assmann, Avis, Schocken, Kravitz, & Cordal, 2003). L. S. Cohen, Soares, Vitonis, Otto, and Harlow (2006) conducted a longitudinal study of women who were initially between 36 and 46-years-old, and who had never experienced an episode of major depression. Over a period of about 6 years of study, women who entered the perimenopausal transition developed 2 times the rate of major depression compared to women who remained premenopausal. These authors also found that the experience of significant stressful life events contributed to likelihood of depression, and suggested that the changing hormonal environment may be a risk factor for depressive reactions should stressors be encountered during the perimenopausal period.

Freeman, Sammel, Lin, and Nelson (2006) also conducted a longitudinal study of premenopausal women with no prior history of depression. They found that entering the perimenopausal transition was associated with significantly higher rates of depressive symptoms and diagnoses of depression compared to premenopausal women. They also examined the levels of various hormones of the reproductive cycle and found that higher or more variable levels (comparing each woman's to her own baseline) were predictive of depressive symptoms or diagnoses. For example, fluctuations in estradiol predicted increased likelihood of symptoms and diagnoses.

Taken together, research on puberty, premenstrual mood changes, postpartum depression, and menopausal depression all show some evidence that depression rates may be associated with changes and fluctuations in hormonal activity that occur throughout women's lives. However, the findings also implicate complex interactions among hormones and neurobiological processes that make it difficult to attribute depression to hormones as such. Moreover, Steiner et al. (2003) note that since hormonal changes occur in all women while mood disorders occur in only a minority, genetic factors may also contribute to individual differences in how the hormones affect the body's reactions to stresses in the environment. Hormonal issues may add to the excess rates of depression in women compared to men, but are among multiple contributing factors with complex interactions.

Summary

- Overall, there is no definitive biological theory of the cause of depression, although there is increasingly convergent evidence consistent with a transaction between genetic vulnerabilities, HPA-axis dysregulation, impaired response to stress, and changes in brain structure and functioning focused on the prefrontal cortex and limbic system.
- Twin studies, family patterns, and progress in studies of specific depression-related genes suggest that some depressions have a genetic component, although the genetic vulnerability may be expressed in the context of environmental stress.
- Although antidepressant medications alter neurotransmitter functioning, there is no valid, simple theory that depression is due to excess or deficits of particular neurotransmitters. Rather, there is encouraging preliminary evidence that neurotransmitters may work via acting on longer-term processes such as the regulation of the number of neurotransmitter binding receptors and signaling cascades that influence neurotrophic factors.
- Abnormal levels and regulation of cortisol suggest that depression is related to a defect in the stress response system.
- Sleep abnormalities, as well as cortisol abnormalities and seasonal patterns of depression, are consistent with a model of some depressions as a biological rhythm disturbance.
- Female hormones have been hypothesized as a crucial factor in the excess of female depression, with increasing evidence that hormonal changes may affect vulnerability to develop depressive symptoms.
- Further integrations of biological and psychological models of depression are needed.

Cognitive and life stress approaches to depression 5

Sarah sips her coffee as she gazes out the window onto the busy street. She watches men and women walk briskly toward their destinations, and imagines that their lives are filled with purpose and meaning—but believes that hers will never be—no interesting job to go to, no eager completion of tasks, no important goal to pursue for the future. She watches couples pass the window, laughing and conversing, and feels a pang of loss. "I'll never have a relationship again," she thinks, "no one would want me, and I'll always be alone." As she often does these days, she leaves the coffee shop unrefreshed and feeling even worse than when she came in.

Sarah's reveries are typical of those of depressed people: a relentless focus on the negative aspects of herself, the world, and her future. Such thoughts are usually exaggerations or misperceptions of reality, but invariably they leave the person feeling overwhelmed and hopeless, accentuating or prolonging the symptoms of his or her depression. Many theorists argue that such negative thinking is not only part of the syndrome of depression, but may indeed reveal a vulnerability to develop depression or to experience recurrences—to the extent that such negativity of thinking is part of the person's *typical* way of perceiving the self and the world. In this chapter several of these models that emphasize primarily *cognitive* causes of depression are reviewed and evaluated.

Suppose that we also discover that Sarah's life changed dramatically a month ago, when her fiancé broke off their relationship. She had dreamed of their life together, and was overwhelmed with hurt and anger when he told her he had found someone else. Her feelings rapidly turned into depression. As with Sarah, many people who experience major depressive episodes are reacting to undesirable negative life events. The role of stressful events and adverse life conditions has long been recognized as a contributor to depression, and in the second part of this chapter, we analyse this approach to understanding depression.

Cognitive and information-processing models of depression

Among psychological models of depression, no approach has stimulated more research in the last 40 years than the cognitive model of Aaron Beck (A. T. Beck, 1967, 1976) and several subsequent cognitive approaches (for recent reviews see A. T. Beck, 2005; D. A. Clark, Beck, & Alford, 1999). Although trained in the psychoanalytic perspective on depression that viewed the condition as introjected anger toward a lost relationship, more than anything Beck was struck by the negative thinking of his patients, the expressions of self-criticism and blame, the exaggeration of misfortune, and the beliefs about personal helplessness and futility. He observed that such thoughts were dysfunctional—representing apparent distortions of reality and serving to prolong or exacerbate the symptoms of depression. Therefore, he formulated a cognitive model of depression with three key elements: the *"cognitive triad," faulty information processing*, and *negative self-schemas*.

The *cognitive triad* refers to characteristic thinking that emphasizes negative expectations, interpretations, perceptions, and memories about the self, the world, and the future. Defeated, self-critical, and hopeless thoughts were believed to contribute to the mood, behavioural, physiological, and motivational deficits in depression. Moreover, Beck argued that depressive thinking is typically distorted, that individuals selectively attend to the negative even when alternative positive events and interpretations are plausible, and they greatly overgeneralize and magnify adversity while minimizing or misinterpreting positive information. These information-processing errors in attention and reasoning are not deliberate or conscious, but rather they happen spontaneously and *automatically*. As in the example of Sarah earlier, there is no basis for her to conclude that she will never have a meaningful career or relationship—but her mood colours her thoughts in distorted ways, always emphasizing the negative.

The third component of Beck's model is the idea of a *negative self-schema*. The schema concept has a long history in psychology, generally referring to organized representations of experiences in memory that serve as a kind of mental filter, guiding the selection, interpretation, and recall of information. Schemas are essential to all human information processing, serving the goals of speed and efficiency so that attention can be directed to "meaningful" information instead of laboriously processing all available information. Thus, by selectively attending to or interpreting certain information, schemas help fill in "missing" information based on what is "expected." A schema about "JOHN" for example (tall, dark hair) helps us to rapidly spot him in a crowd, without seeing his face and without inspecting each and every person. Because they are like pre-existing filters or theories, however, errors are possible (e.g., we stop searching for John when we spot a tall, dark-haired man, but later discover that it wasn't John, who was actually sitting down so that we "ignored" him in our search for tall, dark-haired men).

A *self-schema* refers to organized beliefs and propositions about the self, and according to Beck, the depression-prone person holds negative beliefs (or a mixture of negative and positive). These beliefs may be acquired in childhood, possibly as a result of critical or rejecting parents, and because the schema is selective in "taking in" only confirmatory negative information, beliefs are retained despite accumulated evidence to the contrary. That is, a person who believes that it is terribly important to be perfect at all times and believes that he or she is basically incompetent is likely to pay attention to examples that support this belief while ignoring disconfirming information.

Situations that are stressful and remind the individual of circumstances that were originally responsible for the acquisition of negative self-views are especially likely to activate the negative schema. Thus, a child often scolded for making mistakes might react to a poor exam performance with the "incompetence" self-schema. When activated, it directs his or her attention to any perceived flaws and exaggerates their significance, makes memories available that remind him or her of past shortcomings, and leads to thoughts about the future that include expectations of failure.

Beck has modified his views in various ways over time, an important change being the hypothesis that there are individual personality differences that define the types of negative events or instigators of depression, and that different symptom subtypes of depression might result from such personality differences (D. A. Clark et al., 1999). For example, a *sociotropic* personality style defines someone who bases self-worth on connections with and approval from other people. An *autonomous* personality style refers to someone whose sense of worth is based on achievement and independence.

Vulnerability, therefore, pertains to the dysfunctional beliefs and thoughts that are activated when events matching the content of the personality domain occur that are interpreted as depletions of self-worth.

Other cognitive models of depression

In addition to Beck's seminal model of depression, several variants of cognitive theories have been developed in recent years.

Helplessness and hopelessness models of depression. Martin Seligman and his colleagues originally observed that animals who had been exposed to uncontrollable aversive conditions failed to take action to escape such situations when outcomes were no longer uncontrollable, as if they had learned to be helpless. Seligman applied this hypothesis to human depression, suggesting that when one has erroneous expectations that no control is possible (in obtaining desirable outcomes or preventing undesirable ones), one fails to take action and experiences depressive symptoms. Later, the model was refined to include the individual's perceptions of the *causes* of uncontrollable outcomes. Abramson, Seligman, and Teasdale (1978) developed the *attributional model* that linked depression to the tendency to ascribe the causes of negative events to qualities of the self that are perceived to be unchanging and pervasive. In contrast, negative outcomes attributed to unstable or specific causes would produce less negative responses. It was further argued that some people characteristically show a "negative explanatory style" of stable, global, and internal causal attributions for negative events, and transient, local, and external causal attributions for positive events (Abramson et al., 1978). That is, when something bad or undesirable happens, those vulnerable to depression are more likely to believe that it was caused by global and persisting qualities of themselves that presumably are undesirable and unchangeable. This "negative explanatory style" is contrasted with the more typical "self-serving attributional style," where people make more internal, stable, and global attributions for positive events than for negative events. A recent meta-analysis indicates that in healthy controls there is a large self-serving attributional bias—an often illusory emphasis on their positive attributes—which is reduced in groups with psychopathology, most particularly in patients with depression (Mezulis, Abramson, Hyde, & Hankin, 2004).

A further variant of the attributional model is the *hopelessness model* of depression (Abramson et al., 1989; Alloy et al., 1999). In this model, hopelessness (consisting both of negative expectations about the occurrence of a highly valued outcome and perceptions of helplessness to change the likelihood of the outcomes) is the cognition that immediately causes depressive reactions. In turn, hopelessness is the outcome of negative life events that are interpreted negatively, in terms of stable and global causal attributions for the event, or inferred negative consequences of the event and/or inferred negative characteristics of the self given the event's occurrence. The increased use of negative cognitive styles such as hopelessness and the negative explanatory style has been linked to early experiences of childhood sexual and emotional maltreatment, and to personality disorders and more severe depression (Gibb, 2002; Gibb et al., 2001; Rose, Abramson, Hodulik, Halberstadt, & Leff, 1994).

Problem-solving, self-focus, and rumination models. There have been additional approaches to depression that emphasize dysfunctional cognitions. There is not sufficient space to present them all in detail, but they have been influential with many of their elements incorporated into the information-processing or other broad models.

Nezu and colleagues (Nezu, 1987; Nezu & Perri, 1989) proposed a *problem-solving deficit* model of depression in which depression results from and is perpetuated by ineffective skills in problem solving when stressful events occur. Although not exclusively cognitive in its focus on actual problem-solving skills, the model emphasizes several cognitive elements of problem solving such as perceiving and defining problems and difficulties in generating and selecting alternative solutions.

Several investigators have noted that depressed people exhibit a heightened state of self-awareness, or *self-focused attention* (Ingram, 1990; Pyszczynski & Greenberg, 1987). During such inward focus, individuals invariably magnify their negative appraisals of themselves and the significance and meaning of their negative experiences. Pyszczynski and Greenberg (1987) and Ingram (1990) proposed that self-focus increases negative affect and self-criticism, magnifies the perceived negative consequences of undesirable events, and potentially interferes with appropriate social and adaptive functioning, thereby contributing to a vicious cycle. A recent meta-analysis of experimental and longitudinal studies of self-focus has confirmed the negative consequences on affect of self-focus during sad mood (Mor & Winquist, 2002).

A related version of this approach has been proposed by Nolen-Hoeksema, as noted in Chapter 3 (1991) as an explanation for sex differences in depression, and as a theory about vulnerability to depression. She proposed that a *ruminative* response to depression, characterized by repeated focus on self, feelings, symptoms, and the causes, meanings, and consequences of these symptoms and feelings, is a typically passive style of responding to dysphoric feelings that leads to the exacerbation of symptoms. This theory proposes that rumination is unhelpful because it exacerbates existing negative affect, impairs problem solving, increases selective focus on negative interpretations, and impairs motivation to engage in helpful, instrumental actions. Consistent with this theory, a number of naturalistic and experimental studies have supported the idea that rumination, compared with distraction, is associated with more dysphoria, less effective problem solving, and more negative thinking about the self and future, but only in participants who are already dysphoric (Lyubomirsky & Nolen-Hoeksema, 1995; Lyubomirsky, Tucker, Caldwell, & Berg, 1999; Nolen-Hoeksema, 1991; Nolen-Hoeksema, Morrow, & Fredrickson, 1993). Rumination has no effect on mood and cognition in individuals with normal mood; rather it serves to exacerbate an individual's response to existing stress and difficulties. Moreover, prospective longitudinal studies have demonstrated that increased self-reported rumination in response to depressed mood predicts increased risk for future onset of diagnosable depression (Nolen-Hoeksema, 2000; Spasojevic & Alloy, 2001) and increased maintenance of depressed symptoms in currently depressed patients (Kuehner & Weber, 1999; Nolen-Hoeksema, 2000). Recent work has suggested that there are distinct subtypes of rumination, with only the more abstract, evaluative, and self-judgmental form of ruminative self-focus (sometimes called "brooding") implicated in the detrimental consequences of rumination on depressed mood, autobiographical memory, and problem solving (Treynor, Gonzalez, & Nolen-Hoeksema, 2003; Watkins & Moulds, 2005; Watkins & Teasdale, 2001).

Self-concept in depression. A frequent theme in many of the cognitive models of depression is that of negative views of the self, a deep-seated belief that one is defective, unworthy, unwanted, or incapable of obtaining or keeping important sources of meaning and gratification. J. E. Roberts and Monroe (1994) note, however, that overall self-esteem in terms of conscious feelings of self-worth is not a reliable predictor of depression. Instead, they propose a multidimensional approach to characterizing self-esteem, in which dysfunctions of the self that contribute to vulnerability include (1) structural deficits, such as few, rigid, or externally based sources of self-worth; (2) abnormally low self-esteem that is "primed" by either mildly depressed mood or stressful events; and (3) temporal instability and lability of self-esteem. Consistent with this analysis, a number of prospective longitudinal studies have found that instability and variability of self-reported self-esteem, rather than level of self-esteem, predict future depression (A. C. Butler, Hokanson, & Flynn, 1994; Kernis et al., 1998; J. E. Roberts & Gotlib, 1997; J. E. Roberts & Kassel, 1997; J. E. Roberts, Kassel, & Gotlib, 1995a). Furthermore, recent reviews have highlighted how self-esteem that is highly contingent on external validation such as approval and success is a source of increased vulnerability to depressed mood (Crocker & Park, 2004; Crocker & Wolfe, 2001; J. T. Sargent, Crocker, & Luhtanen, 2006). In a later section, self-esteem as a consequence of adverse social conditions—and as a contributor to risk for depression in the face of severe stress—is discussed.

Evaluating cognitive vulnerability models

There are a number of issues that have been pursued in the empirical evaluation of the cognitive models of depression. The following sections are organized around some of the major questions.

Depression and negative cognitions

Of the hundreds of studies testing the question whether depressed people think more negatively than do nondepressed comparisons, the great majority have found that depressed patients do report more negative cognition, dysfunctional attitudes, and negative attributions (reviewed in D. A. Clark et al., 1999). Further, relative to non-depressed controls, depressed patients show information-processing biases on tasks assessing memory, interpretative reasoning, and attention, including retrieving more negative memories (e.g., D. M. Clark & Teasdale, 1982, 1985), and endorsing more negative inter-pretations of ambiguous information (G. Butler & Mathews, 1983; Mogg, Bradbury, & Bradley, 2006; Nunn, Mathews, & Trower, 1997). Experiments investigating deployment of attention suggest that nondepressed individuals attend away from negative stimuli and towards positive stimuli, whereas depressed patients do not show this "protective" bias (McCabe & Gotlib, 1995; McCabe & Toman,

2000). Thus, depressed people do appear to emphasize the negative and to find negative information more accessible—a process that likely contributes to the perpetuation or deepening of their depressed mood. Whether such negative thinking plays a causal, rather than merely descriptive, concomitant, role in depression, however, is a different question, addressed in a later section.

Distortion, bias, or depressive "realism." Although Beck noted that the thinking of depressed people is often illogical and unrealistic (which he termed depressive distortion, implying deviant perception of objective reality), others characterized the thinking as negatively "biased" (consistent negativism across times and situations) rather than distorted. Still others have claimed that depressive thinking is actually more realistic ("sadder but wiser") than that of nondepressed individuals who often have positive illusions and esteem-enhancing positive biases (e.g., Alloy & Abramson, 1979). However, a number of studies have failed to find evidence for depressive realism in real-world settings (e.g., Pacini, Muir, & Epstein, 1998; Strunk, Lopez, & DeRubeis, 2006). Moreover, recent experiments suggest that when "realism" effects appear to occur, they are likely a consequence of depressed people failing to pay attention to task information, rather than of reduced positive bias (Msetfi, Murphy, Simpson, & Kornbrot, 2005).

Negative thinking as a cause of depression

Testing whether cognitive vulnerability "causes" depression has proven to be more problematic than demonstrating that people think more negatively when depressed. Historically, few studies were able to demonstrate that cognitive vulnerability at a one point in time predicted the onset of a later depressive episode or worsening of depressed symptoms when assessed at subsequent points over time, once initial depression level was controlled (e.g., Haaga, Dyck, & Ernst, 1991; Just, Abramson, & Alloy, 2001; Lewinsohn, Steinmetz, Larson, & Franklin, 1981).

However, a recent large-scale study, the Temple-Wisconsin Cognitive Vulnerability to Depression (CVD) Study, utilizing a "behavioural high risk" design in which individuals were selected on the basis of hypothesized psychological risk for depression, found that cognitive vulnerability can predict the onset of depression. A large sample of high-cognitive-risk and low-cognitive-risk undergraduates, defined in terms of scoring in the upper and lower quartiles respectively of the Dysfunctional Attitude Scale (DAS) and the Cognitive Style Questionnaire (CSQ), were followed up prospectively every 6 weeks for 2 years and then every 4 months for an additional 3 years. The DAS assesses the endorsement of inflexible, maladaptive, and perfectionistic beliefs about what is required to demonstrate self-worth, e.g., "If I do not do well all the time people will not respect me." The CSQ is an expanded and modified version of the Attributional Style Questionnaire (ASQ; Seligman, Abramson, Semmel, & Baeyer, 1979), which assesses the tendency to make internal, stable, and global attributions about positive and negative events. For the first 2½ years of follow-up, the high-cognitive-risk group were significantly more likely than low-risk participants to develop a first onset of major depression, even after controlling for initial levels of depression (Alloy et al., 1999; Alloy, Abramson, Whitehouse, & Hogan, 2006b). Similarly, high-cognitive-risk participants with a history of prior depression were more likely to develop recurrences than low-cognitive-risk participants with a history of depression. Further, as noted above, rumination is a form of negative cognition that reliably predicts prospective depression (Nolen-Hoeksema, 2000; Spasojevic & Alloy, 2001). In the CVD study, rumination was found to mediate the effect of negative attributional style on risk for depression (Spasojevic & Alloy, 2001), and rumination in response to stressful events moderated the effect of attributional style in predicting onset of depression (M. S. Robinson & Alloy, 2003).

It is important to note that there is also evidence from longitudinal studies that cognitive vulnerability interacts with negative life events to predict future depression (Hankin & Abramson, 1999; Hankin, Abramson, Miller, & Haeffel, 2004; Reilly-Harrington, Alloy, Fresco, & Whitehouse, 1999; Scher, Ingram, & Segal, 2005). The relationship between vulnerability and stress will be discussed in more detail later in the chapter.

State-dependent cognitions. One implication of the cognitive vulnerability model is that the presence of dysfunctional cognitions or schemas should distinguish between those who are depressed and those who are not—even when the person is not presently depressed. That is, the vulnerability remains, even when the person is not depressed, and presumably increases the risk for future depression. However, despite numerous studies comparing nondepressed and formerly depressed (remitted) groups on various measures of presumed cognitive vulnerability, the great majority of studies found that remitted depressed patients did not differ from nondepressed individuals, or display significantly lower scores following treatment, across a range of measures of depressogenic cognition, including the ASQ and DAS (for detailed reviews see Ingram, Miranda, & Segal, 1998; Scher et al., 2005). The few studies that found elevated cognitive dysfunctions in remitted depressed patients compared to controls involved patients with residual depressive symptoms, suggesting that cognitive dysfunctions may only be found in the presence of depressed mood. Thus, the evidence is not consistent with the assumption that depressogenic cognitions are stable traits that might cause vulnerability to depression. Rather, it has been proposed that negative cognitions may be "latent" and mood-state-dependent, inaccessible unless they are activated or primed by a relevant "challenge," such as the development of a negative mood or the experience of a stressful event (Ingram et al., 1998; Miranda, 1992, 1997; Teasdale, 1983), an idea originally proposed by Beck (1967). This process is called "cognitive reactivity," defined as the extent to which negative cognition is activated in response to negative mood or stress.

Cognitive reactivity

Cognitive-reactivity approaches hypothesize that although remitted depressed patients do not differ from nondepressed persons when assessed under normal conditions, vulnerable individuals will demonstrate greater negative thinking than controls in the context of negative mood and stressful events, because these challenges activate underlying depressogenic schemas. Consistent with this hypothesis, individuals with a history of depression do demonstrate greater dysfunctional attitudes and information-processing biases than controls but only when they are primed prior to assessment (for detailed reviews see Ingram et al., 1998; Scher et al., 2005).

The main experimental approach to priming is to induce depressed mood by having subjects read depressive words or phrases, listen to sad music, or watch sad films. For example, following such a sad mood induction procedure, there was greater endorsement of dysfunctional attitudes as depressed mood increased for currently nondepressed women with a prior history of depression but not for currently nondepressed women with no prior history (Miranda & Persons, 1988). Thus, the women vulnerable to depression (indicated by previous episodes) appeared to possess underlying negative cognitions that became accessible during mildly depressed mood (see also Gemar, Segal, Sagrati, & Kennedy, 2001; Miranda, Gross, Persons, & Hahn, 1998; Miranda, Persons, & Byers, 1990; A. Solomon, Haaga,

Brody, Friedman, & Kirk, 1998; Teasdale & Dent, 1987). Similarly, mood inductions influence information-processing biases in vulnerable groups. Dichotic listening studies have found that when participants are asked to track a story heard in one ear, whilst distracter words play in the other ear, formerly depressed individuals divert their attention towards negative distracting stimuli more than never-depressed individuals, but only when induced into a sad mood (Ingram, Bernet, & Mclaughlin, 1994; Ingram & Ritter, 2000). Likewise, on deployment of attention tasks, formerly depressed individuals do not show the protective bias towards positive stimuli, but only when induced into a sad mood (McCabe, Gotlib, & Martin, 2000).

Importantly, a number of studies have found that degree of cognitive reactivity prospectively predicts levels of depression in longitudinal studies. First, negativity of cognitions during a depressive episode was found to predict who remained depressed and who recovered 5 months later in a sample of 53 depressed women (Dent & Teasdale, 1988). Second, a number of studies have found that level of dysfunctional attitudes interacts with stress to predict depression (reviewed by Scher et al., 2005). Third, a sad mood induction produces greater increases in dysfunctional attitudes in remitted patients treated with pharmacotherapy relative to those treated with cognitive behavioural therapy (CBT; Segal, Kennedy, Gemar, Hood, Pedersen, & Buis, 2006; replicating an uncontrolled study by Segal, Gemar, & Williams, 1999). Furthermore, the magnitude of cognitive reactivity predicted relapse over the next 18 months. The accessibility of the negative thinking during negative mood appears to indicate an underlying cognitive structure that confers vulnerability for depression. Fourth, it is important to note that the measure of rumination found to predict future depression specifically assesses ruminative thinking only in response to feeling sad and is thus a de facto measure of cognitive reactivity.

Models of depressive information processing. These findings of mood-dependent cognitions and cognitive reactivity have influenced the development of the underlying models of information processing in depression. Teasdale (1983, 1988) proposed the differential activation hypothesis, which suggested that individuals differ in the extent to which patterns of negative thinking are activated in response to depressed mood and stressors, i.e., there are individual differences in cognitive reactivity. Borrowing from the associative network model of moods and memory (Bower, 1981), Teasdale hypothesized that emotions and associated cognitions are linked in memory, so that when a mood is activated, representations of events and cognitions that are associated with it in memory may also be made accessible. This hypothesis predicts that degree of cognitive reactivity will be a consequence of earlier learning experiences: a negative event such as an interpersonal rejection will activate more negative cognitions, including recollections of previous rejections and self-criticism, for individuals with more-negative histories than for individuals with less-negative histories. Thus, Teasdale proposed that in response to a sad mood, all individuals will experience an increase in negative thinking, but that for more vulnerable individuals, sad mood activates much more extreme and global negative thoughts, such as "I am a complete failure," which, in turn, lead to a depressive reaction (Teasdale, 1988).

Over time, the differential activation hypothesis has evolved into a more complex model which proposes that depressed mood activates an entire "mental model" that involves globally negative views of the self rather than a set of individual cognitions (Teasdale & Barnard, 1993). Different moods involve different mental models, and a person vulnerable to depression is believed to have acquired a schematic model that contains a global, holistic, dysfunctional sense of the self. A series of experimental studies have found evidence consistent with this view that cognitive vulnerability involves global mental models rather than simply negative thoughts and beliefs becoming more accessible during depressed mood. When depressed participants completed sentence stems related to social approval or personal achievement (e.g., "Always to put others' interests before your own is a recipe for . . ."), they made more completions with positive words ("success") that result in dysfunctional meanings than completions with negative words ("disaster") that result in appropriate meanings (Sheppard & Teasdale, 1996; Teasdale, Lloyd, & Hutton, 1998; Teasdale, Taylor, Cooper, Hayhurst, & Paykel, 1995b).

Specificity of depressive cognitions

Are certain kinds of negative cognitions specific to depression rather than other forms of psychopathology? As indicated earlier, there is considerable evidence that during depressed states individuals are characteristically negative about themselves and circumstances, but maybe negativism is present in many forms of disorder. Studies comparing depressed individuals to other psychiatric patients with nondepressive disorders have been relatively infrequent, and the results have been somewhat mixed. There is some evidence that the negative explanatory style is elevated across a range of patient groups, suggesting that this may be a general index of psychopathology, although many studies have not controlled for comorbid depression in other patient groups (see review in Harvey et al., 2004). There are mixed findings on the DAS, with some studies finding that depressed patients score higher than nondepressed patients (e.g., E. W. Hamilton & Abramson, 1983), and other studies finding no difference (Gotlib, Lewinsohn, Seeley, Rohde, & Redner, 1993; Hollon, Kendall, & Lumry, 1986; Sanz & Avia, 1994).

A particularly stringent test of specificity would compare depressed people with anxious subjects, because both represent an internalized, emotional disorder with exaggerated negative beliefs. Most studies comparing depressed and anxious patients have found that depressed individuals do differ from anxious patients in terms of thought content (see reviews in D. A. Clark et al., 1999; Haaga et al., 1991). Depressed individuals are particularly distinct from anxious persons in the emphasis on personal inadequacy and worthlessness, while anxious people focus on perceived future danger. A recent meta-analysis noted that whilst depressive and anxious cognitive content shared significant variance with both depression and anxiety states, depressive cognitive content about the self did display significant specificity, being more strongly related to depression than anxiety (R. Beck & Perkins, 2001).

However, research on the cognitive specificity of depression is complicated by (1) the high levels of comorbidity between depression and other disorders; and (2) the potential confound between diagnostic criteria and severity of psychopathology, since both more-severe depression and personality disorders are associated with increased negative cognition (Riso et al., 2003; J. M. Smith, Grandin, Alloy, & Abramson, 2006). Further research is needed that contrasts depression with disorders other than anxiety.

Apart from content of negative thoughts, an important cognitive variable specifically associated with depression is the tendency to process information in an *overgeneralized* way. First, depression is characterized by an increased tendency towards overgeneralizations, in which a general rule or conclusion is drawn on the basis of isolated incidents and applied across the board to related and unrelated situations, such that one negative event, such as a failure, is interpreted as indicating a global, characterological inadequacy (A. T. Beck, 1976; Carver & Ganellen, 1983). This thinking style has been found to be specific to depression and not anxiety (Carver & Ganellen, 1983, Carver, Lavoie, Kuhl, & Ganellen, 1988; Ganellen,

1988), to predict increased variability of self-esteem (Hayes, Harris, & Carver, 2004), and to prospectively predict subsequent levels of depression on its own (Dykman, 1996; Edelman, Ahrens, & Haaga, 1994) and as an interaction with stressful life events (Carver, 1998). Moreover, overgeneralization has been found to mediate the effect of failure on subsequent negative affect (J. D. Brown & Dutton, 1995; Kernis, Brockner, & Frankel, 1989; Wenzlaff & Grozier, 1988).

Second, depression is characterized by reduced recall of specific autobiographical memories relative to healthy controls and other psychiatric patients (with the exception of patients with posttraumatic stress disorder; Williams et al., 2007). Both currently and formerly depressed patients recall a greater proportion of overgeneral memories characterized by categoric summaries of repeated events (e.g., "making mistakes" or "playing golf every week") even when asked to recall specific personal memories that occurred at a particular place and time (e.g., "beating my friend Paul at golf last Saturday," Williams, 1996). This increased retrieval of overgeneral memory predicts poorer long-term outcome for depression in prospective studies and is associated with poor problem solving (see Williams et al., 2007 for review). Interestingly, recent research has suggested that rumination is implicated in the development of overgeneral memory recall in depression (Watkins & Teasdale, 2001; Williams et al., 2007), and mediates the effects of overgeneral memory in predicting future depression (Raes, Hermans, Williams, Beyers, Brunfaut, & Eelen, 2006). Rumination is characterized by thinking about the abstract consequences, meanings, and implications of one's experience, and, thereby, involves abstraction across different situations, resulting in categoric mental representations such as overgeneral memory.

Overall evaluation of cognitive models of depression

Much of the increased knowledge about depressive disorders that has been acquired in the past 30 years may be attributed to the extremely active research programmes stimulated by cognitive models of depression. The body of evidence is consistent with a cognitive vulnerability perspective such that the extent to which extreme, global, and overgeneral negative models of the self, the world, and the future are activated in response to negative mood and stressful events determines vulnerability to depression. It is clear that negative cognition is vital in understanding depressive reactions to stressful events, since the meaning, interpretation, and responses to the events are all products of thought, and once instigated, negative thoughts and dysphoric moods profoundly affect each other. Moreover, there is increasing support for a causal role of cognition in the development of depression: An increasing number of prospective studies have found that negative cognitive style, rumination, increased cognitive reactivity, and overgeneralization predict the onset, relapse, and recurrence of major depression and the level of depressive symptoms. Of course, prospective longitudinal studies cannot prove causality: manipulation of cognitive styles through experiment or intervention is necessary to demonstrate a causal role in influencing depression.

Moreover, there are still a number of important methodological and conceptual issues that require resolution. First, the relationship between thought content, as assessed by self-report measures, and thought process, as assessed by information-processing tasks, requires further elucidation. Further, it is important to recognize that the schemas hypothesized to underpin depressive vulnerability are inferred on the basis of thought content and thought process, rather than directly assessed. Second, more research is needed on the mechanisms and causes responsible for the development of negative cognition, rumination, and cognitive reactivity.

Another set of criticisms emphasizes the oversimplicity of the focus on cognition as the major diathesis in depression. Many have drawn attention to the nearly exclusive focus on internal cognitive events to the relative neglect of the environmental and social context in which the person lives. For example, the lives of depressed people are often extremely stressful and deficient in resources. As part of the external context, the role of interpersonal relationships including intimate, social, and family relationships has not been fully integrated into cognitive models. Relatedly, many have called for much more integrative models that account for biological as well as personality, social, environmental, and developmental aspects of depression. In subsequent sections and chapters, several of these alternative and integrative approaches are discussed.

Stressful events and circumstances and their role in depression

It is a commonsense observation that "depressing" events lead to depression. But this simple observation is deceptive, because of issues in conceptualizing and measuring negative events, and in determining the mechanisms and patterns of the association between life events and depression. Nevertheless, it appears that stress plays at least a triggering role in many depressive episodes.

Empirical associations between negative life events and depression

The observation of a link between life's adversities and depression is as old as history, and certainly represents one of the longest lines of empirical research on predictors of depression. In view of the voluminous research literature on stress–depression associations, the following sections largely focus on studies of depressive disorders, rather than symptoms, and highlight several key themes emerging over recent years.

Stressful experiences have variously been defined as recent negative life events, ongoing or chronic difficulties, the minor hassles of daily life, and distal adverse experiences such as childhood maltreatment. While all of these levels of stressful experiences have been empirically linked with depression, the majority of studies have focused on the role of negative life events, especially those occurring in the past 1 to 3 months. Also, empirical support has been based on both questionnaire measures of life events and on interviews. Questionnaires have certain built-in problems that make them less than optimal. For instance, checklists may be limited by differences in individuals' interpretations of the same item ("family member has significant health problem"), inclusion of some items that might actually be symptoms (e.g., "difficulty sleeping"), as well the issue of measuring the stressfulness of events. For instance, if individuals rate their own subjective or perceived stressfulness, their interpretations may be biased by their depressive thinking and by their tendencies to blame events for their depression. Moreover, the meaning of an event to a person's life may be vastly different among individuals depending on the surrounding circumstances in which the event occurs. For instance, the end of a marital relationship, or even the loss of a pet, are events that have enormously different significance depending on the surrounding circumstances. Therefore, interview methods (e.g., G. W. Brown & Harris, 1978) that include queries about the event as well as the context, and provide "objective" scores for stressfulness, based on ratings by independent judges taking context into account and who do not know the person's subjective reactions to the event, have been recommended and used in many studies.

Research using such state-of-the-art interview measures of stressful life events has consistently found higher levels of significant stressors

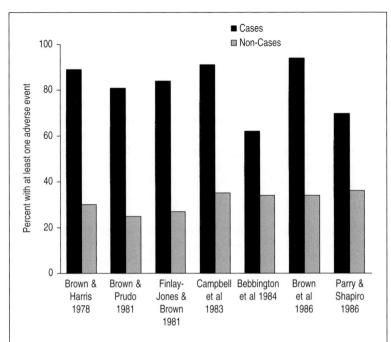

■ Cases
▨ Non-Cases

Figure 5.1.
Rates of severe stress prior to depression comparing depressed and nondepressed adults in a community sample across multiple studies.

From Mazure, C. (1998). Life stressors as risk factors for depression. *Clinical Psychology: Science and Practice, 5,* 291–313. Copyright © (1998) the American Psychological Association, reprinted with permission.

prior to onset of MDEs in patient samples compared to controls, and in community samples (e.g., reviewed in G. W. Brown & Harris, 1989; Mazure, 1998). Mazure's review noted that stressors were 2.5 times more likely in depressed patients compared to controls, and that in community samples, 80% of depressed cases were preceded by major life events. Figure 5.1 displays results from Mazure's review of community studies in which those who were depressed were compared with similar others who were not depressed, and the former group had substantially more recent severe life events than did the nondepressed. Other reviews have also confirmed the association between prior stressors and subsequent depression (e.g., Kessler, 1997; Monroe & Hadjiyannakis, 2002; Paykel, 2003; Tennant, 2002).

In addition to interview studies of patients or depressed community residents (e.g., reviewed in G. W. Brown & Harris, 1989), other research designs have also confirmed a triggering effect of stressors on depression. For instance, Kendler et al. (1999) found that within monozygotic twin pairs who were thus matched and comparable both for genotype and family environment, stressful life events in the past month significantly predicted onset of major depression. Also, "natural" experiments that occur when exposure to a negative event is random and independent of depressive outcomes, such as recent widowhood, or exposure to natural disasters, have also been shown to precipitate depression (reviewed in Kessler, 1997). Taken together, therefore, evidence based on sound methods of stress assessment and novel designs strongly suggests that most episodes of major depression are preceded by stressful life events. An important corollary, however, is that most people do not become depressed even if they experience a negative life event.

Effects of type of stress. In Chapter 6 we review the effects of exposure to early childhood adversity, a particular type of stressful experience that commonly involves the disruption of social bonds and creates enduring stressful conditions that have an impact on biological and psychosocial development. There is also ample evidence that some individuals, faced with current *chronically* negative conditions, such as impaired health, caretaking burdens, social disadvantage, or marital discord may also experience depression and demoralization.

Is there any evidence that particular kinds of stressor content are more likely to precipitate depression? Dating back from Freudian thinking, but also consistent with cognitive models, an extensive line of research has focused on the unique significance for depression of interpersonal "loss," which may include bereavement, separations, endings, or threats of separation, possibly lowering a susceptible person's sense of self-worth. Paykel and Cooper (1992; also Paykel, 2003) reviewed studies showing that such "exit" events often precede depression, and may be more common in depressed samples than in other forms of psychopathology. Tennant (2002; see also Kendler et al., 1995) also suggested that relationship stressors—many of which are loss or threatened loss events—are common in depression, perhaps especially for women. The concept of loss has sometimes been expanded beyond interpersonal exit events to include loss of self-esteem, role loss, or loss of cherished ideas (e.g., G. W. Brown, Harris, & Hepworth, 1995; Finlay-Jones & Brown, 1981).

Personality and depressive reactions to specific life event types. A specific variant of the stressor content question is the hypothesis that individuals may be differentially vulnerable to the depressive effects of particular stressors. A. T. Beck (1983) and others including psychodynamically oriented theorists (e.g., Arieti & Bemporad, 1980; Blatt, Quinlan, Chevron, McDonald, & Zuroff, 1982), proposed that individuals may be particularly vulnerable to some stressors more than others. Specifically, as noted previously in the discussion of depressive cognition, individuals differ in the sources of their self-esteem and sense of mastery, with some individuals experiencing personal worth as deriving from the achievement of highly valued goals and control, while others are more likely to invest themselves and their self-definitions in personal relationships with others. The former type is variously termed *autonomous*, dominant goal-oriented, or self-critical, while the latter may be termed *sociotropic*, dominant-other oriented, or dependent (reviewed in Nietzel & Harris, 1990). Vulnerability, therefore, might consist of personality features or cognitions that include attitudes, beliefs, and values such that a major stressor that is interpreted as representing a depletion in the specific area of an individual's sense of worth or competence would provoke a depressive reaction.

The "specific vulnerability" or personality–event congruency models have stimulated a fair amount of research, most of which supports the model (e.g., reviewed in Nietzel & Harris, 1990). Zuroff, Mongrain, and Santor (2004) noted that dependency-sociotropy is reasonably specifically linked with interpersonal loss events in the prediction of depression, but self-criticism/autonomy has been less clearly supported.

However, it is important to note that the empirical support for the congruency model largely has been broadly based on a variety of cross-sectional and laboratory studies. Relatively fewer personality/schema-matching studies have included longitudinal designs, optimal methods of stress assessment, and clinical evaluations of unipolar depression; exceptions are Hammen, Burge, Daley, Davila, Paley, and Rudolph (1995); Hammen, Ellicott, Gitlin, and Jamison (1989); Hammen and Goodman-Brown (1990); Hammen, Marks, Mayol, and deMayo (1985); D. H. Lam, Green, Power, & Checkley (1996); Segal, Shaw, Vella, and Katz (1992). There are several cross-sectional studies of depressed patients by Mazure, Bruce, Maciejewski, and Jacobs (2000); Mazure, Maciejewski, Jacobs, and Bruce (2002); C. J. Robins (1990); and Spangler, Simons, Monroe, and Thase (1996). These studies varied in methods of assessing personality vulnerability relevant to the congruency hypothesis, and varied in the consistency of results. However, all found some support for the improvement in prediction of depressive reactions to life events by including measures of cognitive or personality vulnerability, and most found support particularly for depression following the matching of interpersonal life events and interpersonal vulnerability. Because the congruency model is one of the most clear diathesis-stress models of depression, and because it has practical treatment and prevention implications, it warrants further study. Further longitudinal studies testing the personality–event congruency hypothesis include a study of dependency within the CVD project (Cogswell, Alloy, & Spasojevic, 2006), which failed to find support for the congruency hypothesis, and a study in late-life depression, which did support the congruency hypothesis (Morse & Robins, 2005).

In addition to the congruency model, it should be noted that the cognitive-diathesis stress approach to depression is also supported by longitudinal evidence that does not include specific matches of personality and life event content. Cognitive vulnerability as indexed generally by dysfunctional attitudes and attributional style interacts with negative life events to predict future depression (Hankin & Abramson, 1999; Hankin et al., 2004; Reilly-Harrington et al., 1999; Scher et al., 2005).

A related refinement of the stress–depression relationship concerns the "match" between a negative life event and ongoing circumstances or role fulfillments that are sources of self-esteem and meaning. G. W. Brown, Bifulco, and Harris (1987) hypothesized that a woman would most likely become depressed if an event represented a loss (such as an important person, belief, role, object, health) that "matched" a particular role to which she was committed or represented a conflict between roles. For example, if Mrs Jones and Mrs Smith both had teenage sons who were arrested for shoplifting (a severe event), Mrs Jones might become depressed because the event represented a "loss" of her views of her son as honest and reliable, and a "match" with her major role commitment to being a mother. Mrs Smith, on the other hand, might not become depressed because she already knew her son had a propensity for getting into trouble and she herself was more invested in her career than homemaking now that the children were older. G. W. Brown et al. (1987) found support for their matching hypothesis (and see also Kendler, Hettema, Butera, Gardner, & Prescott, 2003b).

Stress and types of depression. As noted in Chapter 1, there has been a long history of attempts to distinguish between "biological" and nonbiological subtypes of depression, with one enduring hypothesis that depressions triggered by stressful life events are different in features and underlying etiology from depressions that are not stress related. However, as Chapter 1 indicated, there is little evidence that stress-related (situational) depressions are different clinically or etiologically from those that do not appear to be triggered by life events. Moreover, even depressions that have so-called endogenous clinical features are more likely than not to have been precipitated by stressors (e.g., Harkness & Monroe, 2002).

Gender differences. Noting that much of the research on stress–depression linkages has been conducted on female samples, Mazure (1998) and others have speculated that there may be gender differences in stress exposure that contribute to the overall higher rates of depression in women than men. In Chapter 3 several lines of evidence were reviewed concerning women's possibly greater exposure to stress, including episodic life events, chronic stressful conditions, traumatic events, and social disadvantage. Although the evidence is somewhat mixed on whether women have more exposure than men to episodic stressful life events, there is ample support for the idea that women are more "reactive" to stress—that is, females are more likely to become depressed following stressors than men are (e.g., Maciejewski et al., 2001; Rudolph, 2002; Rudolph & Hammen, 1999; Shih et al., 2006; Spangler et al., 1996; Van Os & Jones, 1999). Overall, findings of gender differences in exposure to stress, and especially reactivity to stress, may provide clues to the greater rates of depression in women. Several theoretical reviews have offered a variety of hypotheses about the mechanisms underlying such patterns, including biological, gender socialization, and cognitive and coping processes (e.g., Cyranowski et al., 2000; Hankin & Abramson, 2002; Nolen-Hoeksema, 2002; Nolen-Hoeksema & Girgus, 1994).

Nature of stress–depression relationships

In addition to the empirical association between stressors and subsequent depression, several topics address the directional, temporal, and conceptual nature of the association. In recent years there has been a movement away from testing the empirical association between depression and stress, toward addressing several newer questions in the field.

Changing relations of stress and depression over time. One such issue concerns the changing relationship over time. Based in part on clinical lore and bolstered by animal models of kindling and sensitization, Post and colleagues (Post, 1992; Post, Rubinow, & Ballenger, 1984) hypothesized that recurrent episodes of mood disorders may become progressively independent of stressors, as a function of neurobiological changes associated with repeated stressors and repeated episodes. Over time the person becomes sensitized or "kindled," and thus likely to experience spontaneous episodes. Post (1992) reviewed studies of first-onset versus recurrent depression, and concluded that evidence supported a pattern of greater stress prior to first onsets than later episodes. However, other reviews and additional studies yielded mixed results (see review in Mazure, 1998; also Daley et al., 2000 and Lewinsohn et al., 1999a on adolescents; Ormel, Oldehinkel, & Brilman, 2001 on later-life depression). Most of the studies include interview measures of episodic stressors, but have methodological problems such as inclusion of bipolar patients and varying definitions of stressors and time frames. The great majority of the studies have not controlled for gender or age, which are known to affect the rates of stressors (female and younger patients typically report higher rates of stressors). Most limiting of all, none of the studies had a within-person design, which is the critical test of the first-onset vs. recurrence hypothesis. In view of the empirical and methodological limitations, therefore, the idea of greater stress before first vs. later depression episodes remains an intriguing hypothesis rather than an established fact.

Other aspects of the "kindling" or stress-sensitization hypothesis have been tested, although more commonly among those with bipolar disorder, which by definition is a recurrent mood disorder. However, a within-person design to evaluate hypothesized changes in the nature of association between stress and unipolar depression over time was undertaken by Kendler, Thornton, and Gardner (2000b), who studied nearly 2400 female twins over 4 waves separated by at least 13 months each. Using SCID-based diagnostic assessments and life event interviews, they computed both between-subjects and within-subjects analyses of the interaction between previous number of episodes and life events occurring prior to the targeted most recent episode. They found evidence in both types of analyses for a diminishing association between life events and depression as the person experienced increasing numbers of episodes (up to about 6–8 episodes). Kendler et al. (2000b) suggested that whether the mechanism involved is biological or psychological, it appears to occur intensively in the first few episodes after initial onset, and then the kindling process slows or stops. Similar within-subject patterns were reported among a subgroup of patients studied by life-charting methods by Ehnvall and Agren (2002). In a further study, Kendler, Thornton, and Gardner (2001a) determined that the increasing independence of stress and depression over repeated episodes was strongest in those with low genetic risk (based on twin methodology). In contrast, those at higher genetic risk (had twin siblings with depression) appeared to be "prekindled" with weaker associations between stressors and depression, similar to those at low genetic risk who had already experienced at least three episodes. Thus, the stress–depression relationship may vary not only over time with increasing numbers of episodes, but may also differ according to genetic risk for depression. A review and conceptual analysis by Monroe and Harkness (2005) also notes the need for testing of alternative versions of the kindling model: whether episodes become independent of stress over time (stress autonomy) or whether episodes are triggered by increasingly lower levels of stress (stress sensitivity). Further studies are needed to confirm and elucidate the patterns in longitudinal studies, and, of course, to clarify the nature of the mechanisms that account for the kindling/sensitization effects.

Effects of depression on stress: Stress generation. Most research on stress–depression associations has examined the effects of stressors on depression, but the opposite direction of influence has also been studied. Hammen (1991b) observed that women with recurrent depression experienced significantly more interpersonal negative events during a 1-year follow-up period than groups of women with bipolar or medical disorders or nonpsychiatric controls. Moreover, the unipolar depressed women were especially likely to experience conflict events—interpersonal disputes with a wide variety of others such as friends, spouses, family, employers, and teachers. Interpersonal and conflict events are among those that occur at least in part because of the actions or characteristics of the individual. This process has been termed "stress generation" (Hammen, 1991b). The implications of stress generation are significant: some individuals seem to contribute to higher levels of stress occurrence, and individuals whose lives are highly stressful are likely to experience recurrences of depression in response to such upsetting events.

The tendency of depressed women to contribute to the occurrence of more interpersonal and conflict stressors has been replicated in numerous samples of adults, adolescents, and children (reviewed in Hammen, 2006). While most of the research has been conducted on female or mixed samples, at least one study found the same pattern occurring in men with histories of depression (Cui & Vaillant, 1997). Most of the research has further indicated that while current depression may contribute to greater difficulty in relationships and hence major negative life events such as fights, break-ups, and estrangement, many studies have found that such elevated rates of negative interpersonal events may occur in formerly depressed people even when they are not currently depressed (e.g., Hammen & Brennan, 2002).

What factors are responsible for the generation of stressful interpersonal events? One hypothesis is that individuals select themselves into potentially stressful circumstances, possibly due to characteristics of their environments or to personal vulnerabilities. Thus, for example, because of poverty and low educational attainment, or because of childhood adversities that affect self-esteem and social skills, an individual may be more likely to "select" (or have available) a marital partner who him- or herself may have limited personal or social resources. Under difficult and stressful circumstances the marriage may be more likely to have conflict, or the children may be exposed to genetic and social environments that contribute to behavioural and school problems that challenge effective parent–child relationships, possibly creating parent–child conflict. Thus, a person may develop depression in response to stressful circumstances and also be "caught" in a difficult family environment that provokes interpersonal stressors leading to further depressive episodes.

Another pathway to stress generation—which may overlap with the social selection approach—is through personal characteristics that contribute to disrupted relationships. Such characteristics may include biological and genetic predispositions, or those that are learned and acquired largely through adverse family backgrounds. It is known that the tendency to experience high levels of stressful life events is partly genetically mediated (e.g., Kendler et al., 1993b, 1999; McGuffin et al., 1988; Plomin et al., 1990). One hypothesis is that the genetically transmitted trait of neuroticism contributes to the occurrence of stressful life events because of the person's difficult temperament and emotionality. Several studies have shown a link between neuroticism and elevated occurrence of stressful life events (e.g., Fergusson & Horwood, 1987; Kendler, Gardner, & Prescott, 2003a; Poulton & Andrews, 1992). Other studies have shown that stress generation among depressed people is associated with parental depression (likely transmitting both genetic and learned maladaptive social problem solving), traits such as excessive reassurance seeking, sociotropy, autonomy, dependency, self-criticism, poor interpersonal problem solving, and comorbid clinical conditions (reviewed in Hammen, 2006).

It is important not to "blame" individuals for creating stressors in their lives, since their vulnerabilities and circumstances may be tragically unwanted. Such individuals may be greatly burdened by the social and family environments in which they find themselves. It would seem that clinical interventions that help depressed individuals find ways to be more effective in dealing with their relationships, and to prevent situations from escalating into major stressors, may help prevent the recurrence of depression in those who are at risk.

Models of the mechanisms in the stress–depression association

It is evident that even in the face of severe stressors, most people do not develop major depression. Therefore, it is presumed that there must be a "diathesis" or vulnerability factor that accounts for why some people get depressed after stressors and others do not. Increasingly, models of the etiology of depression are complex and include multiple, interacting biological, developmental, psychological, and sociodemographic factors (e.g., Hammen, Shih, & Brennan, 2004; Kendler, Gardner, & Prescott, 2002a, 2006a; Kendler, Kessler, Neale, Heath, & Eaves, 1993a; Zuroff, Santor, & Mongrain, 2005, to name a few). Such models are difficult to test because they require large samples, multiple variables including biological markers, and must characterize bidirectional relations among variables.

Chapter 4 discusses biological features of the presumed etiology of depression. In particular, two topics highlight mechanisms potentially underlying the link between stress and depression, one involving abnormalities of the HPA axis and the other noting genetically mediated susceptibility to depressive reactions to stress. HPA-axis abnormalities may explain why some individuals have excessive or prolonged neuroendocrine reactions to stressors, but the mechanisms specifically explaining depression have yet to be clarified. Similarly, there is emerging evidence that certain genetic variants of the serotonin transporter system result in increased likelihood of depression following major stressors, but the precise mechanisms have not been elucidated, and other gene candidates may also play important roles.

In Chapter 6 a variety of developmental and interpersonal features of depression are discussed, and some of these topics reflect vulnerabilities that may be acquired in childhood and family experiences (e.g., insecure attachment) or reflect temperamental and personality features that heighten risk for depression—especially in the context of interpersonal adversities. Early experiences, through both cognitive-psychological and biological pathways, likely influence the appraisal of stressors, the extent of emotional reactivity, and coping capabilities.

The current chapter emphasizes cognitive models of depression, which have always implicitly been diathesis-stress approaches. For some investigators, like Beck and the attributional/hopelessness theorists described earlier, cognitive schemas or dysfunctional explanatory style represent the underlying vulnerability because they predispose the person to interpret an event and its aftermath in hopeless, self-deprecating ways that elicit depression. The nature of the stressor itself is relatively unimportant to these theorists—except that it must be "meaningful" to the individual in the sense that it elicits the interpretation of hopelessness or worthlessness. In these models the objective magnitude of the event may be exaggerated, so that even fairly minor events may trigger depressive reactions if they are subjected to biased interpretation arising from the cognitive vulnerability.

By contrast, George Brown, who is a sociologist, and his colleagues (e.g., G. W. Brown & Harris, 1978) have articulated a model based on characteristics of the stressful life events themselves, and their occurrence in a particular psychosocial context that elicits or reinforces cognitions of hopelessness and low self-esteem. In this model the vulnerability factors are features of the person's current and historical context that promote the experiences of hopelessness. The "meaning" of an event is shaped by context, and factors thought to increase the risk for depression in the face of stressors were empirically identified, based on a large community study of working-class women. They included lack of an intimate or confiding relationship (e.g., a poor marital relationship), loss of the mother before age 11, having 3 or more children at home under the age of 14, and lack of full- or part-time employment outside the home (G. W. Brown & Harris, 1978). According to Brown's model (e.g., G. W. Brown & Harris, 1989), severe events that give rise to a lack of hope for better things induce depression; low self-esteem prior to the event is likely to give rise to hopelessness.

Although Brown's model is different from those of cognitive theorists in its focus on the nature and context of life events, they are somewhat similar in the emphasis on cognitive mediation of the effects of stress. G. W. Brown and Harris (1989), like Beck, emphasize the interpretation of the event as a depletion of the sense of self-worth and identity. To a great extent Brown infers cognitions, with the exception of direct measures of self-esteem (e.g., G. W. Brown, Andrews, Bifulco, & Veiel, 1990), whereas cognitive theorists attempt to measure them directly. However, a major point of disagreement is the extent to which the individual is viewed as having distorted interpretations of events, with Brown and others arguing that it is actual severe negative events and adversity that trigger depression, whereas implicit in the cognitive models is the assumption that it is the biased interpretation of events—even minor, exaggerated misfortunes—that cause depression. Although there have been tests in recent years of cognitive diatheses interacting with life stressors to predict depressive reactions, as noted earlier in the chapter (e.g., Lewinsohn, Joiner, & Rohde, 2001), the inclusion of actual stressors in longitudinal designs of cognitive vulnerability predicting depressive episodes has been relatively rare (but see Hankin & Abramson, 1999; Hankin et al., 2004; Reilly-Harrington et al., 1999; Scher et al., 2005). The search to understand why some people become depressed following stressful events, but most do not, is an ongoing quest.

Summary

- Cognitive models of depression, originating with Beck, emphasize negative thinking as a factor causing or maintaining depression.
- Contemporary versions of cognitive models variously emphasize explanatory style, self-schemas, hopelessness, ruminative response style, and biased information processing, among other factors.
- Cognitive vulnerability models of depression have stimulated considerable research and discussion of measurement and design issues. Such research has led to improved empirical support for the idea that individual differences in the negative perceptions of the self and events play an important role in depression vulnerability, but many unresolved questions remain.
- Negative life events play a triggering role in the occurrence of most episodes of depression, but most people who experience stressful events do not get depressed.
- Research has attempted to explore what kinds of events and circumstances are most likely to provoke depression, suggesting that loss and interpersonal events are especially prevalent causes of depression, but that individual cognitive and personality

factors may determine which kinds of events are most potent predictors for that person.

- The relationships between stress and depression are not just unidirectional with stress precipitating depression. Depression and personal characteristics may create stressful events, and also the nature of the stress–depression relationship may change over the course of multiple episodes.

Social aspects of depression 6

Most forms of psychological disorder affect individuals' interpersonal lives, impairing their social functioning by altering behaviours and the quality of relating to others. Depression is no exception, because the symptoms of depression interfere with normal relationships. But even more importantly, several perspectives emphasize the role of difficulties in relatedness to others as a fundamental causal or risk factor for depression. In this chapter, therefore, various topics are explored. There is no single interpersonal perspective on depression; instead there are diverse topics of study, such as family functioning, attachment, marital adjustment, loss, the effects of stressful interpersonal events, and social skills. As we will see, difficulties in social relatedness have been variously viewed as concomitants of being in a depressed state, consequences of depression that have negative "side effects," and as fundamental causal factors in depression.

In this chapter, the first section is on depression in the family context, further subdivided into sections discussing family-based *causes* of depression and those discussing the *consequences* of depression on family members. The remainder of the chapter discusses nonfamily social relations, reviewing research on ways in which depressed people function in the social world and how their actions affect others—and themselves. Throughout the chapter, the distinction between depression as a cause of interpersonal difficulties and depression as a result of interpersonal problems is somewhat arbitrary. Or perhaps more precisely, the associations are bidirectional: eventually, even if some social difficulties are the result of depression, the problems may perpetuate or create depression because they are stressful for the depressed or depression-vulnerable person. That is, vulnerability to depression may arise in the early family environment; the interpersonal consequences of depression might also contribute to further symptomatology; and deficits in social behaviours set the stage for stressful events and circumstances that may trigger depression.

Depression in the family context

Theoretical models of the family origins of depression

Both psychodynamic and social learning theory models of human development emphasize the importance of experiences in early childhood in the family environment. When those experiences are dysfunctional or when the child lacks crucial experiences such as a close bond with a stable caretaker, he or she may develop in maladaptive ways. Both of these models hypothesize that depression might be a form of psychopathology resulting from certain negative family experiences.

Psychodynamic approaches. The original Freudian psychodynamic approach, which has evolved into a contemporary version called object relations theory, emphasized that depression is similar to bereavement, and results from the loss of an important "object." Loss of an important other person, especially in childhood, produces sadness and other experiences of mourning, but unlike bereavement, according to the traditional psychodynamic model, object loss can cause self-deprecation, guilt, and related symptoms of the depression syndrome due to introjected anger toward an ambivalently loved lost object (the theory of anger turned inward).

More recently, John Bowlby (1978, 1981) articulated a model of the importance of early attachment bonds between the infant and caretaker that has implications not only for depression, but for key elements of individual personality and adaptive functioning. Specifically, Bowlby argued that infants have an innate and fundamental tendency to form attachment bonds to a primary caretaker, in the service of protection and survival. Further, the development of a stable and secure attachment bond is essential for healthy development. An infant with a mother or primary caretaker who is consistently responsive, accessible, and supportive will acquire a "working model" (that is, mental representations) of the self that is positive, will be able to use the relationship as a "secure base" from which to explore the environment and acquire essential skills, and will form beliefs and expectations of other people as trustworthy and dependable. If, however, the attachment bond is insecure due to actual disruption or loss, or to caretaker rejection, unresponsiveness, or inconsistency, the person becomes vulnerable to depression. Insecurely attached children may be highly anxious and needy, or alternatively, may deal with the lack of attachment by being avoidant or rejecting of closeness. In later life, actual or threatened loss of close relationships may trigger not only mourning, but also self-criticism, feelings of abandonment, hopelessness and helplessness, and related depressive symptoms. There is a considerable body of empirical work validating Bowlby's ideas about attachment security in infants and its consequences for healthy or maladaptive development (e.g., reviewed in Blatt & Homann, 1992; see also Cicchetti & Schneider-Rosen, 1986). Studies specifically linking attachment quality and loss to depression are reviewed in a later section.

Cognitive social learning approaches. Based on learning models, this perspective on the role of early family experiences on depression is more general than the attachment model, and has been less well elaborated as a model specifically of depression than has attachment theory. Its essential tenets are that adaptive social skills and inter-personal attitudes and expectations are acquired through learning during childhood. In Chapter 5 we discussed the role of negative cognitions in vulnerability to depression. Parent–child interactions that lead to the child's acquisition of dysfunctional self-schemas or negative explanatory style set the stage for vulnerability to depression in the face of stress. It is hypothesized that several forms of learning in early family life affect depression vulnerability. These may include direct experiences with reward and punishment of the child by parents, as well as learning through observation of the parent. Being treated harshly or subjected to criticism, or not receiving rewards for appropriate socially skilled behaviour, or learning negative views of the self and world from the parent's own attitudes, may all have a negative effect on a developing child's self-esteem, expectations about others, and ability to engage appropriately in relations with others. Since coping with stressors throughout life requires learning appro-priate problem-solving and coping skills, deficiencies in these areas might also create vulnerability for depression. In general, research directly bearing on the childhood acquisition of maladaptive cogni-tions and skills relevant to future depression has been relatively sparse. As reviewed in subsequent sections, however, numerous studies are consistent with the basic perspective of cognitive social learning theory.

In addition to early childhood family causes of vulnerability to depression, the family context is also important from the opposite perspective: the enormous impact of depression on others in the family. Depressed parents commonly have difficulties in their parent-ing roles, and such dysfunctions may contribute to the high rates of depression and other disorders in the children. Marital relationships may also suffer as a result of the depression of one of the partners. In other cases, the depressed individual may experience relating to family members as highly stressful, and this stress may contribute to further depression. Research on the relationship between depression and parental and marital functioning is reviewed below.

Family relationships and early environment as potential causes of depression

We turn first to various lines of research investigating the importance of early family experiences on development of depression.

Early loss and depression.   Various studies have been conducted on the impact of loss of a parent on risk for depression, but many of the studies have not distinguished between types of loss (e.g., death, separation, parental divorce) or age of occurrence. In general, earlier research has shown at best a small or modest association between childhood loss and later adult depression (e.g., G. W. Brown & Harris, 1978; Lloyd, 1980). Two more recent studies showed small specific associations between loss of a parent by death and risk for depression in women only (Maier & Lachman, 2000), or for both genders (Kendler, Sheth, Gardner, & Prescott, 2002b). Kendler et al. (2002b) also found that the risk of depression was greater following maternal death in childhood than death of fathers, and that the risk period was relatively brief, suggesting that the person who develops depression, if at all, experiences depression apparently precipitated by and in close proximity to the death, but has little continuing risk into adulthood.

Increasingly it has been recognized that it is usually not parental loss as such that creates risk for depression, but rather the quality of parental care following the loss. Poor quality of parenting or inconsistent parenting following loss, for example, were found to be predictive of later depression (e.g., Bifulco, Brown, & Harris, 1987; Harris, Brown, & Bifulco, 1986). Other consequences of loss of a parent may include economic hardship, family instability, and stressful conditions that contribute to risk for depression. Kendler et al. (2006a) found that parental loss (defined to include death or separation) predicted depression in a sample of adult men in part because of its association with various risk factors including low self-esteem and low educational attainment. The same authors had previously also demonstrated that prediction of depression in women involved multiple interacting risk factors of which childhood parental loss was a small contributor (Kendler et al., 2002a).

Early adversity and depression. In addition to loss, various studies have tested the idea that early childhood adversities of various kinds may increase vulnerability to develop depression in adulthood. These are relevant to family experience since most such adverse conditions reflect aspects of the family environment. Two research strategies have predominated: studying links between a single specific experience and depression, or studying links between any of many kinds of negative childhood experience. Among single specific experiences (including loss), one of the most studied is abuse—sexual, physical, or emotional maltreatment—typically but not always occurring in the family context. There is ample evidence from mostly retrospective community and clinical studies of a significant association between childhood sexual or physical abuse and adult depression (e.g., J. Brown, Cohen, Johnson, & Smailes, 1999; Kendler, Bulik, Silberg, Hettema, Myers, & Prescott, 2000a; MacMillan, Fleming, Streiner, Lin, Boyle, & Jamieson, 2001), and similar results from prospective studies (e.g., Bifulco, Brown, Moran, Ball, & Campbell, 1998; G. W. Brown & Harris, 1993). Some studies suggest that abuse experiences are especially predictive of chronic or recurrent depression (Bifulco, Moran, Baines, Bunn, & Stanford, 2002a; Lizardi et al., 1995). However, several studies suggest that physical and sexual abuse are related to diverse adult psychological disorders, not specifically to depression. Many of the studies have not distinguished among the specific types of abuse, nor have controlled for factors in the environment that are correlated with the abuse which could themselves influence the likelihood of depression (such as parental mood disorders). In a large study of psychiatric outpatients, Gibb, Butler, and Beck (2003) found that childhood emotional abuse was most specifically related to depression compared with sexual or physical abuse (see also review in Alloy, Abramson, Smith, Gibb, & Neeren, 2006a), but in general further research is needed to establish the nature and outcomes of abuse as it relates to depression.

Additional research has investigated the association between depression and experiencing one or more early adversities from a list of negative childhood events. A large-scale retrospective epidemiological study of community residents who met criteria for major depression found that several childhood adversities (parental drinking, parental mental illness, family violence, parental marital problems, deaths of mother or father, and lack of a close relationship with an adult) were predictive of later *onset* of depression (Kessler & Magee, 1993). Three early adversities—parental mental illness, violence, and parental divorce—were significantly predictive of *recurrence* of depression. In a later similar study, Kessler, Davis, and Kendler (1997a) examined 26 adversities occurring by age 16, and found that although many of the events were associated with adult major depressive disorder, the adversities were also related to a broad array of psychological disorders besides depression. The investigators also noted that exposure to one or more adversities is common, occurring in three quarters of respondents, and that the adversities tend to overlap or cluster with each other. Further, they noted that no claim to causal relationships between adversity and disorders is possible, since there may be unmeasured common variables responsible for both adversity exposure and later disorder. Thus, while childhood traumas and early stressful conditions may contribute to depression, more study of the complex pathways is needed. An example is the multivariate research of Kendler and colleagues (e.g., Kendler et al., 2002a, 2006a), who found evidence of contributions due to childhood adversity, but only in the context of multiple factors including genetic predisposition (which not only may create direct biological risks for depression but also serve to expose children to higher levels of childhood adversity).

The mechanisms by which specific childhood stressors such as physical or sexual abuse have their effects on later depression are not known directly. However, such experiences are highly likely to occur in the context of parental lack of care, plus exposure to an environment in which negative events contribute to dysfunctional cognitions and coping skills that increase vulnerability to depression. Neurobiological mechanisms may also be implicated, with the speculation that severe stress early in life alters the brain's neuroregulatory processes that promote susceptibility to depression (see Chapter 4). Research has also supported the hypothesis that exposure to adverse conditions in childhood may sensitize the youth to stress, such that it may take minimal exposure to later stressful life events to precipitate depression compared to those with no childhood adversity (e.g., Hammen, Henry, & Daley, 2000; Harkness, Bruce, & Lumley, 2006). Such sensitization processes are discussed further in Chapter 5. Although most individuals have a greater probability of developing a depressive reaction when highly stressful events occur, Figure 6.1 illustrates that exposure to early childhood adversity may make a person more likely to develop depression in the face of even relatively mild stressors compared to people who have not had adversity exposure.

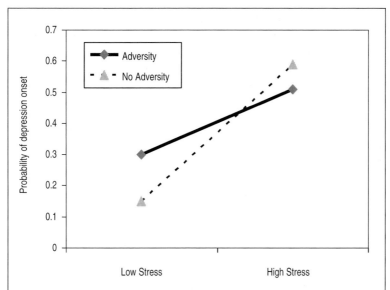

Figure 6.1.
Exposure to harmful family experiences and adverse events in childhood may contribute to vulnerability to develop depression by making people more reactive to relatively mild stressors.

From Hammen, C., Henry, R., and Daley, S. (2000). Depression and sensitization to stressors among young women as a function of childhood adversity. *Journal of Consulting and Clinical Psychology*, *68*, 782–787. Copyright © (2000) American Psychological Association, reprinted with permission.

Attachment and depression. The ideal long-term prospective study to test Bowlby's infant insecure attachment model of adult depression has yet to be conducted. However, several studies, using various methods of assessing "attachment" including self-reported attitudes toward parents, have shown that depressed children and adolescents report less secure attachment to parents, compared with nondepressed groups (e.g., Armsden, McCauley, Greenberg, Burke, & Mitchell, 1990; Kobak, Sudler, & Gamble, 1991). Kobak et al. (1991) and Hammen et al. (1995) also showed that adolescents were more likely to become depressed following stressful life events if they had more insecure attachment representations of their parents or close figures. A retrospective study of clinically depressed women patients found that they reported significantly less attachment to their mothers than did nonpsychiatric controls (Rosenfarb, Becker, & Khan, 1994). Bifulco, Moran, Ball, and Bernazzani (2002b) found that insecure attachment representations predicted onset of depressive episodes over a 1-year follow-up. Attachment in romantic relationships reflected more insecurity in depressed students compared to nondepressed, and attachment representations were significant predictors of quality of relationship functioning (Carnelley, Pietromonaco, & Jaffe, 1994). Thus, in multiple samples and studies with different designs, the construct of insecure attachment is associated with depression. However, because all of the measures used in adult or youth samples are self-reports, there is a need to distinguish among factors that may reflect current depressive thinking and actual quality of the current relationship context, and those that represent relatively stable, infancy-based intrapersonal representations of the self in relation to others.

Quality of parent–child relationships and depression. The discussions of loss, attachment, and early childhood adversity as predictors of vulnerability to depression are aspects of a broader research topic linking depression vulnerability to poor quality of parent–child relationships. Several kinds of research designs have investigated the associations between the quality of the parent–child relationship and depression: retrospective reports by adults (both depressed patients and community samples, measuring depressive symptoms or diagnoses); cross-sectional designs assessing current associations among variables in adults and children or adolescents; longitudinal studies of associations between parental attitudes and behaviours toward the child and later depressive experiences in the child/adolescent. In general, the retrospective studies are fairly consistent: Depressed adults report more adverse relationships with their parents during childhood. For example, a large classic study compared depressed and nondepressed inpatients on perceptions of their own parents (Crook, Raskin, & Eliot, 1981). The depressed patients described both their mothers and fathers as more rejecting, controlling, and as demonstrating hostile detachment, compared with the reports of the nondepressed controls. Other studies of depressed patients have similarly found that depressed adults report that their relations with their parents were marked by lack of caring, warmth, and acceptance, as well as stricter control (e.g., reviewed in Parker & Gladstone, 1996). Related findings have been reported in nonpatient community samples, in which depressed individuals reported more negative views of their parents (e.g., Blatt, Wein, Chevron, & Quinlan, 1979; Holmes & Robins, 1987, 1988). Andrews and Brown (1988), for example, found that women who became clinically depressed following occurrence of major life events were more likely to report lack of adequate parental care or hostility from their mothers, compared to those who did not become depressed (see also G. W. Brown & Harris, 1993). In reviewing the extensive literature on depressed individuals' recollections of parents, Gerlsma, Emmelkamp, and Arrindell (1990) and Alloy et al. (2006a) concluded that parental childrearing styles that included low affection and more control (overprotection) were especially consistently related to depression.

In addition to retrospective reports of their parents by depressed adults, there is direct evidence from contemporary reports and observations that depressed children and adolescents experience difficulties in their relationships with parents (e.g., Asarnow, Tompson, Woo, & Cantwell, 2001; Kobak et al., 1991; Messer & Gross, 1995; Sheeber & Sorenson, 1998; see reviews in Alloy et al., 2006a; Kaslow, Deering, & Racusin, 1994). True prospective studies collect information about parental behaviour prior to onset of depression in the offspring, and are thus free of potential reporting biases due to depression. Such studies are rare, but provide additional evidence of an association between parent–child relationship difficulties and later depression. For example, Lindelow (1999) found that mothers' reports of *lack of positive* parent–child interactions significantly predicted depressive episodes 20 years later—although there was little evidence of an association between overtly negative aspects of parenting and later depression. Additional studies that confirm a predictive role of negative parenting style and offspring depression are reported in a review by Alloy et al. (2006a).

Overall, the evidence suggests that "affectionless control," a combination of low care, lack of warmth or hostility, plus high control or overprotection, is associated with risk for depression. A large review of the relevant studies suggests that there is more evidence that low care predicts depression than does overcontrol, and that the effects may be strongest for same-sex parent–child pairs (Alloy et al., 2006a). The same authors have also reviewed studies addressing the question whether affectionless control is specific to depression or is related to other problems such as anxiety and externalizing disorders as well. Their conclusion is that the evidence is mixed at this point, and that under some conditions hostile and controlling parenting styles may elicit conduct and behavioural problems as well as depression.

A critical issue in determining whether depression is the likely outcome of poor parenting quality is its psychological effects on the child. Many have speculated that criticism and lack of warmth and caring convey a message to the child that he or she is not valued—or that overcontrol conveys a message of incompetence and untrustworthiness. According to Blatt and Homann (1992), certain depressed persons are likely to have had parents who set high standards, and are harshly critical, intrusive, and controlling in an attempt to get their children to meet their high expectations. As a result, the child constantly berates herself or himself, and attacks the self as worthless. Cognitions about worthlessness and unlovability set the stage for depression, as discussed in Chapter 5. In recent years studies have confirmed that higher levels of negative parenting styles including low warmth and negative feedback are associated with negative cognitions in the children. For example, Garber and Flynn (2001) found that mothers' "affectionless control" style predicted children's lower self-esteem 2 years later (see also review in Alloy et al., 2006a). Moreover, studies have indicated that the association between negative parenting style and offspring depression is accounted for by negative cognitions such as low self-esteem, negative explanatory style, and other dysfunctional cognitions (e.g., Liu, 2003; review by Alloy et al., 2006a).

In addition to negative cognitions that may link poor parenting with later depression, biological processes may also be involved. In a novel study, Hooley, Gruber, Scott, Hiller, and Yurgelun-Todd (2005) examined activation of a brain region thought to be implicated in depression, the dorsolateral prefrontal cortex (DLPFC), while formerly depressed women listened to audiotaped critical or praise comments about themselves by their own mothers. Even though the women were no longer depressed, they showed significantly less activation of the DLPFC during criticism than did never-depressed controls, but the two groups did not differ on responses to praise. The authors suggest that vulnerability to depression might involve failure to engage the prefrontal cortex during psychosocial threat such as criticism, possibly leading to more pronounced negative emotion. The origins of such brain differences remain a matter of speculation, but Chapter 4 discusses possible biological mechanisms of the etiology of depression.

Summary. This brief review of research indicates that the quality of early life experiences in the family may contribute to depression. The quality of the attachment bond, the experience of critical, rejecting, or overcontrolling parenting and disrupted family life appear to set the stage for depression. Children exposed to such experiences may become depressed, while adults who experienced such events in childhood may be vulnerable to depressive reactions when faced with stressful experiences. Most of the research to date is correlational, however, with little direct evidence of a causal relationship between early negative events and depression. Nevertheless, the associations are robust and well-replicated, suggesting that disruption of close family relationships may be a critical vulnerability factor for depression. Although research has yet to fully clarify the mechanisms accounting for the associations with depression, it is likely that maladaptive family relationships create children's negative cognitions about the worth and competence of the self, and overwhelm or impair important adaptive skills that would help to avoid or resolve stressful situations. Such experiences contribute to vulnerability to react with depression when a negative event is encountered that is interpreted as a depletion of the self and beyond one's ability to overcome its impact.

Impact of depression on family relationships

Not only do some forms of depression appear to result from inadequate emotional connectedness with parents, but the reverse direction of effects is also important: Depression appears to *create* interpersonal disruptions in families. In the following sections, ways in which depression is associated with dysfunctional family interactions are discussed. In these ways, depression may induce negative reactions in others and promote disturbed interactions; in turn such stressful relationships may contribute to further depression.

At the most basic level of the effects of depression, the symptoms of depression may contribute to difficulties in close relationships. Irritability, loss of energy and enjoyment, sensitivity to criticism, pessimistic or even suicidal thoughts may initially elicit concern from others, but eventually may seem burdensome, unreasonable, or even willful—sometimes eroding the support of spouses, friends, and family (Coyne, 1976). There is ample evidence of an association between depression and poor marital adjustment. In their classic book, Weissman and Paykel (1974) were among the first to characterize the marriages of depressed women as fraught with friction, inadequate communication, dependency, overt hostility, resentment and guilt, poor sexual relationships, and a lack of affection—patterns of negative interactions confirmed by observational studies (e.g., S. L. Johnson & Jacob, 1997). Meta-analyses across multiples studies have indicated significant associations between depressive symptoms or diagnoses and self-reported poor marital satisfaction (Whisman, 2001). Rates of divorce and never-married status are elevated among those with recurring depression (e.g., Coryell, Scheftner, Keller, Endicott, Maser, & Klerman, 1993). Given the overall associations between depression and marital distress, four issues are pertinent: (1) Does marital strife cause depression? (2) Does depression cause marital strife? (3) Are marital problems unique in their relationship to depression? (4) Why is there a link between marital problems and depression?

Marital difficulties cause depression.   Most investigators acknowledge that the relationship between depression and poor marital adjustment is bidirectional—depression causing problems with intimate partners, and marital dysfunction causing depression. Conflict in a marriage or close relationship, or the ending of a desired intimacy are obviously highly stressful experiences that often precipitate depression. There is fairly strong evidence from longitudinal studies that earlier relationship dissatisfaction predicts depressive symptoms or episodes (e.g., Fincham, Beach, Harold, & Osborne, 1997). For instance, Whisman and Bruce (1999) examined reported marital dissatisfaction in over 900 nondepressed married adults in an epidemiological sample, and examined occurrence of major depression in the subsequent 12 months. They found that dissatisfied spouses were nearly 3 times more likely to develop a depressive episode than satisfied spouses, and the effects were similar for men and women.

Research has also confirmed that relationship difficulties affect the course of depression. For instance, spouse expressions of criticism and negative attitudes toward the depressed person (sometimes termed the construct of "expressed emotion") have been shown to predict relapse following treatment or hospitalization, according to a review by Butzlaff and Hooley (1998). Studies of family functioning of hospitalized depressed patients indicate that those with poorer family functioning were less likely to recover by 12 months and to have worse long-term course of depression (Keitner, Ryan, Miller, Kohn, Bishop, & Epstein, 1995; Keitner, Ryan, Miller, & Zlotnick, 1997). Overall, therefore, conflict and dissatisfaction in marital relationships may contribute to the onset and continuing course of depressive disorders.

Depression causes marital difficulties.   As we have seen in discussions of depressive symptoms and cognitions, depression is typically accompanied by characteristically negative interpretations, so that a depressed person might focus on the annoying, less rewarding aspects of the marriage that he or she largely overlooks when not depressed, and he or she may be irritable, withdrawn, and generally not pleasant to be around. It appears that the partner's depression may affect the behaviour and attitudes of the well spouse in negative ways, possibly causing or exacerbating marital unhappiness in both partners (Coyne, 1976). Whisman, Uebelacker, and Weinstock (2004) attempted to tease apart the influence of mood state and marital dissatisfaction in subjects and their partners, and found that not only did current depressed mood predict marital dissatisfaction for the self, but also the spouse's depressed mood predicted the partner's dissatisfaction. Coyne, Thompson, and Palmer (2002) studied attitudes of female depressed patients and their spouses, and found that both partners reported more marital distress, poor conflict-resolution tactics, and less positive expressions of affection, compared to nondepressed couples. A 4-year longitudinal study of newlywed couples confirmed that depressive symptoms predicted lower marital satisfaction levels over time as much as marital satisfaction levels predicted depressive symptoms (Davila, Karney, Hall, & Bradbury, 2003). The romantic relationships of young women assessed over a 5-year period indicated that lower quality of the relationships at the end of the follow-up and the boyfriends' dissatisfaction were significantly correlated with the amount of time the women had spent in major depressive episodes (Rao et al., 1999).

Finally, it should be noted that, although the state of being in a depressive episode may contribute to marital difficulties, there is substantial evidence that even when treated or no longer depressed, many depressed individuals have persisting interpersonal dysfunction including marital dissatisfaction and conflict (e.g., Billings & Moos, 1985; Hammen & Brennan, 2002; Weissman & Paykel, 1974).

Unique association between depression and difficulty in close relationships. Is marital maladjustment more likely to occur with depression than other disorders? Some have speculated that for many people, the vulnerability to develop depression is rooted in dysfunctions in the ability to manage close relationships, possibly originating in insecure attachment bonds or poor parenting in childhood so that the individual has difficulties in trust, closeness, management of conflict, and other interpersonal skills and attitudes. While there is suggestive evidence for many of these ideas as reviewed in this chapter, there is little research on whether intimate relationship difficulties are more associated with depression than with other disorders. However, one study is noteworthy: Zlotnick et al. (2000) used a large epidemiological database to compare people who were currently depressed, nondepressed, and those with other psychiatric disorders on ratings of the quality of relationships with their spouses/partners. The depressed individuals—both men and women—reported significantly fewer positive and more negative interactions with their partners than did the other two groups. Thus, there may be something specific about depression and dissatisfaction in intimate relationships that does not occur or is not as marked among those who have nondepressive disorders.

Mechanisms of marital dysfunction in couples with depression.   Why is there a strong association between depressive disorders and marital difficulties? Little evidence exists to address the issue but there are several speculative hypotheses. Obviously, the symptoms of depression itself, as noted earlier, may impede marital communication and satisfaction. Furthermore, as Coyne (1976) noted, there may be a deteriorating marital process in which initial concern and caring by the well spouse for the depressed spouse eventually is replaced by resentment and impatience—reactions likely perceived by the depressed person as rejection and lack of sympathy, provoking further depression. Because depression is often misunderstood as largely within the sufferer's control, spouses may be perplexed and frustrated when the depressed partner does not quickly bounce back or take the steps the well partner believes will be fruitful ("don't let things bother you so much," "go get a new job if this one is causing you distress"). The burden of caring for a depressed person is stressful, and often overwhelms the caretaker. Spouses and partners are often especially troubled by the restrictions in social and leisure activities, and the depressed persons' withdrawal, worry, and suicidal thoughts (e.g., Coyne et al., 1987; Fadden, Bebbington, & Kuipers, 1987).

Vulnerability to depression itself may include personality predispositions, insecure attachment expectations, and behavioural styles such as overdependency on others that create tension in relationships. These vulnerability features may contribute to dysfunctional relationships—and are reviewed elsewhere in the chapter.

Finally, a further hypothesis is that depressed people tend to marry other people with psychological problems, thus increasing the chances of marital disharmony. A review and meta-analysis of several studies of patients with mood disorders confirmed the significant likelihood that individuals with depressive disorders marry others with depression (Mathews & Reus, 2001). Depressed women patients have also been found to have higher rates of marriage to men with antisocial and substance use disorders (e.g., Hammen, 1991a). Research on nonpatient samples similarly shows spouse similarity for depressive disorders (e.g., Galbaud du Fort, Bland, Newman, & Boothroyd, 1998; Hammen & Brennan, 2002), and wife major depression associated with husband antisocial personality disorder (Galbaud du Fort et al., 1998). While the possible reasons for "nonrandom mating" are beyond the scope of this chapter, the implications of such marital patterns are clear: Marriages in which both partners experience symptoms and vulnerabilities to disorder may give rise to marital discord and instability by contributing to stressful home environments and potentially to limited skills for resolving interpersonal disputes.

Effects of parental depression on children. Over the past two decades research has demonstrated that one of the most profoundly significant effects of depression on the family is the increased risk that children of a depressed parent will develop depressive disorders and other forms of psychopathology. Reviews suggest that approximately half of the offspring of depressed parents develop disorders (e.g., reviewed in Beardslee et al., 1998). Pilowsky and colleagues (2006) reported that 45% of 7- to 17-year-old children of currently depressed women in treatment had a lifetime disorder, including 19% with depressive disorder, a rate similar to that found in a study of 15-year-old offspring of depressed community women (Hammen & Brennan, 2001). When followed up over periods ranging from 3 to 20 years, studies indicate that rates of recurrent depression and other disorders in the offspring are high, and also that the children of depressed parents display substantial psychosocial impairment and health problems (e.g., Hammen, Burge, Burney, & Adrian, 1990; Lewinsohn, Olino, & Klein, 2005; Lieb, Isensee, Hofler, Wittchen, 2002; Timko, Cronkite, Berg, & Moos, 2002; Weissman, Wickramaratne, Nomura, Warner, Pilowsky, & Verdeli, 2006). Research also indicates that even very young children—infants and toddlers—demonstrate impaired cognitive, behavioural, and social adjustment if their mothers are depressed (e.g., Cicchetti, Rogosch, & Toth, 1998; Dawson et al., 2003; Field, Lang, Martinez, Yando, Pickens, & Bendell, 1996; NICHD Early Child Care Research Network, 1999). Most of the research has been based on maternal depression, but depression in fathers also appears to have a negative association with children's outcomes (reviewed in Kane & Garber, 2004). Overall, the research consistently indicates that having a depressed parent is one of the strongest known risk factors for depression.

The reasons for the negative impact of parental depression on children include a variety of genetic and environmental possibilities.

Genetic and neurobiological factors were reviewed in Chapter 4, including gene–environment interactions. It seems clear that whatever modest genetic contributions to offspring depression exist, a considerable amount of the explanation of the effects of parental depression comes from a complex and interacting set of family, environmental stress, cognitive, and interpersonal factors. Goodman and Gotlib (1999) presented an integrative model based on numerous studies, emphasizing a variety of risk factors contributing to depression vulnerability (such as neurobiological, skills deficits, cognitive, affective, and interpersonal factors), that may eventually predict depression and other disorders. Investigators have observed that depression in a parent typically occurs in the context of marital problems, chronic stressful family circumstances, difficult parent–child relationships and maladaptive communication patterns, and parental personality, interpersonal, and cognitive characteristics that impair the child's acquisition of social and problem-solving skills.

Considerable attention, for example, has been directed at quality of parent–child relations in families with a depressed parent. Numerous studies have indicated that the very young children of depressed women develop insecure attachments (e.g, see review in Gelfand & Teti, 1990). Lovejoy et al. (2000) conducted a meta-analysis of studies of parent–child interactions, and identified three commonly studied variables: negative/hostile interactions (negative affect, criticism, negative facial expression); positive behaviours (pleasant affect, praise, affectionate contact); and disengagement (ignoring, withdrawal, silence, gaze aversion). The meta-analyses showed that depressed mothers differed significantly from nondepressed mothers, displaying more negative and disengaged behaviours; depressed mothers also were less positive. Negative interactions were more pronounced among currently depressed women, but studies have suggested that even when no longer depressed the interpersonal styles of formerly depressed women continue to show dysfunctions compared to never-depressed women (e.g., Hammen & Brennan, 2002). As discussed in a previous section, negativity of the mother–child relationship is presumed to result in a variety of consequences for the child, including impaired cognitive development, negative cognitions about the self, and dysfunctional interpersonal strategies, contributing to vulnerability to develop depression under stressful circumstances.

Although difficulties in the parent–child relationship may be one mechanism by which depression is "transmitted" from parent to child, Goodman and Gotlib (1999) caution that many factors may be involved. Hammen et al. (2004), for example, showed that the link between maternal and youth depression in a sample of 15-year-olds was accounted for by stressful family lives (including marital discord and poor relationships with the mother's own family of origin)—conditions that affected quality of the parent–child relationship as well as quality of the child's own social competence, and exposure to stress, which in turn was a proximal cause of depression. Further study of the complex associations among multiple variables in high-risk samples is a fruitful strategy for understanding vulnerability to depression.

Social behaviours of depressed persons

The research on family functioning indicates that depressed people experienced difficulties in their relationships with their parents as children, and with their spouses and children when adults—and that depressed children also experience problems in their interactions with family members. What about more general social relationships with others, including strangers? What is the nature of interpersonal difficulties that depressed people have, and how might social difficulties or vulnerabilities lead to depression? In the following section the extensive research is organized into two major topics: interpersonal characteristics of depressed persons, and the impact of stressors under conditions of interpersonal vulnerabilities.

Interpersonal characteristics of depressed persons

This section explores the extent to which there may be characteristics of depressed people that reflect cognitions or behaviours that have negative consequences on their relationships with other people.

Responses of others to depression. Beginning with the hypothesis of Coyne (1976) noted earlier, numerous studies have examined the proposition that depression elicits negative responses from others. A variety of controlled, simulated laboratory experiments have documented that, indeed, interacting with a depressed person often (although not invariably) results in negative emotional reactions in the other person, relatively more negative verbal and nonverbal interactions, and indicators of rejection in the form of lack of desire for further contact (e.g., Gotlib & Beatty, 1985; Gotlib & Meltzer, 1987;

Hammen & Peters, 1978; Stephens, Hokanson, & Welker, 1987; Strack & Coyne, 1983). Other studies that used "real life" situations such as college roommates have also found that over time the roommates of depressed individuals themselves became more dysphoric (Howes, Hokanson, & Loewenstein, 1985). Furthermore, both roommates reported low enjoyment of their contacts (Hokanson, Rubert, Welker, Hollander, & Hedeen, 1989). In fact, Hokanson, Hummer, and Butler (1991) found that the stably depressed subjects perceived high levels of hostility and unfriendliness in their roommates. Taken together, these patterns are consistent with those from many of the simulated interaction studies with strangers: depressed persons elicited more negative emotions and relatively greater social rejection from non-depressed others.

Mechanisms of interpersonal difficulties in depressed persons. Why does depression elicit negative reactions in others? Coyne and colleagues (e.g., Coyne, Burchill, & Stiles, 1991) speculated that depression induces negative mood, that is aversive to others, leading to rejection. Coyne et al. (1991) also observed that depressed people are often needy and seek reassurance of their worthiness from others, but that neediness or reassurance-seeking may actually provoke negative reactions. Reassurance-seeking may be annoying to others because depressed people may appear to be unreasonable and irrational in their worries, insecurities, and lack of apparent motivation and energy—so that their "inconsolability" is irritating and burdensome to those trying to help. The depressed person may appear to be unable or unwilling to accept the reassurance or take the steps the nondepressed partners think are needed to overcome depression. Several studies have shown that excessive reassurance-seeking may result in increased levels of depression over time, presumably due to the negative reactions and perceived rejection it elicits in others (e.g., Joiner & Schmidt, 1998; Potthoff, Holahan, & Joiner, 1995).

Various deficits in social skills have also been hypothesized to account for negative reactions to depressed people. Studies have indeed shown that both depressed persons themselves, as well as observers, rate them as less socially skilled than nondepressed persons (e.g., reviewed in Segrin, 2000; Tse & Bond, 2004). When people are depressed they are less verbally fluent and have more monotonous speech, and poor eye contact (reviewed in Segrin & Abramson, 1994). Segrin and Abramson (1994) argue that such "depressive" behaviours elicit negative reactions from others because they violate certain norms of communication such as responsiveness, politeness, and expectations of mutual involvement. That is, they fail to engage others and respond with interest and attention, so that interacting with them is aversive and unrewarding.

Certainly, in the depressive state, the symptoms of apathy and anhedonia, social withdrawal, low energy, and negative expectations create obstacles to pleasant and constructive communication. A key question, however, is whether depressed individuals have relatively stable social characteristics that might contribute to vulnerability to develop depression, or whether their social deficiencies are temporary symptoms of the depressive state. While it appears that many of the poor social skills may be associated with the depressed state (e.g., Segrin, 2000; Tse & Bond, 2004), there may also be relatively enduring traits such as dependency, negative interpersonal cognitions, and deficiencies in social problem-solving skills that have the potential to persist and contribute to future depressive experiences.

Personality traits: dependency and introversion. Clinical lore and empirical observations have noted that an important predictor of depression is dependency (or the related construct of sociotropy)—emotional reliance on others—the belief that the affection, acceptance, and support of other people is essential to personal worth. There are two versions of this approach—one emphasizing trait dependency as a vulnerability factor for developing depression, and the other emphasizing a diathesis-stress model that depression occurs when a match between interpersonal stressful life events and underlying dependency motives and cognitions occurs (reviewed in a later section).

There is a long history of studies showing that depressed people have relatively more dependency beliefs than nondepressed people (reviewed by Nietzel & Harris, 1990). Although some studies have suggested that dependency is related to current depression, a review by Zuroff et al. (2004) concluded that levels of dependency are relatively stable over time. High levels of dependency predict future onset or relapse of major depression (e.g., Alnaes & Torgersen, 1997; Sanathara, Gardner, Prescott, & Kendler, 2003). Attempting to further understand the nature of dependency, L. A. Clark et al. (1994) examined its correlates, and reported that dependency appears to be a characterological dimension of inhibited expression, particularly of difficulty expressing hostility and anger. Dependency traits are generally more elevated in women than men (Bornstein, 1992). The implications of these findings for excess depression in women are apparent: to the extent that women are relatively more socialized both to orient toward others and to suppress expressions of aggression, they may thereby acquire a vulnerability to depressive experiences.

In addition to dependency, a large quantity of research has linked the personality dimensions of neuroticism and introversion–extraversion to depression. Although neuroticism is not specifically an interpersonal behaviour, it is a higher order personality dimension with implications for social behaviours because it is considered a "difficult" temperament, defined by negative emotionality and high reactivity to stress. Persons scoring high on neuroticism, for example, may actually contribute to the occurrence of interpersonal life events and chronic problems. Neuroticism is a powerful predictor of depressive episodes, according to a review by Enns and Cox (1997; see also Fanous et al., 2002; Schmitz, Kugler, & Rollnik, 2003). Although the level of neuroticism may decline with reductions in depression symptoms, recent longitudinal studies have supported the idea that relatively higher levels of neuroticism persist (e.g., L. A. Clark, Vittengl, Kraft, & Jarrett, 2003; Santor, Bagby, & Joffe, 1997).

Another higher order personality factor is introversion—the preference for solitary activities and discomfort in social situations, which is also related to the construct of childhood behavioural inhibition. Studies of adults indicate that introversion is consistently associated with depression both during the episode and in remission (e.g., Hirschfeld, Klerman, Clayton, & Keller, 1983; see Barnett & Gotlib, 1988). Introverted behaviours and cognitions would imply that a person might be vulnerable to develop depression, because he or she may have difficulties in his or her interpersonal relationships, perhaps experience less enjoyment of social situations and relationships, and have less self-confidence in social occasions. Gladstone and Parker (2006), for example, found that individuals who reported childhood social withdrawal and fearfulness were significantly more likely to develop major depression by adulthood, especially when they developed social anxiety. Thus, introverted and inhibited temperament that led to social fears and anxiety predicted depression. We might speculate that depression results from stressful events and circumstances associated with difficulties in experiencing comfortable social contacts and relationships—a topic to which we now turn.

Stress and social functioning

Most models of depression are "diathesis-stress" models, positing that stressful life events or circumstances provoke or challenge the person's underlying vulnerabilities, triggering depression. There are several specific ways in which research has demonstrated the importance of interpersonal functioning or social characteristics in predicting individuals' responses to stressors.

Specific vulnerability to interpersonal life events.   As noted in Chapter 5, both cognitive (e.g., A. T. Beck, 1983) and psychodynamic (e.g., Arieti & Bemporad, 1980; Blatt, 1974) theorists have hypothesized that different subtypes of depression are associated with different life stress vulnerabilities and express somewhat different symptoms. Specifically, one form of vulnerability is the dependent or sociotropic person who is especially likely to base the sense of personal worth and competence on close relations with other people and to become depressed when faced with interpersonal rejection or loss. It was noted in Chapter 5 that reasonably strong empirical support has been reported for the predictive association of sociotropy or dependency and depression when the person has experienced a stressor with interpersonal content. Sociotropic persons do not become depressed when they encounter a negative life event, such as an achievement failure, that does not match their domain of vulnerability.

Note that the "specific vulnerability" process is hypothesized to be the same for men and women, but since women may be more likely to subscribe to dependent values and beliefs—and since interpersonal events may be more common than achievement events (Hammen et al., 1985)—such matching may particularly have implications for the preponderance of depression in women. That is, if women are more likely to be socialized to value close connections with others and to be dependent on others' approval and love, they are more vulnerable to depression in the wake of interpersonal losses, conflict, and rejections.

Hammen and colleagues (Hammen et al., 1995) also explored the matching of interpersonal life events to vulnerability due to negative cognitions about attachment relationships (that is, beliefs about ability to depend on others, fear of abandonment). In a longitudinal study of young adult women, relatively more "insecure" attachment beliefs, combined with high levels of interpersonal stress, predicted subsequent depression. Taken together, studies suggest that stressful interpersonal life events may trigger depressive reactions in individuals who have particular vulnerabilities due to maladaptive traits and cognitions that affect their skills and beliefs about themselves in relations with others.

Social support.   A considerable body of research indicates that the availability of supportive relationships with others—or the perception of such support—plays an important role in whether individuals will become depressed. Presumably, individuals who experience close bonds, acceptance, and caring will feel greater self-esteem and a sense of efficacy, helping to guard against depression. Individuals with low levels of social resources are more likely to become depressed. A multinational community survey in Europe found that higher levels of depression were associated with perceptions of lower social support (Dalgard et al., 2006). A large-scale sample of medical and psychiatric patients indicated that the extent of depressive symptoms decreased over a 2-year period as a function of availability of perceived support, and that if support was available, patients were less likely to develop a new episode (Sherbourne, Hays, & Wells, 1995). There is mixed evidence for gender differences in the association between depression and social support, but when differences are found they typically indicate that women's depression is more likely than men's depression to be associated with lower levels of social support (e.g., Kendler, Myers, & Prescott, 2005c).

In addition to the association of low levels of social support and depression, some have specifically predicted that social support "buffers" the ill effects of negative life events on depression (e.g., G. W. Brown & Harris, 1978; S. Cohen & Wills, 1985). Such research suggests that among those who have stressful life events, only those with low support will become depressed. Despite the plausibility of the hypothesis, however, recent research has fairly consistently failed to find evidence of "buffering" (Burton, Stice, & Seeley, 2004; Wade & Kendler, 2000). Instead, both high levels of stress regardless of support and low levels of support regardless of stress are associated with development of depression.

One of the remaining challenges in the social support–depression link is to clarify the mechanisms. As noted, much of the research involves individuals' reports of availability of supportive relationships or social network size, as well as subjective appraisals of how much support they get from such relationships. The subjective appraisal of the helpfulness or availability of others is often found to be lower for depressed people than comparison groups (e.g., reviewed in Gotlib & Hammen, 1992). Such appraisals may be distorted by the negative thinking associated with depressive symptoms, although some studies report that even when no longer symptomatic, depressed individuals report restricted networks or perceptions of less support (e.g., Billings & Moos, 1985, Billings, Cronkite, & Moos, 1983).

The source of limited support among depressed people is not fully understood. It may be due to social skill deficits or other characteristics of the individual as discussed above. As Coyne et al. (1987) have speculated, depressed individuals may alienate those close to them because of their excessive demands for support—a process that elicits rejection and promotes isolation and negative self-perceptions that in turn serve to intensify or maintain depression.

Social problem solving. Several investigators have proposed that deficient problem-solving and coping skills may contribute to depressive reactions to stressors (e.g., Nezu, 1987). Several studies have shown that depressed individuals do indeed display less effective solutions to hypothetical problems (e.g., Gotlib & Asarnow, 1979). Nezu and Ronan (1985; Nezu, 1987) suggested that depressed individuals are particularly deficient in generating and implementing solutions to interpersonal problems.

However, it is unclear whether depressed persons evidence specifically social problem-solving difficulties or more general deficits in coping responses to stressors. An examination of depressed individuals' coping strategies has found that they are relatively less likely to elect active problem-solving approaches to difficulties, and instead rely more than nondepressed people on avoidant and emotion-focused coping (e.g., Billings et al., 1983; Billings & Moos, 1984)—although when no longer depressed their coping behaviours may not differ significantly from those of control subjects (e.g., Billings & Moos, 1985). Avoidance coping, such as trying not to think about one's problems, predicted poorer depressive outcomes and greater likelihood of a recurrence of depression over a 2-year period in a large sample of medical and psychiatric patients (Sherbourne et al., 1995). As noted in earlier chapters, females in particular have been shown to rely on "ruminative" reactions to their depressive symptoms, intensifying self-focused, passive strategies rather than active problem solving or distraction (Nolen-Hoeksema, 1991). Lyubomirsky and Nolen-Hoeksema (1995) found that a consequence of ruminative self-focus among depressed subjects was less effective problem solving and poorer generation of means to solve hypothetical interpersonal problem scenarios (see also Lyubomirsky et al., 1999; Watkins & Moulds, 2005).

Generation of interpersonal stressors. An additional strategy for exploring social factors in vulnerability to depression has been to examine the extent to which individuals contribute to the occurrence of negative life events that are interpersonal in nature. As noted in Chapter 5, there is ample evidence that individuals with histories of depression contribute to the occurrence of stressors, thus risking triggering further depressive episodes. These patterns have been especially noted in women contributing to interpersonal stressors and events with conflict content (reviewed in Hammen, 2006). As we noted in Chapter 5, studies continue to explore the origins and mechanisms of stress generation. However, its consequences are painfully clear: Difficulties in interpersonal relationships are potent predictors of depressive reactions and may contribute to a vicious cycle of depression and stress.

Summary

- Difficulties in social relationships may be a key element of many depressions: disrupted social connectedness may cause depression, and depression disrupts relationships, potentially causing depression continuation or recurrence.
- Early adverse experiences reflecting disrupted bonds between children and parents appear to be associated with vulnerability for later depression. Early loss, adversity, insecure attachment, and difficulties in the parent–child relationship have been linked to vulnerability for later depression.
- Depression affects the family. Not only are the symptoms of depression difficult for other family members to cope with, but also depression takes a toll on marital relationships and is a risk factor for development of depression and negative outcomes in offspring of depressed parents.
- The social behaviours of depressed people appear to have a negative impact on others, potentially leading to rejection. While heightened when the person is in a depressed state, some behaviours and traits commonly displayed by depressed people, such as dependency and reassurance-seeking, may persist even when the person is not depressed.
- Maladaptive interpersonal styles and vulnerabilities may contribute to the occurrence of stressful life events and chronic difficulties that result in further depression. Furthermore, people who are vulnerable to depression may be deficient in key problem-solving and support-eliciting skills that help them to cope with the effects of stressful life events.

Biological treatment of depression 7

Stephanie experienced two bouts of major depression that each lasted for about 6 months. During one episode she sought counselling, but discussions of her life difficulties didn't seem to relieve the symptoms of depression, and she dragged herself through the bleak days and endless nights until the depression just seemed to wear away. Recently, when she began to sink into yet another depressive episode, she sought treatment from a medical doctor who prescribed a common antidepressant medication. Within a week her energy improved and she slept more soundly, and within 2 weeks her mood was definitely better and she began to feel able to face some of the difficult personal events that had precipitated the depression.

As we discuss in this chapter, there are several well-established biological interventions as well as several more experimental approaches to treatment. This chapter discusses antidepressant medications, electroconvulsive therapy (ECT), transcranial magnetic stimulation (TMS), light therapy, sleep deprivation, and physical exercise.

Comment on treatment of depression

Before discussing biological or psychotherapy approaches to treating depression, it is important to emphasize a singular fact about treatment in general. The majority of individuals with major depression or dysthymic disorder do not seek treatment for their condition. And of those who do seek help, surveys have generally found that only about 50% of individuals with such disorders seek treatment from a mental health specialist, with others visiting general practitioners or seeking assistance from family or friends (Narrow, Regier, Rae, Manderscheid,

& Locke, 1993). Furthermore, there is substantial delay between the first onset of depression and initial help seeking, with only one third of the people who seek help doing so in the same year as the first onset of depression, leading to a median delay for treatment seeking of at least 5 years (Kessler, Olfson, & Berglund, 1998a; Olfson, Kessler, Berglund, & Lin, 1998). Unfortunately, as we have seen, the consequences of depression are extremely negative in terms of impaired functioning, reduced health, and impact on others. Moreover, individuals whose depression goes unrecognized and untreated may actually burden the primary care sector and inflate health care costs for medical problems (G. Simon, Ormel, VonKorff, & Barlow, 1995).

The reasons for failure to seek treatment for depression are numerous. Commonly depression is unrecognized as such by the individual, who might attribute symptoms to medical conditions or to stress and circumstances—leading either to seeking medical treatment or to the expectation that the distress is simply an aspect of the stress to be endured. Western culture particularly emphasizes self-reliance, and many with depression feel guilty about "weakness" and forego seeking help because they believe depression requires firmer will or personal effort—"stiff upper lip" and so forth. Although women are given greater latitude in help seeking, both women and men typically believe that depression is under their own control (if only they were stronger) or that with the help of friends and family they will get by. An additional factor may be lack of resources, or negative expectations about the possible outcome of treatment even if it is sought. Depression itself magnifies pessimistic beliefs that treatment cannot help.

Antidepressant medications

There has been a huge expansion in the prescription of antidepressant medications to treat mood disorders over the last 25 years. The surge in antidepressant use appears to be associated with the development of new drugs (27 now approved in the USA) and direct marketing to the public, plus increased awareness of their potential usefulness.

Despite their increased use, however, antidepressants continue to be *underutilized* among depressed outpatients compared with the frequency of depressive disorders, according to large-scale surveys of patients in treatment (Wang, Lane, Olfson, Pincus, Wells, & Kessler, 2005; Wells, Katon, Rogers, & Camp, 1994). Moreover, even when they are prescribed for patients, they are often administered in sub-therapeutic dosages. Analysis of the content of treatment in comparison to published treatment guidelines shows that no more than 30% of patients receiving treatment get even minimally acceptable treatment (Katz, Kessler, Lin, & Wells, 1998; Wang, Berglund, & Kessler, 2000).

Like many drugs used in the treatment of mental disorders, the discovery of antidepressant medications was partly fortuitous, an observed side effect of drugs used to treat medical conditions. Medications that were known to deplete certain neurotransmitters in the brain appeared to cause depression, while those that increased specific neurotransmitters reduced depression. These early effects were focused largely on the monoamine neurotransmitters: norepinephrine (noradrenaline), dopamine, and serotonin. In the 1950s, two classes of medications came to be introduced into widespread use, the *tricyclic antidepressants* (named for their chemical structure) and the *monoamine oxidase inhibitors* (MAOIs). Since 1987, a second generation of antidepressants with a different chemical structure has been developed. The most popular of these newer antidepressants are the *selective serotonin reuptake inhibitors* (SSRIs), such as fluoxetine (Prozac), which block the presynaptic reuptake of serotonin, thereby increasing its availability to the postsynaptic neuron and enhancing serotonergic function. However, there are also a number of novel antidepressants with unique action on multiple neurotransmitters (e.g., Buproprion, Venlafaxine, and Nefazodone).

A recent experimental treatment is the use of antiglucocorticoid drugs as antidepressants. Antiglucocorticoid drugs improve the regulation of the HPA stress response, in particular by reducing the elevated levels of the stress hormone, cortisol, that are found in depression (Wolkowitz & Reus, 1999; Wolkowitz et al., 1999). There is some preliminary evidence for antiglucocorticoid drugs having modest efficacy as an adjunct to other antidepressants (Jahn, Schick, Kiefer, Kellner, Yassouridis, & Wiedemann, 2004) and as a treatment for psychotic depression (DeBattista et al., 2006), although more large-scale data are necessary before antiglucocorticoids can be accepted as an important class of antidepressants. Table 7.1 lists several of more than 20 currently available antidepressants.

Use of antidepressants. Antidepressants are especially recommended for moderate-to-severe levels of depression. Some medications are initially taken at low dosages and build up to a therapeutic level over time adjusted for the person's needs and reactions, while some of the

TABLE 7.1

Selected antidepressant medications: Chemical and brand names

Generic (chemical) name	Brand name
Tricyclic antidepressants	
Imipramine	Tofranil
Amitriptyline	Elavil
Clomipramine	Anafranil
Desipramine	Norpramin
Monoamine oxidase inhibitors	
Phenelzine	Nardil
Isocarboxazid	Marplan
Selective serotonin reuptake inhibitors	
Fluoxetine	Prozac
Sertraline	Zoloft
Paroxetine	Paxil
Citalopram	Celexa
"Novel" antidepressants	
Buproprion	Wellbutrin
Nefazodone	Serzone
Venlafaxine	Effexor

newer drugs have a standard dosage for everyone that starts immediately. Although it was previously judged that the positive effects of antidepressants are not seen for at least 2 weeks, recent reviews suggest that symptomatic improvement occurs during the first two weeks of treatment, and that symptoms continue to improve over the next 6 weeks but at a decreasing rate (Posternak & Zimmerman, 2005; Taylor, Freemantle, Geddes, & Bhagwagar, 2006). For example, in one trial, greater than 50% of all eventual responders to fluoxetine responded within the first 2 weeks, greater than 75% started to respond by week 4, and 90% responded by week 6 (Nierenberg et al., 2000). Given the cumulative response to antidepressants over the first 2 to 6 weeks, depressed people need to be informed that they will not recover immediately. Furthermore, these findings suggest that if a patient has not responded within 4 to 8 weeks, she or he is unlikely to respond to continuation of that antidepressant at the same dose (Gelenberg & Chesen, 2000).

The treatment of current symptoms is referred to as *acute* treatment, but it is only one phase of the recommended course. Once symptoms have diminished, *continuation* treatment is recommended for at least 6 to 9 months in order to prevent relapse of the current episode, and then the medication may be discontinued by tapering off the dosage, as abrupt discontinuation may cause unpleasant side effects. A recent prospective, placebo-controlled study of the optimal length of continuation of antidepressant medication comparing different intervals of treatment discontinuation found that patients successfully treated with antidepressants should continue the antidepressant for at least another 26 weeks to minimize the risk of relapse (Reimherr et al., 1998). A third phase of medication treatment, called *maintenance*, is strongly recommended for individuals who have a history of recurrent episodes of depression. In contrast to the generally agreed period of treatment for continuation, there is less agreement on the ideal duration of maintenance treatment, as no long-term studies have compared the relative efficacy of different durations of maintenance in preventing recurrence, leaving open the question of whether medications should be prescribed indefinitely for those at risk for recurrent depression.

Mechanisms of action.   The tricyclic drugs have complex effects, various ones altering functions of norepinephrine (noradrenaline), dopamine, serotonin, and related neurotransmitter systems. Depending on their specific mechanisms, they may bind to a receptor site in specific neurons, achieving effects by causing a reaction directly or by blocking the effects of naturally occurring substances (for example the MAOIs block the effects of substances that break down the monoamine neurotransmitters, increasing their availability). Alternatively, antidepressant medications may cause the release of more of a particular neurotransmitter, or by blocking the reuptake of a neurotransmitter back into the neuron and thereby increasing the amount of the neurotransmitter that is available in the synapse. In some cases, the medication alters the neurotransmitter receptors, by changing their sensitivity or increasing their numbers. The older tricyclic medications often had effects on several different neurotransmitters, as do several of the novel antidepressants, whereas the SSRIs tend to be more selective, only acting on serotonin.

However, it is now clear that the therapeutic effect of antidepressants is not simply due to increasing levels of neurotransmitter, because the effects on neurotransmitter levels are relatively immediate after the first dose of antidepressant, whereas patients do not show any therapeutic benefit for several weeks. The current speculation is that the mechanism of antidepressant action is via increased levels of neurotransmitters in the synapse activating an intracellular signaling cascade, which ultimately influences neuro-genesis—the ability of neurons in key brain areas to grow and form new connections. The neurotransmitters activate secondary messenger proteins and transcription factors (e.g., cAMP response element binding protein, CREB), which in turn regulate the expression of specific target genes, including the increased expression of neurotrophic factors (e.g., brain-derived neurotrophic factor, BDNF) necessary for the survival, differentiation, growth, and function of particular neurons (Carlezon, Duman, & Nestler, 2005; Duman, Heninger, & Nestler, 1997; Newton et al., 2002; Russo-Neustadt & Chen, 2005; Shelton, 2000). Such factors are important in neuronal plasticity, that is, the growth and formation of new synaptic connections, underlying learning and memory, and are decreased by exposure to stress (Duman et al., 1997; Duman & Monteggia, 2006). In animal models, the expression of neurotrophic factors in key limbic brain regions implicated in depression (e.g., hippocampus, amygdala) is increased by the administration of antidepressants at a time course consistent with that required for the observed antidepressant effect in humans (Hashimoto et al., 2004) and appears necessary for the behavioural effects of antidepressants (Santarelli et al., 2003). Furthermore, antidepressant medications, ECT, TMS, and exercise all increase the up-regulation of BDNF, whereas adult depression is associated with reduced BDNF, whether assessed through the analysis of postmortem hippocampus or through blood serum levels in antidepressant-naïve patients (Duman & Monteggia, 2006; Shimizu et al., 2003).

Effectiveness of antidepressants. All of the current antidepressant medications are about equally effective. Therefore, the consideration of which drug to take depends on previous response to medications, the type of symptoms displayed, life circumstances, as well as side effects. *Individuals* may respond significantly better to one than another, and therefore sometimes a period of trial-and-error is needed to find an effective drug.

How effective are antidepressants in the treatment of *acute* depression? Numerous studies comparing antidepressants to placebo in controlled *blind* trials report response rates for a single antidepressant of between 60% and 70%, compared with about 30% for placebos (reviewed in Thase & Kupfer, 1996), where response is defined as a 50% or more decrease in symptoms on a clinical interview. Note that the definition of "response" is a crucial factor in evaluating treatment success. Importantly, many of the patients who respond to antidepressant medication still experience some symptoms of depression (known as residual depression). In fact, only 20% to 30% of patients treated with antidepressants achieve symptomatic remission (defined as minimal levels of symptoms) (e.g., Nierenberg et al., 1999; Rush et al., 2006a; Trivedi et al., 2006b). Also, many studies do not evaluate how people function in their life roles as parents, employees, and mates. Individuals may achieve reductions in their depression but still have difficulties in managing their lives successfully.

An important issue concerns the choice of treatment for patients who do not fully respond to the initial treatment. For nonresponders, the clinical recommendation is to *switch* to another antidepressant with a different mode of action (Hirschfeld et al., 2002), whereas for partial responders, the clinical recommendation is to first increase antidepressant dose, followed by *augmentation* of the antidepressant with another medication that facilitates the action of the original drug without itself being an antidepressant (e.g., lithium; Bauer, Bschor, Kunz, Berghofer, Strohle, & Muller-Oerlinghausen, 2000) or the addition of another antidepressant (*combination therapy*). However, these treatment recommendations have rarely been tested in randomized controlled trials. An important large-scale (over 3600 patients initially recruited), multisite, multistep, complex, randomized controlled trial investigating this issue is the Sequenced Treatment Alternative to Relieve Depression (STAR*D) trial, which tests the efficacy of switching and augmenting treatment for outpatients who did not initially respond to the SSRI citalopram (M. Fava et al., 2003; Rush et al., 2004). Within the STAR*D project, stepped trials have suggested that augmentation (Trivedi et al., 2006a) and switching to another antidepressant (Rush et al., 2006b) can have clinical benefits after unsuccessful treatment with citalopram, producing remission rates of approximately 25%, although there was no placebo control condition. Confirming the value of the switching strategy, a recent trial found that switching from a tricyclic to a SSRI or vice versa benefited more than 50% of chronically depressed patients who had not responded to the original antidepressant (Thase et al., 2002b). A recent review suggests that combination therapy can be useful treatment for otherwise treatment-refractory patients, particularly if the antidepressants act on different neurotransmitter systems (Dodd, Horgan, Malhi, & Berk, 2005).

A recent review of 31 randomized trials concluded that *continuation treatment* with a range of antidepressants reduced the risk of relapse compared to treatment discontinuation, with the average rate of relapse 18% for active treatment compared to 41% for placebo (Geddes et al., 2003). This treatment effect persisted as long as 36 months, although the majority of studies were only of 12 months' duration.

There is increasing evidence for the effectiveness of long-term, or *maintenance*, psychopharmacology. A number of randomized placebo-controlled trials using tricyclics (Frank et al., 1990; Kocsis et al., 1996; Kupfer et al., 1992; Reynolds et al., 1999), SSRIs (Keller et al., 1998; Lepine, Caillard, Bisserbe, Troy, Hotton, & Boyer, 2004), and novel antidepressants such as venlafaxine (Montgomery, Entsuah, Hackett, Kunz, & Rudolph, 2004), mirtazapine (Thase, Nierenberg, Keller, & Panagides, 2001), and nefazodone (Gelenberg et al., 2003) compared the maintenance of antidepressant medication for between 1 and 5 years after a clinically significant response versus pill placebo for patients with recurrent or chronic depression. In all of these trials, patients receiving placebo were at least twice as likely to experience recurrence as patients on maintenance anti-depressant. However, few trials have examined the effects of main-tenance beyond 1 to 2 years, thereby limiting definitive conclusions, with the exception of the seminal work by Frank et al. (1990) and Kupfer et al. (1992).

As a final issue when considering effectiveness, it has been noted that between 60% and 80% of the response to antidepressants is duplicated by placebo treatment (Khan, Detke, Khan, & Mallinckrodt, 2003), which if the effects of medication and placebo are additive, would suggest that much of the effectiveness of antidepressants is due to a placebo effect with the medication only having a relatively small direct biological effect (Enserink, 1999; Kirsch, 2000). It has been hypothesized that positive expectations and hope associated with belief in the medication working could itself produce beneficial treatment effects. Furthermore, the awareness of side effects could itself enhance the placebo effect by promoting positive expectancy of treatment response, because the experience of a side effect could lead to attributions that the medication has a powerful biological effect. Thus, one limitation of existing antidepressant trials is that there is a greater frequency of side effects in the medication condition than in the inert pill placebo condition, confounding antidepressant effects with placebo effects. This analysis suggests that trials require an active placebo comparison that produces side effects mimicking those of antidepressants. Meta-analyses that evaluated studies that com-pared different antidepressant medications against each other as well as against active and inert placebos provide a partial answer to this issue. The results suggested that drug effects were considerably more modest than previously claimed—and, indeed, only mildly more effective than active placebo (Greenberg, Bornstein, Greenberg, & Fisher, 1992; Moncrieff, Wessely, & Hardy, 1998), although these conclusions are disputed by Quitkin, Rabkin, Gerald, Davis, and Klein (2000).

Side effects.   Common side effects include dry mouth, nausea, blurry vision, weight gain and sexual dysfunction (e.g., erectile difficulties). Some drugs are sedating (causing drowsiness, being slowed down), and some are stimulating (causing anxiety, tremor, rapid heart beat, insomnia). Some antidepressants can be lethal if taken in overdose. It has therefore been recommended that an antidepressant should be chosen to optimize the fit between potential side effects and the symptoms and needs of the individual patient. For example, it would be logical to prescribe stimulating medications to lethargic, psychomotor-retarded patients and sedating medications to anxious, agitated, and insomniac patients, although a recent trial found no added benefit of matching antidepressant with symptom profile (Simon, Heiligenstein, Grothaus, Katon, & Revicki, 1998).

At the most serious extreme, a few medications may cause seizures in rare cases or cardiac irregularities, or other problems. Constant medical evaluation is important; however, most antidepressant medications do not have known therapeutic levels in the blood that can be monitored. MAOI drugs have a unique and potentially life-threatening side effect; suddenly increased blood pressure, stroke, or even death may occur if the person taking such medications also ingests foods or other drugs containing *tyramine*. Tyramine is an amino acid found in many aged foods such as cheese, smoked or pickled fish or meats, red or fortified wines, and other foods and medications. Thus, people on MAOI drugs must restrict their diets accordingly.

The SSRI drugs have become popular because of their *relatively milder* side effects, although there is no evidence that they are any more effective than any other antidepressants. There has been considerable media attention about fluoxetine (Prozac), with it attracting extreme claims that on the one hand it is a "wonder drug" but that on the other hand it causes suicidal feelings and behaviours. Given these concerns, the safety of antidepressants was reviewed by the U.S. Food and Drug Administration (FDA), who issued a public health advisory in 2004, recommending close observation for the emergence of suicidal thoughts and behaviours in all patients treated with antidepressants, especially when treatment starts or dose is increased. This advisory acknowledged that the available evidence did not indicate any increase in suicide risk in adults treated with antidepressants but noted that the early activating effects of antidepressants can sometimes transiently increase suicide risk. Meta-analyses of the data from pharmacotherapy trials have found no difference between antidepressants and placebo in risk of suicide, arguing against antidepressants causally increasing suicide risk (Khan, Leventhal, Khan, & Brown, 2002; Khan, Warner, & Brown, 2000; Storosum, van Zwieten, van den Brink, Gersons, & Broekmans, 2001). However, because clinical trials typically exclude those at high risk for suicide, it is possible that such trials underestimate the risk for suicide. To address this issue, Simon and colleagues used computerized records from a large prepaid health plan in the USA (over 65,000 people) to examine the relationship between antidepressant use in the community and suicide attempts assessed by hospitalizations and death certificates (Simon, Savarino, Operskalski, & Wang, 2006). This study found that the risk of suicide was 1 in 3000 for patients receiving antidepressants and that there was no increase in suicide risk during the first month of antidepressant treatment, although there was an increase in suicide risk during the month preceding the start of antidepressants, perhaps because increased suicidal ideation and behaviour lead to the initiation of treatment. The SSRIs had no greater risk of suicide than the older antidepressants. Similarly, an analysis of county records across the United States found no relationship between antidepressant prescription and suicide rate, with increases in SSRI prescription associated with decreases in the suicide rate, probably reflecting better treatment of depression in those counties prescribing more SSRIs (Gibbons, Hur, Bhaumik, & Mann, 2005).

An additional "side effect" of medications is noncompliance. At least 40% of patients prescribed antidepressants discontinue them within the first month and only 25% continued antidepressant medication for more than 90 days (Olfson, Marcus, Tedeschi, & Wan, 2006). Given the evidence that continuation of medication is important for full acute response and for preventing relapse, many patients are reducing their chances of staying well (Melfi, Chawla, Croghan, Hanna, Kennedy, & Sredl, 1998). Reasons for noncompliance range from unpleasant side effects to psychological concerns about reluctance to use chemicals to control moods or resistance to defining oneself as having a psychiatric problem. There is some evidence that treatment compliance is higher for SSRIs than for MAOIs and tricyclics, perhaps reflecting their milder side effects (e.g., Olfson et al., 2006).

Predicting response.   Can we tell who will respond well to antidepressants? There are currently few robust indicators to predict treatment response (Esposito & Goodnick, 2003; Nierenberg, 2003), although patients with more severe symptoms respond better to antidepressants relative to placebo than patients with less severe symptoms (Khan et al., 2002). There is little evidence that patients with more of the physical symptoms of depression (i.e., "endogenous" depression) respond better to antidepressants, or that depression associated with psychological causes such as negative life events responds worse to antidepressants. In recent years, advances in the genetic understanding of depression (see Chapter 4) have led to the hope that it may be possible to determine genetic markers that indicate differential antidepressant treatment responsiveness and susceptibility to side effects, for example by assessing gene markers of enzymes involved in metabolizing specific antidepressants (e.g., for preliminary evidence of this see Rau et al., 2004; Rausch et al., 2002). Such genotyping has the potential to make treatment choice rational rather than based on trial and error (Roses, 2000).

It is thought that very severe depressions, agitated depression, and depressions with psychotic features do not respond well to antidepressants alone, and may require additional treatment with hospitalization and, possibly, ECT. Also, "atypical" depression, depression involving significant personality disorders, and persons with more severe histories of repeated or prolonged episodes, do not respond as well to tricyclics or SSRIs, and instead seem to respond better to MAOIs or combination therapy (Joyce & Paykel, 1989; Liebowitz et al., 1988; McGrath, Stewart, Janal, Petkova, Quitkin, & Klein, 2000).

Finally, it should be recalled that relatively few depressions arise "endogenously" in the absence of personally significant life difficulties. Consequently, while medications might be useful to reduce the depression which itself is debilitating, they have little effect on the underlying "depressive" circumstances. Thus, many individuals may need psychotherapeutic interventions to deal with such problems. In Chapter 8 the effectiveness of therapies for depression is discussed— including research that has pitted antidepressants and psychotherapy against each other to study their comparative effects.

Antidepressants in treatment of children and adolescents. Not all antidepressants appear to be useful for child and adolescent depression, although there is growing evidence that SSRIs are beneficial. Whilst there are positive findings from open trials, methodologically superior placebo-controlled, double-blind studies find that tricyclic antidepressants are no more effective than placebo in children and adolescents (see review by Sommers-Flanagan & Sommers-Flanagan, 1996). However, in a controlled study of 96 children and adolescents (age 7 to 17) with major depression, there was a significant improvement on clinician ratings of depressive symptoms for fluoxetine compared to placebo, although there was no difference for self-reported symptoms (Emslie et al., 1997). This beneficial effect of SSRIs for adolescent depression has been replicated in two subsequent controlled trials (Emslie et al., 2006; M. B. Keller et al., 2001).

However, there is a need for caution in the use of antidepressants with children and adolescents because of potentially dangerous side effects including cardiac complications and increased suicide risk. Both the British Medicine and Healthcare products Regulatory Agency (MHRA) and the U.S. FDA have issued warnings about the potential risk of suicide for children treated with SSRIs, with the MHRA recommending against the use of all SSRI antidepressants except fluoxetine in children and adolescents. A recent meta-analysis of 24 controlled drug trials in adolescents found that SSRIs significantly, albeit modestly, increased the risk of suicidal ideation and nonfatal self-injury compared to placebo (Hammad, Laughren, & Racoosin, 2006). Nonetheless, care needs to be taken in interpreting these findings given the low levels of suicidality reported, and, because suicidal ideation does not necessarily lead to a suicide attempt.

St John's wort. In the last decade, there has been increasing interest in complementary medicine approaches to depression (Ernst, Rand, & Stevinson, 1998), particularly in the use of extracts of the herb St John's wort (*Hypericum perforatum*) as an antidepressant. Meta-analyses of over 20 randomized trials report that Hypericum extracts were superior to placebo and as effective as antidepressants in response rate for mild-to-moderate depression (Kim, Streltzer, & Goebert, 1999; Linde, Ramirez, Mulrow, Pauls, Weidenhammer, & Melchart, 1996). However, many studies were not methodologically rigorous or properly controlled and did not use patients diagnosed with major depression (Kim et al., 1999). In a more rigorous, double-blind, randomized, placebo-controlled trial of 375 patients with mild-to-moderate major depression, St John's wort was found to be safe and more effective than placebo (Lecrubier, Clerc, Didi, & Kieser, 2002). However, a similar controlled trial found no treatment difference between St John's wort, sertraline, and placebo for patients with major depression, although the failure to find an active effect of the SSRI raises questions as to the sensitivity of the study (J. R. T. Davidson et al., 2002). Likewise, another trial found that St John's wort and placebo had equivalent effects on reducing levels of depressive symptoms, although St John's wort achieved significantly higher levels of remission than placebo (14% vs. 5%; Shelton et al., 2001).

Other nonpharmacological biological treatments

Additional biological interventions sometimes used to treat depression include ECT, TMS, phototherapy for SAD, sleep deprivation, and exercise.

Electroconvulsive therapy

ECT often strikes people as a barbaric, inhumane treatment that should be entirely abolished. Indeed, in past decades it was misused, applied to many patient groups without evidence of effectiveness, and caused physical damage to many persons. Nowadays its use in the USA and Europe is subject to stringent restrictions and is highly variable according to location, hospital, and patient characteristics, reflecting the ambivalence that many psychiatrists experience about it.

Use and effectiveness. ECT has not disappeared for one very good reason. It is extremely effective in the treatment of severe, otherwise-untreatable, depressions. It is the treatment of choice where there are prominent psychotic features of depression, and especially where severe depression has not responded to medication, and in life-threatening situations where rapid response is needed. A recent meta-analysis of controlled trials concluded that ECT is significantly more effective than placebo (in the form of simulated or sham ECT, 6 trials) and more effective than antidepressants (18 trials; Carney et al., 2003).

ECT is currently administered under medically safe conditions, in which patients are first given sedatives, muscle relaxants, or other agents to control potentially damaging physical side effects. The typical course averages 6 to 9 treatments spaced 2 or 3 times per week. The electrical current must be supplied above a threshold necessary to induce a seizure in order to achieve therapeutic effects. Recent evidence suggests that ECT delivered to both hemispheres of the brain simultaneously (bilateral) is more effective than ECT delivered to one hemisphere only (unilateral), and that ECT at a dose substantively higher than the seizure threshold is more effective than low-dose ECT (Carney et al., 2003; McCall, Reboussin, Weiner, & Sackheim, 2000). High-dose right unilateral ECT (500% over seizure threshold) was as effective as bilateral ECT, but with less cognitive side effects such as impairment of memory (Lisanby, Maddox, Prudic, Devanand, & Sackeim, 2000; Sackeim et al., 2000). In a double-blind study, no difference in clinical outcomes was found between ECT administered twice per week versus 3 times per week for 4 weeks, although the cognitive side effects of twice-per-week ECT were milder (Lerer et al., 1995). Thus, it may be that the dose, location, and timing of ECT can be adjusted to optimize treatment effects whilst minimizing side effects.

Despite its short-term efficacy, one limitation of ECT is that it has high relapse rates (Fink, 2001; Sackeim et al., 2000), with one study finding that nearly all remitted patients relapse within 6 months after ECT without further active treatment (Sackeim et al., 2001). The use of continuation antidepressants following a course of ECT is recommended to reduce relapse (Sackeim et al., 2001).

How does ECT work? Its mechanisms are not fully understood. There is preliminary evidence that the therapeutic effects of ECT are related to decreased cerebral blood flow and reduced regional brain metabolism in specific neural regions particularly the frontal and anterior cortex, as well as to localized activation of seizures within the prefrontal cortex (Nobler et al., 1994, 2001; Sackeim, 2004). Recent evidence indicates that ECT, like antidepressants, influences the intracellular signaling cascade and neurogenesis through the up-regulation of factors such as BDNF (Duman & Monteggia, 2006).

Side effects of ECT. One of the major issues in the use of ECT is whether it causes damage to the recipient, in terms of functions or structure of the brain. Numerous studies of memory functioning reveal that reterograde amnesia (loss of memory for events going back months to years) is common. The amnesia typically improves during the months after treatment, although amnesia for events that immediately preceded the ECT often remains (Coleman et al., 1996;

Squire, 1977). Reviews examining neuroimaging techniques for viewing the brains of ECT recipients, as well as controlled animal studies of neuronal consequences of ECT administration, conclude that there is no evidence that ECT causes structural brain damage (Devanand, Dwork, Hutchinson, Bolwig, & Sackeim, 1994; Fink, 2001).

Transcranial magnetic stimulation (TMS)

In TMS, high-intensity current is pulsed through electromagnetic coils placed on the scalp, producing a time-varying high intensity magnetic field, which induces an electric current in brain neural tissue (George, Lisanby, & Sackeim, 1999). Thus, like ECT, TMS induces electrical stimulation in the brain, although it has the advantages of being more focal and localized than ECT, since magnetic fields are not deflected or weakened by intervening scalp and tissue. Furthermore, TMS does not require anesthesia, muscle relaxants, or analgesics. Single pulses of TMS can be used to excite or inhibit localized brain function, temporarily influencing behaviour and cognition, and is therefore a useful tool for mapping brain function.

For the treatment of mood disorders, repeated, rhythmic pulses of TMS are used, called repetitive TMS (rTMS). There is some evidence that rTMS has a small-to-moderate antidepressant effect, although most trials are limited by small sample size, the lack of a long-term follow-up and the lack of a double-blind (George et al., 1999; Martin, Barbanoj, Schlaepfer, Thompson, Perez, & Kulisevsky, 2003). A recent meta-analysis of 33 studies found that rTMS has a modest effect size relative to sham treatment, where the coils are held at an angle to the scalp that prevents any active effect (Hermann & Ebmeier, 2006). There is evidence from controlled trials that both high-frequency rTMS of the left dorsolateral prefrontal cortex (DLPFC), and low-frequency rTMS of the right DLPFC reduce depressive symptoms when compared to sham rTMS (Berman et al., 2000; Fitzgerald, Benitez, de Castella, Daskalakis, Brown, & Kulkarni, 2006; Fitzgerald, Brown, Marston, Daskalakis, de Castella, & Kulkarni, 2003; Klein et al., 1999). Since high-frequency stimulation is hypothesized to have an excitatory effect on cortical activity, whereas low-frequency stimulation is hypothesized to have an inhibitory effect, both forms of rTMS may work by increasing left DLPFC cortical activity relative to right DLFPC activity. The principal side effects of rTMS are muscle-tension headaches, caused by the stimulation of facial and scalp muscles, found in 5% to 25% of patients, which usually are only temporary, and the risk of epileptic seizure, although this seems to be limited to high-frequency rTMS.

Phototherapy for seasonal mood disorders

Phototherapy, or light therapy, is a treatment for the SAD subtype of depression. Speculating that SAD may be a "hibernation-like" response resulting from circadian rhythm dysfunction during diminished exposure to light during Winter, investigators reasoned that increasing exposure to bright light might reverse the depressive symptoms. The basic treatment consists of having the depressed person sit near a source of bright (2500–10,000 lux) light for a period of time daily. A recent review and meta-analysis of 13 controlled trials in SAD found that light therapy was an efficacious treatment compared with placebo (Golden et al., 2005). Light therapy is also as effective as fluoxetine in patients with Winter SAD, although with the advantages of an earlier response onset and fewer side effects (R. W. Lam et al., 2006). Recent studies have suggested that morning light is more effective than evening light in the treatment of winter depression in parallel designs (Eastman, Young, Fogg, Liu, & Meaden, 1998; Lewy et al., 1998; Terman, Terman, Lo, & Cooper, 2001). Although improvements in symptoms occur relatively rapidly (within a few days or a week), the benefit is temporary, such that people with SAD may need to continue the treatments throughout the Winter.

The mechanism of action of phototherapy is assumed to relate to circadian rhythm dysregulation. Consistent with the hypothesis that Winter depressions are triggered by phase delays in the circadian system with respect to the sleep–wake or light–dark cycle, exposure to morning light appears to achieve antidepressant effects by phase-advancing the circadian rhythm, whereas evening exposure, which produces delays in the melatonin rhythm, has less antidepressant effect (Lewy et al., 1998, 2006; Terman et al., 2001).

Sleep deprivation

Sleep deprivation (SD) is an experimental treatment based on the association between sleep disturbances and depression, as well as atypical REM sleep patterns in some depressed patients. Manipulations of the sleep–wake cycle, including total or partial sleep deprivation, in which depressed patients are kept awake throughout the night, and phase advance, in which the sleep cycle is advanced by 6 hours, produces marked mood improvements the night of SD or on the following day in 40% to 60% of patients with mood disorders (Giedke & Schwarzler, 2002; Wirz-Justice & Van den Hoofdakker, 1999). However, these positive benefits are very temporary, with 50% to 80% of responders relapsing after a night's sleep or even after naps. It may be that these treatment benefits can be maintained by the combination of SD with antidepressants or light therapy, although approximately 50% of medicated patients still relapse after SD. To date, SD has not been examined in large-scale controlled studies, and is not a commonplace treatment. The therapeutic effect of sleep deprivation is postulated to be linked to changes in disturbed circadian and disturbed sleep–wake dependent phase relationships.

Effects of physical exercise on depression

Increasing attention has focused on the beneficial effects of exercise in treating depression. Although this research is included in this chapter on biological treatments, it must be emphasized at the outset that the actual mechanisms accounting for the positive effects of exercise might be psychological (rewarding effects of positive activity, social contact, distraction, improved self-esteem, changes in cognitions) as much as those due to actual physical changes in energy, endorphin and monamine concentrations, and physical arousal.

A meta-analysis of 14 controlled-outcome studies of physical exercise on depression found that exercise significantly reduced depressive symptoms compared to no treatment (Lawlor & Hopker, 2001). However, this review concluded that these studies were limited in a number of ways: treatment allocation was not adequately concealed, possibly affecting patients' expectations; outcome was not assessed blind; few studies used an intention-to-treat analysis that accounts for dropouts; the majority of studies did not recruit clinical populations; and there was no follow-up of outcomes postintervention. Perhaps the best of these studies was a randomized controlled trial that compared 4 months of aerobic exercise (30 min of moderate aerobic exercise 3 times a week), sertraline, and exercise plus sertraline in 156 participants with major depression, and which found that all 3 groups significantly improved and did not differ from each other postintervention (Blumenthal et al., 1999). The remitted subjects in the exercise group had fewer relapses than the other groups at 6 months follow-up (Babyak et al., 2000). More recently, another well-controlled randomized trial with participants with major depression found that 12 weeks of individual moderate-to-high dose aerobic exercise reduced symptoms of depression significantly more than a low-dose exercise programme or a placebo control consisting of flexibility exercise (Dunn, Trivedi, Kampert, Clark, & Chambliss, 2005). These studies confirm the efficacy of exercise for mild-to-moderate depression, whilst suggesting that exercise needs to exceed a threshold level to be of value.

Summary

- Antidepressant medications have greatly increased in use in recent years, but continue to be frequently misadministered in terms of dosage and application to suitable cases.
- There is solid evidence of therapeutic effectiveness of antidepressant medications, although all have about the same level of demonstrated effectiveness. Rates of "success" differ, however, depending on how outcomes are defined, and many people continue to have residual symptoms and incomplete recovery.
- There are concerns about the acceptability of antidepressants to patients, with recognized unpleasant side effects and low rates of continuation of medication.
- Based on research findings, treatment guidelines recommend that antidepressants be continued for up to 6 months after recovery to prevent relapse, and that antidepressant treatment be maintained long-term or indefinitely for patients with histories of recurrent depression.
- The efficacy of antidepressants is not proof of an underlying biochemical etiology of depression.
- Other biological treatments for depression include electroconvulsive therapy, transcranial magnetic stimulation, light therapy, sleep deprivation and, possibly, physical exercise.

Psychological treatment of depression 8

Psychotherapy for depression used to be regarded as difficult and unrewarding (and often unproductive), because of the relentless negativism, lack of energy, and low motivation of the depressed patients. However, over the last 25 years, a number of systematically tested and effective psychological treatments for depression have been developed, providing optimism for both therapists and patients. In the sections to follow, two of the most widely used and most empirically validated treatment methods are discussed in greater detail, *cognitive behavioural therapy* and *interpersonal therapy*. Their methods are briefly described, and research is reviewed on their effectiveness, range of application, and mechanisms of effectiveness.

Cognitive behavioural treatment of depression

Developed by Aaron Beck, a psychoanalytically trained psychiatrist, the theory behind cognitive behavioural therapy (CBT) emphasizes the role of maladaptive cognitions in the origin, maintenance, and worsening of depression (A. T. Beck, 1967), as described in Chapter 5. When people think negatively, they feel depressed, and therefore therapy attempts to identify and alter the negative thoughts and beliefs, whilst also altering dysfunctional behaviours that might be contributing to depression.

Treatment methods

CBT is intended to be time-limited, relatively brief (approximately 20 sessions over 16 weeks), active, collaborative, here-and-now focused on current problems and current dysfunctional thinking (as described in A. T. Beck, Rush, Shaw, & Emery, 1979). Homework assignments are used between sessions to practise skills necessary to master the techniques of the treatment, observe thoughts and behaviour, test hypotheses, and acquire new skills.

Some of the key ingredients of the therapy are behavioural activation, graded task assignments, thought-catching and cognitive restructuring, identification and challenging of underlying maladaptive beliefs, and problem solving and specific behavioural techniques as needed to deal with particular life difficulties. *Behavioural activation* employs the well-known commonsense idea that being active leads to rewards that are an antidote to depression. It assists the client in identifying pleasurable or mastery activities and then helps the person overcome obstacles to performing them, followed by accurate assessment of their value. Often depressed individuals fail to participate in previously enjoyable activities because of a loss of interest and pleasure, or they anticipate that activity would be too difficult, take too much energy, or would fail to produce pleasure. The therapist and client collaborate to identify potentially pleasurable or meaningful activities, and then anticipate and deal with possible actual or cognitive obstacles to undertaking them. The client is encouraged to experiment with activity and test the hypothesis that engagement in activities that provide a sense of mastery or pleasure causes improvement in mood. In combination with this technique, *graded task assignments* help clients to engage in successively more rewarding yet demanding activities that lead to increased pleasure or mastery experiences; such activities can also tackle current problems (e.g., lack of rewarding job, relationship difficulties) that contribute to depression. Behavioural activation and graded task assignments are especially likely to be employed to treat symptoms directly, usually at the initial stages of treatment.

Thought-catching of "automatic negative thoughts" is the fundamental tool for changing maladaptive, depressogenic thoughts. Clients are taught to observe the link between thoughts and feelings, and to clarify their own emotion-related thoughts. Using a written form typically divided into columns, individuals keep records of emotion-arousing experiences, the automatic negative thoughts associated with them, and their realistic thoughts or challenges to the maladaptive thoughts. Several techniques are taught to clients to challenge each negative thought, such as "is there a distortion?," "what's the evidence?," "is there another way to look at it?," and "what if (the worst is really true)?" Usually, one or more of these challenges helps the client to replace the dysfunctional thought with a more realistic one. Often the realistic thoughts lead to specific behavioural activities to try out new ways of behaving or to collect behavioural data to test one's beliefs ("behavioural experiments"). The negative thoughts are hypothesized to occur at different levels, ranging from surface-level interpretations of events ("if he didn't phone me it means he doesn't like me"), to deeper, pervasive, core beliefs and assumptions ("if someone doesn't like me it means I'm no good"). Later stages of therapy would be more likely to deal with the deeper level assumptions and schemas.

The therapy is intended not only to alleviate the symptoms of depression and resolve immediate difficulties in the client's environment, but also to teach skills that can be used to resolve problems or deal with emerging depressive symptoms. Thus, an important goal of the therapy is to reduce the likelihood of recurrence of depression.

Behavioural activation. In recent years, the behavioural activation (BA) component of CBT has been developed into a psychological therapy in its own right. BA initially developed as a result of a trial examining the contribution of the different components of CBT: 150 depressed outpatients were randomly assigned to BA, BA plus modification of automatic negative thoughts, or "full" CBT which consisted of BA, modification of negative thoughts, plus changing core dysfunctional schemas. At the end of treatment as well as at a 6-month and 2-year follow-up, there were no differences between the treatments, with all reducing symptoms (Gortner, Gollan, Dobson, & Jacobson, 1998; Jacobson et al., 1996). Thus, the BA component was as successful in reducing depression as was full CBT.

Since this initial trial, BA has been elaborated into a full treatment, focusing on understanding the function and context in which depression occurs and targeting avoidance behaviours in depression (Martell, Addis, & Jacobson, 2001). BA proposes that attempts to escape or to avoid aversive situations or emotional states (e.g., arguments, risk of failure, or embarrassment) lead to the maintenance of depression, because avoidance narrows the range of an individual's behaviour, reducing contact with positive reinforcers. BA focuses on the context and functions of thoughts and behaviours rather than their form or content, concentrating on variability in feelings and behaviour across situations in order to determine what differences in environment and behaviour influence the patient's feelings and his or her success at achieving goals. Thus, within BA, monitoring pleasure and mastery, a weekly activity schedule, task rehearsal, and role-playing are used to assess and then influence how changes in behaviour are related to changes in affect.

Evaluating outcome of CBT

Outcome studies have addressed various questions: effects of treatment on acute symptoms, relapse prevention or long-term outcomes, effects of severity on outcome, and comparisons between CBT and medications or other psychotherapies.

Acute phase treatment. Studies of the effectiveness of CBT in reducing acute depression are too numerous to identify individually. Instead, we focus on several key studies and recent meta-analyses. Several individual studies are noteworthy because of their large sample sizes and superior methodology. For example, the NIMH Treatment of Depression Collaborative Research Program (TDCRP; Elkin, Parloff, Hadley, & Autry, 1985; Elkin et al., 1989) randomly assigned 250 outpatients with major depression to either CBT, interpersonal psychotherapy (IPT; Klerman, Weissman, Rounsaville, & Chevron, 1984), imipramine plus clinical management (involving brief support and advice to patients along with the pills), or pill placebo plus clinical management, in a multisite study. Although recovery, defined by minimal symptoms on a psychiatric rating scale for depression, was disappointing following CBT (36%), this was significantly better than for patients assigned to pill placebo treatment (21%). A number of other large-scale studies (reported in greater detail later) find similar rates of recovery from depression for CBT, ranging from 32% to 43% and replicate the finding that CBT is an active treatment superior to pill placebo (e.g., DeRubeis et al., 2005; Dimidjian et al., 2006; Hollon et al., 1992).

Similarly, a number of meta-analyses of controlled trials of CBT have tended to find that CBT is an effective treatment. A first meta-analysis of 28 CBT studies concluded that CBT is significantly better than no therapy, behaviour therapy, or pharmacotherapy or other forms of psychotherapy, regardless of duration of treatment (Dobson, 1989). A second meta-analysis reviewed 57 studies (with 47 studies not included in Dobson, 1989) for the treatment of depression, including cognitive, cognitive behavioural, behavioural, medication, and general verbal therapies (L. A. Robinson, Berman, & Neimeyer, 1990). Overall, treatments for depression were superior to no-treatment control groups, although the effects of treatment were not significant for comparisons with placebo controls. Cognitive behavioural interventions were superior to general verbal and to behavioural methods, but did not differ from cognitive-only treatments. A third meta-analysis (Gloaguen, Cottraux, Cucherat, &

Blackburn, 1998) examined 48 randomized controlled trials, comparing CBT with at least one comparison group for patients with depression. This meta-analysis concluded that CBT was superior to waiting-list or placebo control groups, antidepressants, and a heterogeneous grouping of other therapies (including psychodynamic therapies, IPT, supportive counseling, and relaxation), but of equivalent efficacy to behaviour therapy. These conclusions need to be treated with caution, because statistical differences between trials made it questionable whether the different trials could be pooled together in the meta-analysis. Furthermore, this meta-analysis was critiqued on the basis that the grouping of other therapies did not distinguish between "bona fide" treatments with a good rationale for treating depression versus non bona fide treatments that had no good theoretical grounding. When the Gloaguen et al. (1998) data were reanalysed making this distinction, CBT was found to be superior to non bona fide treatments (e.g., supportive counseling) but of equivalent efficacy to bona fide treatments (e.g., IPT; Wampold, Minami, Baskin, & Tierney, 2002).

Taken as a whole, the outcome research supports the general effectiveness of CBT. Nevertheless, there are additional issues to consider in the following sections: Does CBT work better than other treatments including medication? Does it work better for less severe depression? Does it succeed in reducing relapse rates over a follow-up period?

CBT compared to other treatments. There are three major comparisons: CBT vs. medications; CBT alone vs. CBT combined with medications; CBT vs. other psychotherapy. As noted above, studies of CBT have generally found it to be at least equivalent to, and, in some studies, superior to behaviour therapies or pharmacotherapy. The comparison of CBT with pharmacotherapy is of critical importance, since antidepressant medications represent the standard treatment option of persons with clinically significant depression. Outcome studies comparing CBT with pharmacotherapy need to include a pill placebo control condition in order to determine whether the pharmacotherapy has produced an efficacious response (Hollon, Shelton, & Davis, 1993). Recently, a number of methodologically sophisticated trials have affirmed the efficacy of CBT when compared to antidepressants and pill placebo (DeRubeis et al., 2005; Dimidjian et al., 2006; Elkin et al., 1985; Jarrett, Schaffer, McIntire, Witt-Browder, Kraft, & Risser, 1999).

In a large-scale trial, Jarrett and colleagues found that CBT is equivalent to antidepressant medication (phenelzine) and superior to pill placebo for patients with atypical major depression (Jarrett et al., 1999). Similarly, a recent large-scale trial of patients with moderate-to-severe depression randomized to CBT, pharmacotherapy (paroxetine), or pill placebo across two treatment sites, found that after 8 weeks, response rates in the CBT and pharmacotherapy groups were not significantly different (43% vs. 50%), with both superior to pill placebo (25%; DeRubeis et al., 2005). At 16 weeks, the rates of recovery were 46% for pharmacotherapy and 40% for CBT, indicating that CBT can be as effective as antidepressants for the initial treatment of moderate-to-severe major depression. There was a site by treatment interaction during this trial, with superior performance of CBT at one treatment site versus the other, with the better performing CBT site acknowledged as having more experienced CBT therapists.

Another recent large-scale trial randomly allocated 241 patients with major depression to CBT, BA (behavioural activation), pharmacotherapy (paroxetine), or pill placebo (Dimidjian et al., 2006). For patients with more severe depression (but not for patients with less severe depression), antidepressant medication produced significantly greater improvement per treatment week than pill placebo, confirming that pharmacotherapy was adequately implemented. For patients with less severe depression, CBT, BA, and antidepressants all produced significant improvements and were equally efficacious. However, for patients with more severe depression, BA and antidepressant medication produced significantly more improvement than CBT, with BA and antidepressant medication not differing. Figure 8.1 illustrates the effects of CBT, BA, and antidepressant medication on rates of response and remission in the patients with more severe depression.

A recent "mega-analysis" pooled together the actual raw data from four randomized controlled trials comparing CBT with pharmacotherapy for severe depression, in a procedure that maximizes statistical power. This analysis found that, whilst the effect sizes favoured CBT over medication, there was no overall significant difference between the two treatment modalities, indicating that CBT is as efficacious as pharmacotherapy (DeRubeis, Gelfand, Tang, & Simons, 1999).

Another possible comparison is between CBT or pharmacotherapy versus the combination of the two. A recent systematic review of 16 randomized controlled trials comparing combined pharmacotherapy and psychological treatment versus pharmacotherapy alone for depression found that combined treatment improved outcomes significantly more than medication treatment alone, in part due to a

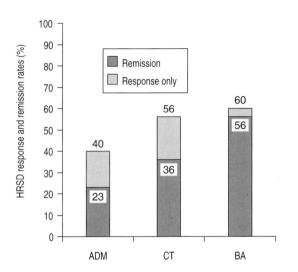

Figure 8.1.

Response and remission rates at posttreatment based on the Hamilton Rating Scale for Depression (HRSD) for the high-severity subgroup for antidepressant medication (ADM), cognitive therapy (CT), and behavioural activation (BA). Total bar represents response; lower bar represents remission.

Data source: Adapted from Dimidjian, S., Hollon, S. D., Dobson, K. S., Schmaling, K. B., Kohlenberg, R. J., Addis, M. E., et al. (2006). Randomized trial of behavioral activation, cognitive therapy, and antidepressant medication in the acute treatment of adults with major depression. *Journal of Consulting and Clinical Psychology, 74,* 658–670. Copyright by the American Psychological Association (APA). Reprinted with permission.

reduction in patients dropping out of therapy (Pampallona, Bollini, Tibaldi, Kupelnick, & Munizza, 2004). Of the 16 trials, 11 involved CBT as the psychological treatment, suggesting additional benefit from combining both medication and CBT. An important individual trial examined Cognitive-Behavioral Analysis System of Psychotherapy (CBASP) with and without the antidepressant nefazodone in the treatment of 681 patients with chronic depression, defined as a major depression lasting at least 2 years or a current major depression superimposed on pre-existing dysthymia (M. B. Keller et al., 2000). CBASP integrates elements of both CBT and interpersonal therapy. It differs from classical CBT in a very explicit focus on the consequences of patients' interpersonal behaviour, by analysing whether patients' interpretations and behaviours help or hinder movement towards their goals (McCullough, 2000). CBASP and nefazodone in combination produced more remission than either nefazodone or CBASP alone.

The other major comparison studies have pitted CBT against IPT or psychodynamic-interpersonal therapy. IPT (discussed further in a later section) was compared with CBT, imipramine, and pill placebo (plus clinical management) in the TDCRP as noted above. In general, there were few differences between CBT and IPT, and it appeared that overall both were as effective as medication (Elkin et al., 1989).

Shapiro and colleagues (1994) compared CBT with psychodynamic-interpersonal therapy (which used psychodynamic methods such as interpretations with a focus on interpersonal issues) on a sample of 117 depressed patients, and half of the participants were assigned to either 8 or 16 weeks of treatment (Shapiro, Barkham, Rees, Hardy, Reynolds, & Startup, 1994). Overall, the two psychotherapies were equally effective in symptom reduction. A further study compared brief (3-session) variants of CBT versus psychodynamic-interpersonal therapy for subsyndromal depression (Barkham, Shapiro, Hardy, & Rees, 1999), finding no difference between the therapies at 3 months, although CBT had better outcomes at 1-year follow-up.

CBT and level of severity of depression. An important question is whether CBT is more effective for patients with less severe depression. The TDCRP had reported that while overall patients responded about equally well to the active treatments, among patients who were most severely depressed, medication and IPT were superior to pill placebo and to CBT, with CBT only doing as well as placebo control on several outcome measures (Elkin et al., 1989). Among the less depressed, however, there were no differences across the treatment conditions. The TDCRP results could reflect CBT being no better than pill placebo for the treatment of severe depression. Alternatively, the TDCRP may have obscured important differences across sites of the study that were due to differential competence or preference for one or other of the psychotherapies. Reanalysis of the original data suggests that CBT performed at levels comparable to other studies (Elkin, Gibbons, Shea, & Shaw, 1996). Interestingly, as noted earlier, Dimidjian et al. (2006) found that CBT did not do as well as BA and antidepressants for severe patients, whereas all the active treatments were equivalent for less severe patients. Nonetheless, the DeRubeis et al. (1999) mega-analysis found that severity of depression did not influence the outcome of CBT. Moreover, as noted earlier, in a trial explicitly designed to test the conclusions of the TDCRP, DeRubeis et al. (2005) found that CBT was as effective as antidepressant medication for severe depression, particularly at the treatment site noted for experience with CBT. Taken together, these studies suggest that CBT is as effective for mild-to-moderate depression as other active treatments, and probably as effective for severe depression, but only when delivered by experienced therapists. The National Institute for Health and Clinical Excellence (NICE) of the British National Health Service recommends CBT as a treatment of choice for mild depression, as an option for moderate depression, and to be used in combination with medication for severe depression.

Relapse prevention. Given that relapse and/or recurrence is a major problem for patients with major depression (Judd, 1997), treatments that reduce relapse are a major priority. Since CBT teaches patients the skills to manage their own depression, it might provide some protection against further episodes of depression. There are three ways that CBT may prevent relapse. First, a course of CBT for a current episode of depression may successfully treat the acute symptoms and then provide ongoing benefit even after the therapy is discontinued (*prophylactic* effects of acute-phase CBT). Second, CBT may be used as a sequential intervention to teach self-management skills following a successful acute response to pharmacotherapy. Third, following successful acute-phase treatment, further sessions of CBT may continue to maintain the treatment gains longer term (i.e., *maintenance* or continuation CBT).

A recent review concluded that CBT has enduring effects that reduce the risk of symptom return following the end of treatment (Hollon, Stewart, & Strunk, 2006b). In general, studies report that after 1- or 2-year follow-up, relapse rates following CBT treatment for depression (30%) were lower than for pharmacotherapy (60%) when both treatments are stopped at termination (see Gloaguen et al., 1998).

It has been speculated that the natural course of a depressive episode may last 6 to 9 months beyond the remission of symptoms, a period during which the person is vulnerable to relapse. Pharmacotherapy might merely suppress the symptoms in the short term, and if discontinued after remission, would leave the patient open to relapse of symptoms. Thus, CBT might show superiority compared to what amounts to the premature withdrawal of medication (Hollon et al., 1993). Indeed, patients maintained on antidepressants have similar rates of relapse to patients who received CBT (M. D. Evans et al., 1992). Therefore, outcome trials to evaluate the long-term effectiveness of CBT require a long-enough follow-up to assess its effects on recurrence and a treatment condition that includes the continuation of antidepressant medication. A number of trials have now examined longer-term follow-up and/or continuation of antidepressants, and suggest that CBT produces similar rates of relapse to continuation of antidepressants, reduces rates of relapse compared to discontinuing antidepressants, and further reduces rates of relapse when added to "treatment-as-usual" (TAU; usually antidepressant medication).

First, in a trial for recurrent major depression comparing acute pharmacotherapy followed by maintenance antidepressants, acute CBT followed by maintenance CBT, and acute pharmacotherapy followed by maintenance CBT, all three groups showed equivalent clinical improvements during both phases of treatment (Blackburn & Moore, 1997). CBT alone is therefore as effective at preventing the recurrence of depression as continued antidepressant medication. Second, the 12-month follow-up to the DeRubeis et al. (2005) trial examined relapse in the 104 patients who had responded to CBT or pharmacotherapy in the acute trial (Hollon et al., 2005). The patients who responded to antidepressants were randomly allocated to continuation antidepressant or withdrawal onto pill placebo, and compared to the patients who had completed acute-phase CBT. The CBT-treated patients were significantly less likely to relapse during the 12 months than patients withdrawn from medication (30.8% vs. 76.2%) and no more likely to relapse than patients who continued their antidepressant (30.8% vs. 47.2%).

Third, several trials have demonstrated the value of CBT treatments at preventing relapse when used as an adjunct to acute pharmacotherapy for depression. Fava and colleagues developed a version of CBT to be used for *residual* symptoms that remained after depressed patients had been treated with medication. Following pharmacotherapy, patients were withdrawn from antidepressants and assigned to CBT versus "clinical management." This therapy protocol involved a combination of CBT focused on residual symptoms of depression, lifestyle modification, and well-being therapy. Residual symptoms of depression are known to predict increased risk of relapse and therefore targeting such symptoms may well help reduce future episodes of depression. In a trial for patients with recurrent depression (> 3 episodes of depression), CBT resulted in significantly fewer residual symptoms postintervention and significantly less relapse and recurrence over 2-year (25% vs. 80%) and 6-year follow-ups (40% vs. 90%) than standard clinical management, in the absence of antidepressant medication (G. A. Fava, Grandi, Zielezny, Canestrari, & Morphy, 1994; G. A. Fava, Grandi, Zielezny, Rafanelli, & Canestrari, 1996; G. A. Fava, Rafanelli, Grandi, Canestrari, & Morphy, 1998; G. A. Fava, Ruini, Rafanelli, Finos, Conti, & Grandi, 2004). Similarly, in a large-scale controlled trial, compared to TAU (clinical management plus antidepressants), TAU plus CBT reduced relapse over the subsequent 2 years in 158 patients with recent major depression that was partially remitted with antidepressant treatment (Paykel et al., 1999).

A second approach to preventing relapse has specifically targeted patients with a history of recurrent depression who are currently in remission. Based on the hypothesis that these patients tend to be caught up in depressive rumination at times of potential relapse, it was proposed that mindfulness meditation, which fosters a relationship to thoughts and feelings antithetical to such rumination, might prevent future episodes of depression (Teasdale, Segal, & Williams, 1995a). Therefore, elements of a mindfulness-based stress reduction programme (Kabat-Zinn, 1990) were incorporated into CBT to create mindfulness-based cognitive therapy (MBCT). MBCT is delivered in weekly group training sessions, in which participants practise and develop a moment-by-moment nonjudgmental awareness of sensations, thoughts, and feelings, through the use of formal and informal meditation exercises. For example, mindfulness-meditation exercises include focusing attention on the breath and then returning the attention to the breath whenever the individual notices that his or her attention has been drawn away. These awareness exercises are further practised during homework (for full details on the treatment see Segal, Williams, & Teasdale, 2002). MBCT therefore differs from the classic rational focus on "challenging and changing" cognitions emphasized in CBT; rather it emphasizes an acceptance of one's thoughts and feelings, and the development of a broader perspective in which thoughts and feelings are viewed as "mental events" rather than "realities." In two randomized controlled trials, for patients with a history of three or more episodes of major depression, MBCT significantly reduced risk of relapse over 1 year compared to TAU (Ma & Teasdale, 2004; Teasdale, Segal, Williams, Ridgeway, Soulsby, & Lau, 2000). There was a suggestion that MBCT was not effective, and possibly unhelpful, for patients with a history of two or less previous episodes of depression, indicating a differential effect across recurrence of depression.

Bockting and colleagues compared the relapse prevention effects of TAU plus group CBT therapy versus TAU for 187 recurrently depressed patients currently in remission following treatment. For patients with 5 or more previous episodes, CBT significantly reduced relapse over a 2-year follow-up compared to TAU (72% to 46%; (Bockting et al., 2005). Taken together, these studies suggest that the addition of CBT to medication, whether sequentially or simultaneously might be a useful option to prevent relapse, especially for patients with residual symptoms or histories of recurrent depression.

A third approach to preventing relapse and recurrence is main- tenance treatment in which further sessions of CBT are provided as booster sessions. In the first controlled trial of maintenance CBT, 84 medication-free patients with recurrent major depression who had responded to acute-phase CBT were randomized to either continua- tion CBT or to a control condition consisting of evaluation sessions without CBT (Jarrett, Kraft, Doyle, Foster, Eaves, & Silver, 2001). Over the 8 months of the intervention period, continuation CBT signifi- cantly reduced relapse compared to the control condition (10% vs. 31%), and over the 2-year follow-up, continuation CBT significantly reduced rates of recurrence compared to the control condition in patients with earlier onset of major depression and residual symp- toms. In a follow-up to the CBASP study (D. N. Klein et al., 2004a), 82 patients who had successfully responded to acute-phase CBASP for chronic depression were randomized to monthly CBASP or to assessment only for a year. Across the 12 months, there were signi- ficantly fewer recurrences of depression in the continuation CBASP condition than in the assessment-only condition (10.7% vs. 32.0%). Thus, in two moderately sized trials, continuation CBT is associated with a significantly lower probability of relapse than assessment only.

In recent years, several randomized controlled trials have shown that compared to standard clinical management (including the prescription of mood stabilizers), standard clinical management plus CBT can reduce the recurrence of future *bipolar* episodes in patients with bipolar disorder (D. H. Lam et al., 2003; D. H. Lam, Hayward, Watkins, Wright, & Sham, 2005; Perry, Tarrier, Morriss, McCarthy, & Limb, 1999; Scott, Garland, & Moorhead, 2001). Importantly, these trials have focused on CBT as an adjunct to mood stabilizers rather than as a separate intervention for bipolar disorder.

Predictors of effectiveness of CBT. What patient characteristics predict whether someone will respond to CBT (a prognostic indicator) and whether someone will respond better to CBT than to another treat- ment (a prescriptive indicator)? Various patient variables predict poor outcome to CBT (see review by K. E. Hamilton & Dobson, 2002), including increased severity and chronicity of the depression, younger age at onset, greater number of previous episodes, not being married, and perfectionistic beliefs, although these variables tend to predict poor outcome for all interventions.

There is evidence that more dysfunctional attitudes pretreatment predict a poorer response to CBT, both at acute-phase improvement (e.g., Jarrett, Eaves, Grannemann, & Rush, 1991; K. E. Keller, 1983;

Sotsky et al., 1991) and for rates of relapse at 1-year follow-up (Thase et al., 1992). Likewise, in a naturalistic study of CBT for depressed outpatients with and without a diagnosis of personality disorder, increased maladaptive avoidant and paranoid beliefs predicted worse outcome to CBT, although personality disorder did not (Kuyken, Kurzer, DeRubeis, Beck, & Brown, 2001).

Are there predictors of superior response to different interventions for depression? Married patients appear to do better with CBT than single patients (Jarrett et al., 1991), whereas single patients do better in IPT than in CBT (Barber & Muenz, 1996). An analysis of the CBASP study found that CBASP alone was superior to antidepressant alone for patients with chronic depression who also had a history of childhood trauma such as loss of parents at an early age, physical or sexual abuse, or neglect (Nemeroff et al., 2003). This study suggests that there may be a differential response in favour of CBT for patients with histories of early difficulties or trauma.

Applications of cognitive therapy

CBT for depression has been successfully applied across a number of different populations and settings, including elderly populations (Laidlaw, 2001; Laidlaw, Thompson, Gallagher-Thompson, & Dick-Siskin, 2003; Thompson, Coon, Gallagher-Thompson, Sommer, & Koin, 2001), low-income women from ethnic minorities (Miranda et al., 2003, 2006), and in private practice (Persons, Bostrom, & Bertagnolli, 1999). CBT in combination with antidepressant medication has been found to be more efficacious for *inpatients* than medication alone in producing treatment response and maintaining gains during 12-month follow-ups (Stuart, Wright, Thase, & Beck, 1997; Thase & Wright, 1991; Wright, 2003). Relatively few studies have evaluated the success of CBT for *dysthymic disorder*, although the handful of small sample studies does seem to indicate positive response to CBT (Markowitz, 1994) and the M. B. Keller et al. (2000) study indicates the value of CBASP for depression plus dysthymia.

CBT has been applied to individuals mostly, but also to marital couples, and in groups (e.g., L. A. Robinson et al., 1990). CBT for depressed spouses performed as well as marital therapy for couples in alleviating depression (Beach & O'Leary, 1992; Emanuels-Zuurveen & Emmelkamp, 1996; Jacobson, Fruzzetti, Dobson, Schmaling, & Salusky, 1991), and resulted in approximately the same relapse rates at a 1-year follow-up (Jacobson, Fruzzetti, Dobson, Whisman, & Hops, 1993).

CBT for depression has even been administered by computer and shown to be as effective as therapist-administered treatment, with both treatments superior to a wait-list control (Selmi, Klein, Greist, Sorrell, & Erdman, 1990; Wright et al., 2005). Further, a computerized, interactive, multimedia program for treating depression produced significantly greater improvement in depression and anxiety compared to TAU in general practice patients (Proudfoot, Goldberg, Mann, Everitt, Marks, & Gray, 2003). Telephone-administered CBT was found to be more effective than telephone-administered supportive therapy in a controlled trial of patients with multiple sclerosis and depression (Mohr et al., 2005).

Mechanisms of change in cognitive behavioural therapy

Investigations of the different components of CBT suggest that specific and concrete elements of CBT, such as thought challenging and homework, are its most effective ingredients. For example, *changing* chronically depressed patients' distorted thoughts led to improved mood, compared to a control condition in which simply *exploring* the thoughts did not (Teasdale & Fennell, 1982). Concrete methods, including setting an agenda, asking for specific examples, labeling cognitive errors, and examining evidence, predicted subsequent symptom reduction when assessed early in CBT treatment (DeRubeis & Feeley, 1990; Feeley, DeRubeis, & Gelfand, 1999). However, neither the therapeutic alliance nor less focused, more abstract approaches, such as exploring the meaning of thoughts and discussing the therapy, predicted improvement. Similarly, improvements in the specific skill of situational analysis during the first 6 weeks of CBASP therapy predicted level of depression at the end of treatment (Manber et al., 2003). Adherence to homework was linked to better outcome (Burns & Nolen-Hoeksema, 1991).

The role of cognitive change. The cognitive model (A. T. Beck, 1976) predicts that CBT should produce specific changes on measures of cognitions, that these changes in cognitions are unique to CBT, and that these changes in cognitions should predict symptomatic improvement. Barber and DeRubeis (1989) discussed several possible mechanisms of cognitive change in CBT that could mediate symptom improvement. One model is "accommodation", meaning that CBT effects a change in the basic cognitive schemata, either in content or process or both. A second possible model of change is "activation–deactivation" in which the maladaptive schemas are not *changed*, but are deactivated while more adaptive schemas are activated. The third model of change is "compensatory skills," in which CBT does not alter the tendency to think in depressive ways, but rather provides a set of skills that help individuals to deal with the thoughts when they do arise. The overall pattern of results is most consistent with the compensatory skills model.

First, the majority of studies using questionnaires to assess changes in negative cognition found that cognitive changes were as likely to occur in noncognitive interventions such as pharmacotherapy or IPT as in CBT, suggesting that change in cognition is simply a consequence of symptom improvement (Imber et al., 1990; Simons, Garfield, & Murphy, 1984; Whisman, Miller, Norman, & Keitner, 1991; for exceptions see Rush, Beck, Kovacs, Weissenburger, & Hollon, 1982). An alternative interpretation is that the causal role of cognitions may differ between treatments: In both CBT and pharmacotherapy, cognitions will change as a consequence of mood change, but only in CBT will change in cognition also cause change in mood (Hollon, DeRubeis, & Evans, 1987). Consistent with this interpretation, a regression analysis of treatment trial data found that change in cognition in the first half of treatment predicted change in depression in the second half of treatment for the CBT group but not for the medication treatment group, suggesting that the cognitive processes did play a mediating role in symptom change in CBT but not in pharmacotherapy (DeRubeis, Evans, Hollon, Garvey, Grove, & Tuason, 1990). These results indicate that cognitive change alone is not causally sufficient to produce symptom change, perhaps because changes in cognitions need to lead to changes in behaviour or compensatory skills, such as encouraged during CBT, in order to produce symptom change. These data are thus not supportive of the accommodation hypothesis, which would predict that change in cognition alone would produce symptom improvement.

Second, as noted earlier, the component trial of CBT found that BA alone was as effective at treating depression as the more "cognitive" treatments (Gortner et al., 1998; Jacobson et al., 1996). This result raises the possibility that cognitive change is not necessary for improvement during CBT, and, indeed, that behavioural change or the development of new coping skills may be sufficient to produce improvement. Nonetheless, this finding could still be consistent with a cognitive account since behavioural change could indirectly lead to changes in beliefs.

Third, as noted in detail in Chapter 5, patients who recovered through pharmacotherapy showed greater increases in dysfunctional attitudes following a negative mood induction than those who recovered through CBT, with such "cognitive reactivity" predicting relapse over the next 18 months (Segal et al., 1999, 2006). This result is strongly consistent with the "compensatory skills" model, suggesting that patients treated with CBT learn skills to prevent sad-mood-activating negative cognitions. Similarly, the association between depressive symptoms and negative cognition posttreatment was weaker for patients who received CBT (in addition to pharmacotherapy) than for patients who did not receive additional CBT, whereas there was no effect of additional family therapy (Beevers & Miller, 2005). So, as symptoms of depression increased, negative cognition increased more slowly for patients treated with CBT, consistent with the hypothesis that CBT teaches compensatory skills. Similarly, in patients with residual depression, CBT reduces an absolutist all-or-nothing thinking style, which, in turn, was found to mediate the effects of CBT on preventing relapse, consistent with the notion that CT helps patients to acquire compensatory skills (Barber & DeRubeis, 1989; Teasdale, Scott, Moore, Hayhurst, Pope, & Paykel, 2001). "Metacognitive awareness," defined as the ability to view thoughts as mental events in a wider context of awareness, predicted the time to relapse for patients with residual depression. Furthermore, CBT that successfully reduced relapse also increased metacognitive awareness (Teasdale, Moore, Hayhurst, Pope, Williams, & Segal, 2002). Thus, these findings in both acute and residual depression are consistent with the active mechanism of CBT being the development of compensatory skills to reduce the link between negative mood and negative cognition.

Interpersonal psychotherapy

Klerman et al. (1984) describe IPT based generally on the interpersonal therapy model of Harry Stack Sullivan, which assumes that depression can result from, and lead to, difficulties in the interpersonal relationships among depressed persons and their significant others. IPT, therefore, attempts both to alleviate depressive symptoms and to improve interpersonal functioning by "clarifying, refocusing, and renegotiating the interpersonal context associated with the onset of depression" (Weissman & Klerman, 1990).

Treatment methods

IPT is a brief, weekly time-limited therapy of 12 to 16 weeks, administered individually. Three general phases are described. The first few sessions are devoted to assessment and forming treatment goals. During this phase the patient is taught the "sick role," learning about depression as an illness and receiving encouragement to continue regular activities but without the expectation of performing normally. The second phase identifies and targets interpersonal problems thought to contribute to the depression, and the third, or termination, phase focuses on consolidating what has been learned and anticipating using the skills during times of future difficulty. The therapy is oriented toward the here-and-now, rather than the early origins of depressive vulnerabilities or interpersonal difficulties.

Improving the depressed patient's interpersonal functioning is accomplished by exploring with the patient one or more of the following problem areas commonly associated with the onset of depression: grief, role disputes, role transition, or interpersonal deficits. Information is gathered concerning the patient's functioning in these areas. Klerman et al. (1984) discuss specific goals and procedures to deal with each of the four problem areas. *Grief* refers to abnormal bereavement (distorted, delayed, or chronic) and the need to resolve loss by accurate perception and by replacing some of the lost activities or resources. *Role disputes* and *role transitions* refer to difficulties with others in managing or changing important areas of functioning and self-definition, such as marital conflict, occupational difficulties, dealing with a child moving out of the home, and the like. The therapy aims at identification of the problem, clarification of expectations, negotiation of disputes, and improvement of communication. *Interpersonal deficits* refer to relatively depression-related problems in interpersonal functioning, such as communication or forming friendships; therapy helps the person identify the problem and its consequences and acquire new behaviours. In general, IPT therapists make use of nondirective exploration, encourage expression of affect, teach the patient more effective methods of interpersonal communication, and attempt to alter depressive behaviours through insight, providing information, and role-playing.

As an example of IPT, a woman might report depression occurring in the context of dealing with a rebellious teenage daughter; she feels upset because the teenager is disrespectful and disobedient, and the mother cannot control her actions, causing great worry. The woman also feels that her husband ignores the problem and does not support her. IPT would draw a link between the depression and the woman's goals and disputes in the parental role. Through exploration, support, and problem-solving activity, IPT helps the woman to see the extent to which her own self-esteem is tied to the approval of her daughter and the daughter's achievements. The mother is encouraged to have realistic expectations for her child's behaviour and to pursue alternative means of bolstering her own self-esteem (such as working outside the home). She is aided in developing reasonable standards of conduct for her daughter, and consistency in disciplining the girl (instead of being lenient as a way to avoid the child's anger at her).

Evaluating the outcome of IPT

A number of studies have examined the efficacy of IPT in the treatment of acute major depression. IPT is as effective as pharmacotherapy in reducing depressive symptomatology, and is more effective than pharmacotherapy in improving social functioning both acutely and at 1-year follow-up (Weissman, 1979; Weissman, Klerman, Prusoff, Sholomskas, & Padian, 1981). As discussed in greater detail earlier, the TDCRP trial indicated that IPT was as effective as CBT and pharmacotherapy in the reduction of depressive symptoms; moreover, patients treated by IPT achieved more rapid gains in interpersonal functioning (Elkin et al., 1989). Interestingly, IPT also had the lowest attrition rate in the study. IPT has also been found to be superior to a waiting-list control in reducing depressive symptoms in women with postpartum depression (O'Hara, Stuart, Gorman, & Wenzel, 2000).

With respect to long-term outcomes, as noted above, IPT and CBT were approximately equal in percentage of patients who relapsed during the follow-up of the TDCRP, and somewhat superior to medication alone. Frank et al. (1990) tested the use of IPT for the *maintenance* of gains after successful medication treatment. Patients were assigned to one of five maintenance treatments: monthly IPT alone, monthly IPT combined with high-dosage continuation medication, medication alone, IPT plus placebo, or placebo alone. The results showed that at 3 years, mean survival time without relapse was greatest for patients in the combined IPT plus medication treatment, and even patients who received only monthly IPT stayed well almost twice as long as patients receiving only placebos (Frank et al., 1990). Similarly, for patients older than 59 years, over a 3-year follow-up, maintenance antidepressant, combined monthly maintenance IPT and antidepressant, and combined monthly maintenance IPT and pill placebo, all increased the time to recurrence relative to pill placebo alone (Reynolds et al., 1999). Combined IPT and medication was superior to IPT alone and approached significance for superiority to antidepressant alone.

A large-scale randomized controlled trial investigated the efficacy of IPT alone, antidepressant alone (sertraline), and combined antidepressant and IPT for 707 patients with dysthymic disorder, with an 18-month follow-up (Browne et al., 2002). Antidepressant and antidepressant combined with IPT were more effective than IPT alone, although IPT alone produced significant improvements in depressive symptoms. However, a further trial comparing 16 weeks of IPT, brief supportive psychotherapy, pharmacotherapy, and pharmacotherapy plus IPT for early-onset dysthymia found no differences between the different treatments in rates of remission (Markowitz, Kocsis, Bleiberg, Christos, & Sacks, 2005a). Together, these studies suggest that IPT may have only modest and nonspecific treatment effects in dysthymia (Markowitz, 2003).

An adaptation of IPT for *bipolar disorder*, incorporating a focus on stabilizing social rhythms (Interpersonal and Social Rhythm Therapy), has been found to reduce recurrence in patients with that condition (Frank et al., 2005). This therapy is based on the social zeitgeber hypothesis, which proposes that unstable or disrupted daily routines lead to disturbed circadian function, which, in turn, can lead to episodes of mania or depression in vulnerable individuals.

Treating children and adolescents

Most approaches to treating children and adolescents target several areas of functioning as common difficulties contributing to depressive symptoms in youngsters. These include social and academic difficulties, social problem-solving difficulties including the management of emotions, maladaptive family relationships, poor self-esteem or other dysfunctional cognitions about the self and others.

Cognitive behavioural treatment of depression in children

CBT for children involves the same *behavioural techniques*, such as activity scheduling, and similar *cognitive interventions*, including the identifying and challenging of negative thoughts, as applied to depressed adults, although therapy is modified to make it accessible for children. Many programmes emphasize the active involvement of parents, with parents participating in *parent training* at the same time the child is in the programme (Stark, Rouse, & Kurowski, 1994). Their training includes learning the same rationales, tasks, and skills as the child in order to facilitate the child's learning. *Family intervention* can also be an essential component, since many of the children's difficulties may originate in families where parents are themselves experiencing psychological disturbances, or dysfunctional inter-actions. Specific difficulties in the parent–child relationship may become the target of the intervention.

Evaluation of CBT for depressed children. A number of studies have examined the efficacy of CBT administered in school settings for children who have elevated depressive symptoms, but who are not selected on diagnostic criteria for major depression (e.g., Kahn, Kehle, Jenson, & Clark, 1990; Stark, Reynolds, & Kaslow, 1987; Stark, Rouse, & Livingston, 1991; Weisz, Thurber, Sweeney, Proffitt, & LeGagnoux, 1997). In general, these trials find that CBT is superior to no treatment or waiting-list controls (see reviews and meta-analyses by Curry, 2001; Michael & Crowley, 2002; Weisz, McCarty, & Valeri, 2006). The most comprehensive and methodologically sophisticated of these meta-analyses found a small but meaningful effect size for seven randomized controlled studies examining interventions for children aged less than 13 years (Weisz et al., 2006). However, most of these trials are limited in having relatively small sample sizes, comparing CBT to no-treatment or waiting-list control groups rather than to an active control condition, only examining selected samples in uni-versity research clinics rather than in "real-world" clinics, and lacking any long term follow-ups (e.g., Kahn et al., 1990; Stark et al., 1987, 1991). There is also a need for further studies in populations meeting criteria for major depression, and for component studies evaluating the specific ingredients that might be relatively more active, such as parent training, relaxation training, social skills training and the like.

Interventions with depressed adolescents

A number of treatment programs for adolescent depression have now been developed, adopting either CBT or IPT approaches. An early meta-analysis of 6 studies of CBT for adolescent depression suggest that CBT is an effective treatment, with a large effect size of 1.02

posttreatment (Reinecke, Ryan, & Dubois, 1998). However, the Weisz et al. (2006) meta-analysis of 28 studies of psychotherapy for adolescent depression found a small effect size of 0.33. Noteworthy studies include the Oregon Coping with Depression (CWD-A) program and the Treatment for Adolescents with Depression (TADS) Study (March et al., 2004).

The CWD-A is an adaptation of the adult Coping with Depression course (Lewinsohn & Clarke, 1984). A key focus is on learning effective problem-solving skills, which are hypothesized to reduce depression in the short run, but also prevent further episodes in the future (Lewinsohn, Clarke, Hops, & Andrews, 1990). Youngsters attend classes twice a week for 8 weeks in groups of 4 to 8 adolescents meeting with a group leader. Homework assignments are given regularly, and workbooks provide readings, tasks, and forms to be used for homework. The course includes self-monitoring and self-reinforcement training, social skills training (such as conversation techniques, planning social activities, communication, assertiveness, negotiation), problem-solving skills training, behavioural activation, anxiety reduction, identifying and challenging negative thoughts and dysfunctional beliefs, and future planning to prevent relapse. A *parent programme* includes parents attending a weekly 2-hour session in which they learn the skills that their child is learning, with information on how to encourage the youth's practising of relevant skills during the course.

In a randomized controlled trial of 59 depressed adolescents aged 14 to 18, both the CWD course for adolescents (CWD-A) and the CWD course for both adolescents and their parents (CWD-A+P) significantly reduced symptoms of depression relative to a waiting-list control group, and maintained these improvements over a 2-year follow-up, with the two versions of the CWD not significantly differing from each other (Lewinsohn et al., 1990). The effectiveness of CWD-A has been replicated in a large-scale controlled trial in which adolescents with diagnoses of major depression or dysthymia were randomly allocated to CWD-A, CWD-A+P, or waiting-list control (Clarke, Rohde, Lewinsohn, Hops, & Seeley, 1999). Postintervention, 65% of the CWD-A and 69% of the CWD-A+P groups no longer met criteria for depression, compared to 48% of the waiting-list control group. Recently, CWD-A was found to be more effective than a life-skills attention control condition (rates of recovery 39% vs. 19%, respectively) in a sample of adolescents with comorbid major depression and conduct disorder referred from the juvenile justice system (Rohde, Clarke, Mace, Jorgensen, & Seeley, 2004).

Brent and his colleagues compared individual CBT for adolescents, systemic behaviour family (SBFT) therapy, and individual nondirective supportive therapy (NST) for 107 adolescent patients with major depression (Brent et al., 1997). SBFT involved engagement of the family in therapy, communication, and problem-solving skills, whereas NST focused on empathic discussion of feelings and problems rather than skills training. Remission was significantly greater for CBT (65%) than for SBFT (38%) and NST (39%).

In the TADS study, 439 adolescents with major depression, aged 12- to 17-years, were randomized to 12 weeks of antidepressant medication only, individual CBT only, combined CBT and medication, or pill placebo (March et al., 2004). Critically, this was the first study to compare CBT for adolescents with antidepressant medication and pill placebo. There was no difference between CBT and placebo in treatment effect, and medication alone was superior to CBT alone, although combined CBT–medication treatment was significantly better than placebo.

Interpersonal Psychotherapy for Adolescents (IPT-A). IPT was adapted for use with depressed adolescents (IPT-A), by including a focus on the interpersonal problems typically encountered by teenagers within the problem areas (grief, role disputes, role transitions, and interpersonal deficiencies). In addition, they added a fifth area of interpersonal problems, single-parent families, because it is an area often associated with difficult challenges for youth (Moreau, Mufson, Weissman, & Klerman, 1991). In three randomized controlled trials, IPT-A for major depression has been shown to produce significantly better outcomes than clinical monitoring for predominantly female and Latino adolescents (Mufson, Weissman, Moreau, & Garfinkel, 1999), than waiting-list control for Puerto Rican adolescents (Rossello & Bernal, 1999), and than treatment-as-usual in school-based health clinics (Mufson, Dorta, Wickramaratne, Nomura, Olfson, & Weissman, 2004). In the Rossello and Bernal (1999) trial, both IPT and CBT significantly reduced depressed symptoms compared to waiting-list control.

Prevention of depression in children and adolescents

Given the recurrent and persistent life-long nature of depression, there is an increasing focus on preventing the initial onset of depression. Because the initial onset of depression is typically between the ages of 16 and 20, this means developing interventions to prevent depression in childhood and adolescence. There are several different approaches to prevention. *Selective prevention* targets individuals who manifest some vulnerability or risk factor for depression, such as children of depressed mothers. *Indicated prevention* targets individuals who have already demonstrated subsyndromal symptoms of the disorder, such as minor depression. *Universal prevention* targets all individuals in a particular population unselected for risk status, with the advantage that it is more broadly accessible, less stigmatizing, and has fewer drop-outs, but the disadvantage that the intervention may be delivered to a large proportion of individuals at low risk for depression who do not need any additional help. A recent meta-analysis of prevention in adolescent depression examined 30 studies and found that the overall effect size for all interventions was small (0.3; Horowitz & Garber, 2006). Selective and indicated prevention were found to be more effective than universal prevention, both immediately postintervention and at follow-ups. However, the review noted that many of the studies have only examined relatively short follow-ups (6 months) and the longer-term effect of prevention (2 to 5 years) needs to be investigated. There is also the question of how much the interventions produced a treatment effect (reducing existing depressive symptoms relative to control) rather than a prevention effect (preventing the increase of depressive symptoms relative to control). Only a handful of studies found a "true" prevention effect in which control groups showed an increase in depressive symptoms, whereas the active intervention showed no increase or decrease in depressive symptoms (e.g., Jaycox, Reivich, Gillham, & Seligman, 1994).

Noteworthy studies of selective and indicated prevention include an intervention based on the CWD program (Clarke, Hawkins, Murphy, Sheeber, Lewinsohn, & Seeley, 1995). The programme, called the "Coping with Stress" course, focused largely on cognitive techniques to identify and challenge dysfunctional thoughts in adolescents selected for high self-reported depression scores. After treatment and over a 12-month follow-up period, those in the prevention group had a significantly lower rate of developing a depression diagnosis (14.5%) compared with those in the control group (25.7%). The CWD program was further examined as a selective prevention for an at-risk population consisting of the adolescent children of depressed patients (Clarke et al., 2001). Over a 2-year follow-up, there were significantly fewer episodes of depression in the CWD group (9.3%) compared to usual care (28.8%).

Another important indicated intervention is the Penn Resiliency Programme (PRP), a group-format, school-based programme to teach adaptive cognitions and coping styles to 10- to 13-year-old children who are at risk because of high depressive symptoms and/or exposure to parental conflict (Jaycox et al., 1994). Compared with the no-treatment control group, students in the PRP reported fewer depressive symptoms up to a 2-year follow-up (Gillham, Reivich, Jaycox, & Seligman, 1995). In a further primary-care based study for 11- to 12-year-old children with elevated depressive symptoms, over a 2-year follow-up, PRP prevented symptoms of depression, anxiety, and adjustment disorders in high-symptom participants but did not prevent the onset of major depression compared to usual care (Gillham, Hamilton, Freres, Patton, & Gallop, 2006). However, a study of rural schoolchildren in Australia using school staff failed to find any benefit for PRP (C. Roberts, Kane, Thomson, Bishop, & Hart, 2003).

A number of studies have examined universal prevention approaches to adolescent depression. One study distinguished by its large sample size, methodological rigour, and long-term follow-up is the Problem-Solving for Life (PSFL) Intervention (Spence, Sheffield, & Donovan, 2003, 2005) which investigated a teacher-implemented, classroom-based intervention to prevent depression in 1500 adolescents across 16 high schools in Western Australia. Students were matched in pairs to PSFL or to a monitoring control. PSFL involved cognitive restructuring and training in problem-solving skills. Participants were split into high-risk and low-risk groups on the basis of their level of depression symptoms. Postintervention, PSFL resulted in greater reductions in depressive symptoms and better problem solving than the control group for both high- and low-risk groups, although the effect was greater in the high-risk groups. However, there were no significant differences between the two treatment conditions for depressive symptoms or onset of major depression at 12 months (Spence et al., 2003) or 2-, 3-, and 4-year follow-ups (Spence et al., 2005). A further trial comparing this universal prevention approach with a selective intervention approach, a combination of universal and selective approaches and a no-intervention control, across 36 schools and 2479 students, with a 1-year follow-up, found no difference between any of the intervention conditions and the no-intervention control on depressive symptoms, anxiety, or coping skills (Sheffield et al., 2006). These large-scale trials thus raise questions about the value of universal prevention programmes for adolescent depression.

Summary

- Cognitive behavioural treatment of depression stresses changing maladaptive cognitions, as well as behavioural methods to reduce depression and to improve dysfunctional skills and problem solving.
- CBT is significantly more effective than no treatment, and appears to equal medication and IPT in reducing depression in the acute phase; it appears to be more successful than medication in the long-term prevention of relapse and recurrence, although there is still scope for improvement given that most patients show a return of depression.
- The active ingredients that make CBT successful appear to be those specific techniques that help patients to learn compensatory skills that break the link between negative mood and negative thinking.
- Interpersonal psychotherapy for depression is focused on exploring the role of interpersonal problems as the cause of depression, working through unresolved emotions associated with losses, transitions, and bereavements, and on making active changes in relationships.
- IPT is significantly more effective than no treatment, and appears to be the equal of medication and CBT in achieving short-term results. Like CBT, IPT has been shown to have maintenance effects in preventing recurrence.
- There is preliminary evidence that combined medication and psychotherapy is superior to either alone, particularly for severe depression.
- Both CBT and IPT have been extended to treat depression in children and adolescents, with some mild-to-moderate success. There is evidence that selective and indicated approaches may be more effective than universal approaches to preventing depression.

Further reading

Allen, N. B., & Badcock, P. B. T. (2003). The social risk hypothesis of depressed mood: Evolutionary, psychosocial, and neurobiological perspectives. *Psychological Bulletin, 129*, 887–913.

Clark, D. A., Beck, A. T., & Alford, B. A. (1999). *Scientific foundations of cognitive theory and therapy of depression*. New York: Wiley.

Davidson, R. J., & Irwin, W. (1999). The functional neuroanatomy of emotion and affective style. *Trends in Cognitive Sciences, 3*, 11–21.

Davidson, R. J., Lewis, D. A., Alloy, L. B., Amaral, D. G., Bush, G., Cohen, J. D., et al. (2002). Neural and behavioral substrates of mood and mood regulation. *Biological Psychiatry, 52*, 478–502.

Goodman, S., & Gotlib, I. (1999). Risk for psychopathology in the children of depressed mothers: A developmental model for understanding mechanisms of transmission. *Psychological Review, 106*, 458–490.

Goodwin, F. K., & Jamison, K. R. (2007). *Manic-depressive illness: Bipolar disorders and recurrent depression* (2nd ed.). New York: Oxford University Press.

Gotlib, I. H., & Hammen, C. L. (Eds.). (2007). *Handbook of depression* (2nd ed.). New York: Guilford.

Hankin, B. L., & Abramson, L. Y. (2001). Development of gender differences in depression: An elaborated cognitive vulnerability-transactional stress theory. *Psychological Bulletin, 127*, 773–796.

Harvey, A. G., Watkins, E., Mansell, W., & Shafran, R. (2004). *Cognitive behavioural processes across psychological disorders*. Oxford: Oxford University Press.

Hollon, S. D., Stewart, M. O., & Strunk, D. (2006). Enduring effects for cognitive behavior therapy in the treatment of depression and anxiety. *Annual Review of Psychology, 57*, 285–315.

Kendler, K. S., Gardner, C. O., & Prescott, C. A. (2006). Toward a comprehensive developmental model for major depression in men. *American Journal of Psychiatry, 163*, 115–124.

Levinson, D. F. (2006). The genetics of depression: A review. *Biological Psychiatry, 60*, 84–92.

Plomin, R., DeFries, J. C., Craig, I. W., & McGuffin, P. (2003). *Behavioral genetics in the postgenomic era*. Washington, DC: American Psychological Association.

Segal, Z. V., Williams, J. M. G., & Teasdale, J. D. (2002). *Mindfulness-based cognitive therapy for depression: A new approach to preventing relapse*. New York: Guilford.

Sloman, L., & Gilbert, P. (2000). *Subordination and defeat*. Mahwah, NJ: Lawrence Erlbaum Associates, Inc.

Teasdale, J. D., & Barnard, P. J. (1993). *Affect, cognition, and change: Re-modelling depressive thought*. Hove, UK: Lawrence Erlbaum Associates Ltd.

Weisz, J. R., McCarty, C. A., & Valeri, S. M. (2006). Effects of psychotherapy for depression in children and adolescents:
A meta-analysis. *Psychological Bulletin, 132*, 132–149.

Wong, M. L., & Licinio, J. (2001). Research and treatment approaches to depression. *Nature Reviews Neuroscience, 2*, 343–351.

References

Abramson, L. Y., Metalsky, G. I., & Alloy, L. B. (1989). Hopelessness depression: A theory-based subtype of depression. *Psychological Review, 96*, 358–372.

Abramson, L. Y., Seligman, M. E. P., & Teasdale, J. D. (1978). Learned helplessness in humans: Critique and reformulation. *Journal of Abnormal Psychology, 87*, 49–74.

Agosti, V., & Stewart, J. W. (2001). Atypical and non-atypical subtypes of depression: Comparison of social functioning, symptoms, course of illness, co-morbidity and demographic features. *Journal of Affective Disorders, 65*, 75–79.

Allgood-Merten, B., Lewinsohn, P. M., & Hops, H. (1990). Sex differences and adolescent depression. *Journal of Abnormal Psychology, 99*, 55–63.

Alloy, L. B., & Abramson, L. Y. (1979). Judgment of contingency in depressed and nondepressed students: Sadder but wiser? *Journal of Experimental Psychology: General, 108*, 441–485.

Alloy, L. B., Abramson, L. Y., Smith, J. M., Gibb, B. E., & Neeren, A. M. (2006a). Role of parenting and maltreatment histories in unipolar and bipolar mood disorders: Mediation by cognitive vulnerability to depression. *Clinical Child and Family Psychology Review, 9*, 23–64.

Alloy, L. B., Abramson, L. Y., Whitehouse, W. G., & Hogan, M. E. (2006b). Prospective incidence of first onsets and recurrences of depression in individuals at high and low cognitive risk for depression. *Journal of Abnormal Psychology, 115,* 145–156.

Alloy, L. B., Abramson, L. Y., Whitehouse, W. G., Hogan, M. E., Tashman, N. A., Steinberg, D. L., et al. (1999). Depressogenic cognitive styles: Predictive validity, information processing and personality characteristics, and developmental origins. *Behaviour Research and Therapy, 37*, 503–531.

Alnaes, R., & Torgersen, S. (1997). Personality and personality disorders predict development and relapses of major depression. *Acta Psychiatrica Scandinavica, 95*, 336–342.

Alpert, J. E., Uebelacker, L. A., Mclean, N. E., Nierenberg, A. A., Pava, J. A., Worthington, J. J., et al. (1997). Social phobia, avoidant personality disorder and atypical depression: Co-occurrence and clinical implications. *Psychological Medicine, 27*, 627–633.

American Psychiatric Association. (2000). *Diagnostic and statistical manual of mental disorders* (4th ed., text revision). Arlington, VA: American Psychiatric Association.

Andrade, L., Caraveo-Anduaga, J. J., Berglund, P., Bijl, R. V., De Graaf, R., Vollebergh, W., et al. (2003). The epidemiology of major depressive episodes: Results from the International Consortium of Psychiatric

Epidemiology (ICPE) Surveys. *International Journal of Methods in Psychiatric Research, 12,* 3–21.

Andrews, B., & Brown, G. W. (1988). Social support, onset of depression and personality: An exploratory analysis. *Social Psychiatry and Psychiatric Epidemiology, 23,* 99–108.

Aneshensel, C. S., Frerichs, R. R., & Clark, V. A. (1981). Family roles and sex differences in depression. *Journal of Health and Social Behavior, 22,* 379–393.

Angold, A., & Costello, E. J. (1993). Depressive comorbidity in children and adolescents: Empirical, theoretical, and methodological issues. *American Journal of Psychiatry, 150,* 1779–1791.

Angold, A., Costello, E. J., Erkanli, A., & Worthman, C. M. (1999). Pubertal changes in hormone levels and depression in girls. *Psychological Medicine, 29,* 1043–1053.

Angold, A., Costello, E. J., & Worthman, C. M. (1998). Puberty and depression: The roles of age, pubertal status and pubertal timing. *Psychological Medicine, 28,* 51–61.

Angold, A., & Rutter, M. (1992). Effects of age and pubertal status on depression in a large clinical sample. *Development and Psychopathology, 4,* 5–28.

Angst, J., Sellaro, R., Stassen, H. H., & Gamma, A. (2005). Diagnostic conversion from depression to bipolar disorders: Results of a long-term prospective study of hospital admissions. *Journal of Affective Disorders, 84,* 149–157.

Arieti, S., & Bemporad, J. (1980). The psychological organization of depression. *American Journal of Psychiatry, 137,* 1360–1365.

Armsden, G. C., McCauley, E., Greenberg, M. T., Burke, P. M., & Mitchell, J. R. (1990). Parent and peer attachment in early adolescent depression. *Journal of Abnormal Child Psychology, 18,* 683–697.

Asarnow, J. R., Tompson, M., Woo, S., &

Cantwell, D. P. (2001). Is expressed emotion a specific risk factor for depression or a nonspecific correlate of psychopathology? *Journal of Abnormal Child Psychology, 29,* 573–583.

Aubrey, J. M., Gervasoni, N., Osiek, C., Perret, G., Rossier, M. F., Bertschy, G., et al. (2007). The DEX/CRH neuroendocrine test and the prediction of depressive relapse in remitted depressed outpatients. *Journal of Psychiatric Research, 41,* 290–294.

Babyak, M., Blumenthal, J. A., Herman, S., Khatri, P., Doraiswamy, M., Moore, K., et al. (2000). Exercise treatment for major depression: Maintenance of therapeutic benefit at 10 months. *Psychosomatic Medicine, 62,* 633–638.

Barber, J. P., & DeRubeis, R. J. (1989). On second thoughts: Where the action is in cognitive therapy. *Cognitive Therapy and Research, 13,* 441–457.

Barber, J. P., & Muenz, L. R. (1996). The role of avoidance and obsessiveness in matching patients to cognitive and interpersonal psychotherapy. Empirical findings from the treatment for depression collaborative research program. *Journal of Consulting and Clinical Psychology, 64,* 951–958.

Bardone, A., Moffitt, T., Caspi, A., Dickson, N., & Silva, P. (1996). Adult mental health and social outcomes of adolescent girls with depression and conduct disorder. *Development and Psychopathology, 8,* 811–829.

Barkham, M., Shapiro, D. A., Hardy, G. E., & Rees, A. (1999). Psychotherapy in two-plus-one sessions: Outcomes of a randomized controlled trial of cognitive-behavioral and psychodynamic-interpersonal therapy for subsyndromal depression. *Journal of Consulting and Clinical Psychology, 67,* 201–211.

Barnett, P. A., & Gotlib, I. H. (1988). Psychosocial functioning and depression: Distinguishing among antecedents, concomitants, and consequences. *Psychological Bulletin, 104,* 97–126.

Bauer, M., Bschor, T., Kunz, D., Berghofer, A., Strohle, A., & Muller-Oerlinghausen, B. (2000). Double-blind, placebo-controlled trial of the use of lithium to augment antidepressant medication in continuation treatment of unipolar major depression. *American Journal of Psychiatry, 157,* 1429–1435.

Beach, S. R. H., & O'Leary, K. D. (1992). Treating depression in the context of marital discord: Outcome and predictors of response of marital therapy versus cognitive therapy. *Behavior Therapy, 23,* 507–528.

Beardslee, W. R., Versage, E. M., & Gladstone, T. R. (1998). Children of affectively ill parents: A review of the past 10 years. *Journal of the American Academy of Child and Adolescent Psychiatry, 37,* 1134–1141.

Beck, A. T. (1967). *Depression: Clinical, experimental and theoretical aspects.* New York: Harper & Row.

Beck, A. T. (1976). *Cognitive therapy and emotional disorders.* New York: Meridian.

Beck, A. T. (1983). Cognitive therapy of depression: New perspectives. In P. J. Clayton & J. E. Barrett (Eds.), *Treatment of depression: Old controversies and new approaches* (pp. 265–290). New York: Raven.

Beck, A. T. (2005). The current state of cognitive therapy: A 40-year retrospective. *Archives of General Psychiatry, 62,* 953–959.

Beck, A. T., Brown, G., Berchick, R., Stewart, B. L., & Steer, R. A. (1990). Relationship between hopelessness and ultimate suicide: A replication with psychiatric outpatients. *American Journal of Psychiatry, 147,* 190–195.

Beck, A. T., Rush, A. J., Shaw, B. F., & Emery, G. (1979). *Cognitive therapy of depression.* New York: Guilford.

Beck, A. T., Steer, R. A., Ball, R., & Ranieri, W. F. (1996a). Comparison of Beck Depression Inventories-IA and -II in psychiatric outpatients. *Journal of Personality Assessment, 67,* 588–597.

Beck, A. T., Steer, R. A., & Brown, G. K. (1996b). *The Beck Depression Inventory* (2nd ed.). San Antonio, TX: The Psychological Corporation.

Beck, A. T., Steer, R. A., & Garbin, M. G. (1988). Psychometric properties of the Beck Depression Inventory: Twenty-five years of evaluation. *Clinical Psychology Review, 8,* 77–100.

Beck, A. T., Ward, C. H., Mendelson, M., Mock, J., & Erbaugh, J. (1961). An inventory for measuring depression. *Archives of General Psychiatry, 4,* 561–574.

Beck, R., & Perkins, T. S. (2001). Cognitive content-specificity for anxiety and depression: A meta-analysis. *Cognitive Therapy and Research, 25,* 651–663.

Beekman, A. T., Geerlings, S. W., Deeg, D. J., Smit, J. H., Schoevers, R. S., de Beurs, E., et al. (2002). The natural history of late-life depression: A 6-year prospective study in the community. *Archives of General Psychiatry, 59,* 605–611.

Beevers, C. G., & Miller, I. W. (2005). Unlinking negative cognition and symptoms of depression: Evidence of a specific treatment effect for cognitive therapy. *Journal of Consulting and Clinical Psychology, 73,* 68–77.

Belle, D. (1990). Poverty and women's mental health. *American Psychologist, 45,* 385–389.

Benca, R. M., Obermeyer, W. H., Thisted, R. A., & Gillin, J. C. (1992). Sleep and psychiatric disorders: A meta-analysis. *Archives of General Psychiatry, 49,* 651–668.

Berman, R. M., Narasimhan, M., Sanacora, G., Miano, A. P., Hoffman, R. E., Hu, X. S., et al. (2000). A randomized clinical trial of repetitive transcranial magnetic stimulation in the treatment of major depression. *Biological Psychiatry, 47,* 332–337.

Bifulco, A. T., Brown, G. W., & Harris, T. O. (1987). Childhood loss of parent, lack of adequate parental care and adult depression: A replication. *Journal of Affective Disorders, 12,* 115–128.

Bifulco, A. T., Brown, G. W., Moran, P., Ball, C., & Campbell, C. (1998). Predicting depression in women: The role of past and present vulnerability. *Psychological Medicine, 28,* 39–50.

Bifulco, A. T., Moran, P., Baines, R., Bunn, A., & Stanford, K. (2002a). Exploring psychological abuse in childhood: II. Association with other abuse and adult clinical depression. *Bulletin of the Menninger Clinic, 66,* 241–258.

Bifulco, A. T., Moran, P., Ball, C., & Bernazzani, O. (2002b). Adult attachment style: I. Its relationship to clinical depression. *Social Psychiatry and Psychiatric Epidemiology, 37,* 50–59.

Billings, A. G., Cronkite, R. C., & Moos, R. H. (1983). Social–environmental factors in unipolar depression: Comparisons of depressed patients and nondepressed controls. *Journal of Abnormal Psychology, 93,* 119–133.

Billings, A. G., & Moos, R. H. (1984). Coping, stress, and social resources among adults with unipolar depression. *Journal of Personality and Social Psychology, 46,* 877–891.

Billings, A. G., & Moos, R. H. (1985). Psychosocial processes of remission in unipolar depression: Comparing depressed patients with matched community controls. *Journal of Consulting and Clinical Psychology, 53,* 314–325.

Birmaher, B., Williamson, D. E., Dahl, R. E., Axelson, D. A., Kaufman, J., Dorn, L. D., et al. (2004). Clinical presentation and course of depression in youth: Does onset in childhood differ from onset in adolescence? *Journal of the American Academy of Child & Adolescent Psychiatry, 43,* 63–70.

Blackburn, I. M., & Moore, R. G. (1997). Controlled acute and follow-up trial of cognitive therapy and pharmacotherapy in out-patients with recurrent depression. *British Journal of Psychiatry, 171,* 328–334.

Bland, R. C., Newman, S. C., & Orn, H. (1986). Recurrent and nonrecurrent depression: A family study. *Archives of General Psychiatry, 43,* 1085–1089.

Blatt, S. J. (1974). Levels of object representation in anaclitic and introjective depression. *Psychoanalytic Study of the Child, 29,* 107–157.

Blatt, S. J., & Homann, E. (1992). Parent–child interaction in the etiology of dependent and self-critical depression. *Clinical Psychology Review, 12,* 47–91.

Blatt, S. J., Quinlan, D., Chevron, E., McDonald, C., & Zuroff, D. (1982). Dependency and self-criticism: Psychological dimensions of depression. *Journal of Consulting and Clinical Psychology, 50,* 113–124.

Blatt, S. J., Wein, S. J., Chevron, E. S., & Quinlan, D. M. (1979). Parental representations and depression in normal young adults. *Journal of Abnormal Psychology, 88,* 388–397.

Blazer, D. G. (2003). Depression in late life: Review and commentary. *Journal of Gerontology, 58A,* 249–265.

Blazer, D. G., Kessler, R. C., McGonagle, K. A., & Swartz, M. S. (1994). The prevalence and distribution of major depression in a national community sample: The National Comorbidity Survey. *American Journal of Psychiatry, 151,* 979–986.

Blazer, D. G., Kessler, R. C., & Swartz, M. S. (1998). Epidemiology of recurrent major and minor depression with a seasonal pattern: The National Comorbidity Survey. *British Journal of Psychiatry, 172,* 164–167.

Blazer, D. G., Swartz, M., Woodbury, M.,

Manton, K. G., Hughes, D., & George, L. K. (1988). Depressive symptoms and depressive diagnoses in a community population: Use of a new procedure for analysis of psychiatric classification. *Archives of General Psychiatry, 45*, 1078–1084.

Bloch, M., Rotenberg, N., Koren, D., & Klein, E. (2005). Risk factors associated with the development of postpartum mood disorders. *Journal of Affective Disorders, 88*, 9–18.

Blumenthal, J. A., Babyak, M. A., Moore, K. A., Craighead, E., Herman, S., Khatri, P., et al. (1999). Effects of exercise training on older patients with major depression. *Archives of Internal Medicine, 159*, 2349–2356.

Bockting, C. L. H., Schene, A. H., Spinhoven, P., Koeter, M. W. J., Wouters, L. F., Huyser, J., et al. (2005). Preventing relapse/recurrence in recurrent depression with cognitive therapy: A randomized controlled trial. *Journal of Consulting and Clinical Psychology, 73*, 647–657.

Bockting, C. L., Spinhoven, P., Koeter, M. W., Wouters, L. F., Schene, A. H., & Depression Evaluation Longitudinal Therapy Assessment Study Group. (2006). Prediction of recurrence in recurrent depression and the influence of consecutive episodes on vulnerability for depression: A 2-year prospective study. *Journal of Clinical Psychiatry, 67*, 747–755.

Bornstein, R. F. (1992). The dependent personality: Developmental, social, and clinical perspectives. *Psychological Bulletin, 112*, 3–23.

Borowsky, I. W., Ireland, M., & Resnick, M. D. (2001). Adolescent suicide attempts: Risks and protectors. *Pediatrics, 107*, 485–493.

Bower, G. H. (1981). Mood and Memory. *American Psychologist, 36*, 129–148.

Bowlby, J. (1978). Attachment theory and its therapeutic implications. *Adolescent Psychiatry, 6*, 5–33.

Bowlby, J. (1981). Psychoanalysis as a natural science. *International Review of Psycho-Analysis, 8*, 243–256.

Boyce, W. T., & Ellis, B. J. (2005). Biological sensitivity to context: I. An evolutionary-developmental theory of the origins and functions of stress reactivity. *Development and Psychopathology, 17*, 271–301.

Brent, D. A., Holder, D., Kolko, D., Birmaher, B., Baugher, M., Roth, C., et al. (1997). A clinical psychotherapy trial for adolescent depression comparing cognitive, family, and supportive therapy. *Archives of General Psychiatry, 54*, 877–885.

Breslau, J., Aguilar-Gaxiola, S., Kendler, K. S., Su, M., Williams, D., & Kessler, R. C. (2005a). Specifying race-ethnic differences in risk for psychiatric disorder in a USA national sample. *Psychological Medicine, 35*, 1–12.

Breslau, J., Kendler, K. S., Su, M., Gaxiola-Aguilar, S., & Kessler, R. C. (2005b). Lifetime risk and persistence of psychiatric disorders across ethnic groups in the United States. *Psychological Medicine, 35*, 317–327.

Breslau, N., Roth, T., Rosenthal, L., & Andreski, P. (1996). Sleep disturbance and psychiatric disorders: A longitudinal epidemiological study of young adults. *Biological Psychiatry, 39*, 411–418.

Brieger, P., Ehrt, U., & Marneros, A. (2003). Frequency of comorbid personality disorders in bipolar and unipolar affective disorders. *Comprehensive Psychiatry, 44*, 28–34.

Broadhead, W. E., Blazer, D. G., George, L. K., & Tse, C. K. (1990). Depression, disability days, and days lost from work in a prospective epidemiologic survey. *Journal of the American Medical Association, 264*, 2524–2528.

Brody, A. L., Saxena, S., Stoessel, P.,

Gillies, L. A., Fairbanks, L. A., Alborzian, S., et al. (2001). Regional brain metabolic changes in patients with major depression treated with either paroxetine or interpersonal therapy: Preliminary findings. *Archives of General Psychiatry, 58*, 631–640.

Bromberger, J. T., Assmann, S. F., Avis, N. E., Schocken, M., Kravitz, H. M., & Cordal, A. (2003). Persistent mood symptoms in a multiethnic community cohort of pre-and peri-menopausal women. *American Journal of Epidemiology, 158*, 347–356.

Brouwer, J. P., Appelhof, B. C., van Rossum, E. F. C., Koper, J. W., Fliers, E., Huyser, J., et al. (2006). Prediction of treatment response by HPA-axis and glucocorticoid receptor polymorphisms in major depression. *Psychoneuroendocrinology, 31*, 1154–1163.

Brown, C., Schulberg, H. C., Madonia, M. J., Shear, M. K., & Houck, P. R. (1996). Treatment outcomes for primary care patients with major depression and lifetime anxiety disorders. *American Journal of Psychiatry, 153*, 1293–1300.

Brown, G. K., Beck, A. T., Steer, R. A., & Grisham, J. R. (2000). Risk factors for suicide in psychiatric outpatients: A 20-year prospective study. *Journal of Consulting and Clinical Psychology, 68*, 371–377.

Brown, G. R., & Anderson, B. (1991). Psychiatric morbidity in adult inpatients with childhood histories of sexual and physical abuse. *American Journal of Psychiatry, 148*, 55–61.

Brown, G. W., Andrews, B., Bifulco, A. T., & Veiel, H. O. (1990). Self-esteem and depression: I. Measurement issues and prediction of onset. *Social Psychiatry and Psychiatric Epidemiology, 25*, 200–209.

Brown, G. W., Bifulco, A., & Harris, T. O. (1987). Life events, vulnerability and onset of depression: Some refinements. *British Journal of Psychiatry, 150*, 30–42.

Brown, G. W., & Harris, T. O. (1978). *Social origins of depression.* New York: Free Press.

Brown, G. W., & Harris, T. O. (1989). Depression. In G. W. Brown & T. O. Harris (Eds.), *Life events and illness* (pp. 49–93). New York: Guilford.

Brown, G. W., & Harris, T. O. (1993). Aetiology of anxiety and depressive disorders in an inner-city population: 1. Early adversity. *Psychological Medicine, 23*, 143–154.

Brown, G. W., Harris, T. O., & Hepworth, C. (1995). Loss, humiliation and entrapment among women developing depression: A patient and non-patient comparison. *Psychological Medicine, 25*, 7–21.

Brown, G. W., & Moran, P. M. (1997). Single mothers, poverty and depression. *Psychological Medicine, 27*, 21–33.

Brown, J., Cohen, P., Johnson, J. G., & Smailes, E. (1999). Childhood abuse and neglect: Specificity of effects on adolescent and young adult depression and suicidality. *Journal of the American Academy of Child Adolescent Psychiatry, 38*, 1490–1496.

Brown, J. D., & Dutton, K. A. (1995). The thrill of victory, the complexity of defeat: Self-esteem and people's emotional-reactions to success and failure. *Journal of Personality and Social Psychology, 68*, 712–722.

Brown, T. A., Campbell, L. A., Lehman, C. L., Grisham, J. R., & Mancill, R. B. (2001a). Current and lifetime comorbidity of the DSM-IV anxiety and mood disorders in a large clinical sample. *Journal of Abnormal Psychology, 110*, 585–599.

Brown, T. A., Di Nardo, P. A., Lehman, C. L., & Campbell, L. A. (2001b). Reliability of DSM-IV anxiety and mood disorders: Implications for the classification of emotional disorders. *Journal of Abnormal Psychology, 110*, 49–58.

Browne, G., Steiner, M., Roberts, J., Gafni, A., Byrne, C., Dunn, E., et al. (2002). Sertraline and/or interpersonal psychotherapy for patients with dysthymic disorder in primary care: 6-month comparison with longitudinal 2-year follow-up of effectiveness and costs. *Journal of Affective Disorders, 68,* 317–330.

Bruce, M. L., Takeuchi, D. T., & Leaf, P. J. (1991). Poverty and psychiatric status: Longitudinal evidence from the New Haven Epidemiologic Catchment Area Study. *Archives of General Psychiatry, 48,* 470–474.

Burke, H. M., Davis, M. C., Otte, C., & Mohr, D. C. (2005). Depression and cortisol responses to psychological stress: A meta-analysis. *Psychoneuroendocrinology, 30,* 846–856.

Burke, K. C., Burke, J. D., Regier, D. A., & Rae, D. S. (1990). Age at onset of selected mental disorders in five community populations. *Archives of General Psychiatry, 47,* 511–518.

Burns, D. D., & Nolen-Hoeksema, S. (1991). Coping styles, homework, compliance and the effectiveness of cognitive-behavioural therapy. *Journal of Consulting and Clinical Psychology, 59,* 305–311.

Burton, E., Stice, E., & Seeley, J. R. (2004). A prospective test of the Stress-Buffering Model of Depression in adolescent girls: No support once again. *Journal of Consulting and Clinical Psychology, 72,* 689–697.

Butler, A. C., Hokanson, J. E., & Flynn, H. A. (1994). A comparison of self-esteem liability and low trait self-esteem as vulnerability factors for depression. *Journal of Personality and Social Psychology, 66,* 166–177.

Butler, G., & Mathews, A. (1983). Cognitive processes in anxiety. *Advances in Behaviour Research and Therapy, 5,* 51–62.

Butzlaff, R. L., & Hooley, J. M. (1998). Expressed emotion and psychiatric relapse. *Archives of General Psychiatry, 55,* 547–552.

Camp, N. J., Lowry, M. R., Richards, R. L., Plenk, A. M., Carter, C., Hensel, C. H., et al. (2005). Genome-wide linkage analyses of extended Utah pedigrees identifies loci that influence recurrent, early-onset major depression and anxiety disorders. *American Journal of Medical Genetics. Part B, Neuropsychiatric Genetics, 135,* 85–93.

Carlezon, W. A., Duman, R. S., & Nestler, E. J. (2005). The many faces of CREB. *Trends in Neurosciences, 28,* 436–445.

Carlson, G. A., & Cantwell, D. P. (1980). Unmasking masked depression in children and adolescents. *American Journal of Psychiatry, 137,* 445–449.

Carnelley, K. B., Pietromonaco, P. R., & Jaffe, K. (1994). Depression, working models of others, and relationship functioning. *Journal of Personality and Social Psychology, 66,* 127–140.

Carney, S., Cowen, P., Geddes, J., Goodwin, G., Rogers, R., Dearness, K., et al. (2003). Efficacy and safety of electroconvulsive therapy in depressive disorders: A systematic review and meta-analysis. *Lancet, 361,* 799–808.

Carver, C. S. (1998). Generalization, adverse events, and development of depressive symptoms. *Journal of Personality, 66,* 607–619.

Carver, C. S., & Ganellen, R. J. (1983). Depression and components of self-punitiveness: High standards, self-criticism, and overgeneralization. *Journal of Abnormal Psychology, 92,* 330–337.

Carver, C. S., Lavoie, L., Kuhl, J., & Ganellen, R. J. (1988). Cognitive concomitants of depression: A further examination of the roles of generalization, high standards, and self-criticism. *Journal of Social and Clinical Psychology, 7,* 350–365.

Caspi, A., Sugden, K., Moffitt, T. E., Taylor,

A., Craig, I. W., Harington, H., et al. (2003). Influence of life stress on depression: Moderation by a polymorphism in the 5-HTT gene. *Science, 301,* 386–389.

Cerel, J., Roberts, T. A., & Nilsen, W. J. (2005). Peer suicidal behavior and adolescent risk behavior. *Journal of Nervous and Mental Disease, 193,* 237–243.

Chang, P. P., Ford, D. E., Mead, L. A., Cooper-Patrick, L., & Klag, M. J. (1997). Insomnia in young men and subsequent depression: The Johns Hopkins Precursors Study. *American Journal of Epidemiology, 146,* 105–114.

Chapman, D. P., Perry, G. S., & Strine, T. W. (2005, January). The vital link between chronic disease and depressive disorders. *Preventing Chronic Disease.* Available from http://www.cdc.gov/pcd/issues/2005/jan/04_0066.htm

Cicchetti, D., Rogosch, F. A., & Toth, S. L. (1998). Maternal depressive disorder and contextual risk: Contributions to the development of attachment insecurity and behavior problems in toddlerhood. *Development and Psychopathology, 10,* 283–300.

Cicchetti, D., & Schneider-Rosen, K. (1986). An organizational approach to childhood depression. In C. M. Rutter, C. Izard, & P. Read (Eds.), *Depression in young people: Clinical and developmental perspectives* (pp. 71–134). New York: Guilford.

Cicchetti, D., & Toth, S. L. (1998). The development of depression in children and adolescents. *American Psychologist, 53,* 221–241.

Clark, D. A., Beck, A. T., & Alford, B. A. (1999). *Scientific foundations of cognitive theory and therapy of depression.* New York: Wiley.

Clark, D. C., & Fawcett, J. (1992). Review of empirical risk factors for evaluation of the suicidal patient. In B. M. Bongar (Ed.), *Suicide: Guidelines for assessment, management, and treatment* (pp. 16–48). New York: Oxford University Press.

Clark, D. M., & Teasdale, J. D. (1982). Diurnal variation in clinical depression and accessibility of memories of positive and negative experiences. *Journal of Abnormal Psychology, 91,* 87–95.

Clark, D. M., & Teasdale, J. D. (1985). Constraints on the effects of mood on memory. *Journal of Personality and Social Psychology, 48,* 1595–1608.

Clark, L. A. (2005). Temperament as a unifying basis for personality and psychopathology. *Journal of Abnormal Psychology, 114,* 505–521.

Clark, L. A., Vittengl, J., Kraft, D., & Jarrett, R. B. (2003). Separate personality traits from states to predict depression. *Journal of Personality Disorders, 17,* 152–172.

Clark, L. A., Watson, D., & Mineka, S. (1994). Temperament, personality, and the mood and anxiety disorders. *Journal of Abnormal Psychology, 103,* 103–116.

Clarke, G. N., Hawkins, W., Murphy, M., Sheeber, L. B., Lewinsohn, P. M., & Seeley, J. R. (1995). Targeted prevention of unipolar depressive disorder in an at-risk sample of high-school adolescents: A randomized trial of a group cognitive intervention. *Journal of the American Academy of Child and Adolescent Psychiatry, 34,* 312–321.

Clarke, G. N., Hornbrook, M., Lynch, F., Polen, M., Gale, J., Beardslee, W., et al. (2001). A randomized trial of a group cognitive intervention for preventing depression in adolescent offspring of depressed parents. *Archives of General Psychiatry, 58,* 1127–1134.

Clarke, G. N., Rohde, P., Lewinsohn, P. M., Hops, H., & Seeley, J. R. (1999). Cognitive-behavioral treatment of adolescent depression: Efficacy of acute group treatment and booster sessions. *Journal of the American Academy of Child and Adolescent Psychiatry, 38,* 272–279.

Cogswell, A., Alloy, L. B., & Spasojevic, J. (2006). Neediness and interpersonal life stress: Does congruency predict depression? *Cognitive Therapy and Research, 30,* 427–443.

Cohen, L. S., Soares, C. N., Vitonis, A. F., Otto, M. W., & Harlow, B. L. (2006). Risk for new onset of depression during the menopausal transition. *Archives of General Psychiatry, 63,* 385–390.

Cohen, P., Cohen, J., Kasen, S., & Velez, C. N. (1993). An epidemiological study of disorders in late childhood and adolescence: I. Age- and gender-specific prevalence. *Journal of Child Psychology and Psychiatry, 34,* 851–867.

Cohen, S., & Wills, T. A. (1985). Stress, social support, and the buffering hypothesis. *Psychological Bulletin, 98,* 310–357.

Coleman, E. A., Sackeim, H. A., Prudic, J., Devanand, D. P., McElhiney, M. C., & Moody, B. J. (1996). Subjective memory complaints prior to and following electroconvulsive therapy. *Biological Psychiatry, 39,* 346–356.

Coryell, W., Akiskal, H., Leon, A., Winokur, G., Maser, J., Mueller, T., et al. (1994a). The time course of nonchronic major depressive disorder: Uniformity across episodes and samples. *Archives of General Psychiatry, 51,* 405–410.

Coryell, W., Endicott, J., & Keller, M. B. (1991). Predictors of relapse into major depressive disorder in a nonclinical population. *American Journal of Psychiatry, 148,* 1353–1358.

Coryell, W., Leon, A. C., Turvey, C., Akiskal, H. S., Mueller, T., & Endicott, J. (2001). The significance of psychotic features in manic episodes: A report from the NIMH collaborative study. *Journal of Affective Disorders, 67,* 79–88.

Coryell, W., Leon, A., Winokur, G., Endicott, J., Keller, M., Akiskal, H., et al. (1996). Importance of psychotic features to long-term course in major depressive

disorder. *American Journal of Psychiatry, 153,* 483–489.

Coryell, W., Scheftner, W., Keller, M., Endicott, J., Maser, J., & Klerman, G. L. (1993). The enduring psychosocial consequences of mania and depression. *American Journal of Psychiatry, 150,* 720–727.

Coryell, W., Winokur, G., Shea, T., Maser, J. D., Endicott, J., & Akiskal, H. S. (1994b). The long-term stability of depressive subtypes. *American Journal of Psychiatry, 151,* 199–204.

Costello, E. J., Costello, A. J., Edelbrock, C., Burns, B. J., Dulcan, M. K., Brent, D., et al. (1988). Psychiatric disorders in pediatric primary care: Prevalence and risk factors. *Archives of General Psychiatry, 45,* 1107–1116.

Costello, E. J., Mustillo, S., Erkanli, A., Keeler, G., & Angold, A. (2003). Prevalence and development of psychiatric disorders in childhood and adolescence. *Archives of General Psychiatry, 60,* 837–844.

Cox, J. L., Murray, D., & Chapman, G. (1993). A controlled study of the onset, duration and prevalence of postnatal depression. *British Journal of Psychiatry, 163,* 27–31.

Coyne, J. C. (1976). Depression and the response of others. *Journal of Abnormal Psychology, 85,* 186–193.

Coyne, J. C., Burchill, S., & Stiles, W. B. (1991). An interactional perspective on depression. In C. R. Snyder & D. Forsyth (Eds.), *Handbook of social and clinical psychology: The health perspective.* Pergamon General Psychology Series, Vol. 162 (pp. 327–349). Elmsford, NY: Pergamon.

Coyne, J. C., Kahn, J., & Gotlib, I. H. (1987). Depression. In T. Jacob (Ed.), *Family interaction and psychopathology: Theories, methods, and findings. Applied clinical psychology* (pp. 509–533). New York: Plenum.

Coyne, J. C., Thompson, R., & Palmer, S. C.

(2002). Marital quality, coping with conflict, marital complaints, and affection in couples with a depressed wife. *Journal of Family Psychology, 16,* 26–37.

Craighead, W. E., Curry, J. F., & Ilardi, S. S. (1995). Relationship of children's depression inventory factors to major depression among adolescents. *Psychological Assessment, 7,* 171–176.

Craighead, W. E., Smucker, M. R., Craighead, L. W., & Ilardi, S. S. (1998). Factor analysis of the children's depression inventory in a community sample. *Psychological Assessment, 10,* 156–165.

Crocker, J., & Park, L. E. (2004). The costly pursuit of self-esteem. *Psychological Bulletin, 130,* 392–414.

Crocker, J., & Wolfe, C. T. (2001). Contingencies of self-worth. *Psychological Review, 108,* 593–623.

Crook, T., Raskin, A., & Eliot, J. (1981). Parent–child relationships and adult depression. *Child Development, 52,* 950–957.

Cross-National Collaborative Group. (1992). The changing rate of major depression: Cross-national comparisons. *Journal of the American Medical Association, 268,* 3098–3105.

Cuellar, A. K., Johnson, S. L., & Winters, R. (2005). Distinctions between bipolar and unipolar depression. *Clinical Psychology Review, 25,* 307–339.

Cui, X. J., & Vaillant, G. E. (1997). Does depression generate negative life events? *The Journal of Nervous and Mental Disease, 185,* 145–150.

Cummings, E. M., & Davies, P. T. (1999). Depressed parents and family functioning: Interpersonal effects and children's functioning and development. In T. E. Joiner & J. C. Coyne (Eds.), *The interactional nature of depression: Advances in interpersonal approaches* (pp. 299–327). Washington,

DC: American Psychological Association.

Curry, J. F. (2001). Specific psychotherapies for childhood and adolescent depression. *Biological Psychiatry, 49,* 1091–1100.

Cyranowski, J. M., Frank, E., Young, E., & Shear, K. (2000). Adolescent onset of the gender difference in lifetime rates of major depression. *Archives of General Psychiatry, 57,* 21–27.

Daley, S. E., Hammen, C., Burge, D., Davila, J., Paley, B., Lindberg, N., et al. (1999). Depression and Axis II symptomatology in an adolescent community sample: Concurrent and longitudinal associations. *Journal of Personality Disorders, 13,* 47–59.

Daley, S. E., Hammen, C., & Rao, U. (2000). Predictors of first onset and recurrence of major depression in young women during the 5 years following high school graduation. *Journal of Abnormal Psychology, 109,* 525–533.

Dalgard, O. S., Dowrick, C., Lehtinen, V., Vazquez-Barquero, J. L., Casey, P., Wilkinson, G., et al. (2006). Negative life events, social support and gender difference in depression. *Social Psychiatry and Psychiatric Epidemiology, 41,* 444–451.

Davidson, J. R. T., Gadde, K. M., Fairbank, J. A., Krishnan, R. R., Califf, R. M., Binanay, C., et al. (2002). Effect of Hypericum perforatum (St John's wort) in major depressive disorder: A randomized controlled trial. *Journal of the American Medical Association, 287,* 1807–1814.

Davidson, J. R. T., Miller, R. D., Turnbull, C. D., & Sullivan, J. L. (1982). Atypical depression. *Archives of General Psychiatry, 39,* 527–534.

Davidson, R. J., & Irwin, W. (1999). The functional neuroanatomy of emotion and affective style. *Trends in Cognitive Sciences, 3,* 11–21.

Davidson, R. J., Lewis, D. A., Alloy, L. B.,

Amaral, D. G., Bush, G., Cohen, J. D., et al. (2002). Neural and behavioral substrates of mood and mood regulation. *Biological Psychiatry, 52,* 478–502.

Davila, J., Karney, B. R., Hall, T. W., & Bradbury, T. N. (2003). Depressive symptoms and marital satisfaction: Within-subject associations and the moderating effects of gender and neuroticism. *Journal of Family Psychology, 17,* 557–570.

Davis, L. L., Rush, J. A., Wisniewski, S. R., Rice, K., Cassano, P., Jewell, M. E., et al. (2005). Substance use disorder comorbidity in major depressive disorder: An exploratory analysis of the Sequenced Treatment Alternatives to Relieve Depression cohort. *Comprehensive Psychiatry, 46,* 81–89.

Dawson, G., Ashman, S. B., Panagiotides, H., Hessl, D., Self, J., Yamada, E., et al. (2003). Preschool outcomes of children of depressed mothers: Role of maternal behavior, contextual risk, and children's brain activity. *Child Development, 74,* 1158–1175.

De Graaf, R., Bijl, R. V., Smith, F., Vollebergh, W. A. M., & Spijker, J. (2002). Risk factors for 12-month comorbidity of mood, anxiety, and substance use disorders: Findings from the Netherlands Mental Health Survey and Incidence Study. *American Journal of Psychiatry, 159,* 620–629.

DeBattista, C., Belanoff, J., Glass, S., Khan, A., Horne, R. L., Blasey, C., et al. (2006). Mifepristone versus placebo in the treatment of psychosis in patients with psychotic major depression. *Biological Psychiatry, 60,* 1343–1349.

Dent, J., & Teasdale, J. D. (1988). Negative cognition and the persistence of depression. *Journal of Abnormal Psychology, 97,* 29–34.

Depue, R. A., & Monroe, S. M. (1986). Conceptualization and measurement of human disorder and life stress research: The problem of chronic disturbance. *Psychological Bulletin, 99,* 36–51.

DeRubeis, R. J., Evans, M. D., Hollon, S. D., Garvey, M. J., Grove, W. M., & Tuason, V. B. (1990). How does cognitive therapy work: Cognitive change and symptom change in cognitive therapy and pharmacotherapy for depression. *Journal of Consulting and Clinical Psychology, 58,* 862–869.

DeRubeis, R. J., & Feeley, M. (1990). Determinants of change in cognitive therapy for depression. *Cognitive Therapy and Research, 14,* 469–482.

DeRubeis, R. J., Gelfand, L. A., Tang, T. Z., & Simons, A. D. (1999). Medications versus cognitive behavior therapy for severely depressed outpatients: Mega-analysis of four randomized comparisons. *American Journal of Psychiatry, 156,* 1007–1013.

DeRubeis, R. J., Hollon, S. D., Amsterdam, J. D., Shelton, R. C., Young, P. R., Salomon, R. M., et al. (2005). Cognitive therapy vs medications in the treatment of moderate to severe depression. *Archives of General Psychiatry, 62,* 409–416.

Devanand, D. P., Dwork, A. J., Hutchinson, E. R., Bolwig, T. G., & Sackeim, H. A. (1994). Does ECT alter brain structure? *American Journal of Psychiatry, 151,* 957–970.

Dimidjian, S., Hollon, S. D., Dobson, K. S., Schmaling, K. B., Kohlenberg, R. J., Addis, M. E., et al. (2006). Randomized trial of behavioral activation, cognitive therapy, and antidepressant medication in the acute treatment of adults with major depression. *Journal of Consulting and Clinical Psychology, 74,* 658–670.

Dobson, K. S. (1989). A meta-analysis of the efficacy of cognitive therapy for depression. *Journal of Consulting and Clinical Psychology, 57,* 414–419.

Dodd, S., Horgan, D., Malhi, G. S., & Berk, M. (2005). To combine or not to combine? A literature review of antidepressant combination therapy. *Journal of Affective Disorders, 89,* 1–11.

Drevets, W. C. (1998). Functional neuroimaging studies of depression: The anatomy of melancholia. *Annual Review of Medicine, 49,* 341–361.

Drevets, W. C. (2001). Neuroimaging and neuropathological studies of depression: Implications for the cognitive-emotional features of mood disorders. *Current Opinion in Neurobiology, 11,* 240–249.

Drevets, W. C., Price, J. L., Simpson, J. R., Todd, R. D., Reich, T., Vannier, M., et al. (1997). Subgenual prefrontal cortex abnormalities in mood disorders. *Nature, 386,* 824–827.

Duman, R. S., Heninger, G. R., & Nestler, E. J. (1997). A molecular and cellular theory of depression. *Archives of General Psychiatry, 54,* 597–606.

Duman, R. S., & Monteggia, L. M. (2006). A neurotrophic model for stress-related mood disorders. *Biological Psychiatry, 59,* 1116–1127.

Duncan, W. C. (1996). Circadian rhythms and the pharmacology of affective illness. *Pharmacology & Therapeutics, 71,* 253–312.

Dunn, A. L., Trivedi, M. H., Kampert, J. B., Clark, C. G., & Chambliss, H. O. (2005). Exercise treatment for depression: Efficacy and dose response. *American Journal of Preventive Medicine, 28,* 1–8.

Dykman, B. M. (1996). Negative self-evaluations among dysphoric college students: A difference in degree or kind? *Cognitive Therapy and Research, 20,* 445–464.

Eastman, C. I., Young, M. A., Fogg, L. F., Liu, L. W., & Meaden, P. M. (1998). Bright light treatment of winter depression: A placebo-controlled trial. *Archives of General Psychiatry, 55,* 883–889.

Eaton, W. W., Armenian, H., Gallo, J., Pratt, L., & Ford, E. (1996). Depression and risk for onset of type II diabetes: A prospective population-based study. *Diabetes Care, 22,* 1097–1102.

Edelman, R. E., Ahrens, A. H., & Haaga, D. A. F. (1994). Inferences about the self, attributions, and overgeneralization as predictors of recovery from dysphoria. *Cognitive Therapy and Research, 18,* 551–566.

Egger, H. L., & Angold, A. (2006). Common emotional and behavioral disorders in preschool children: Presentation, nosology, and epidemiology. *Journal of Child Psychology and Psychiatry, 47,* 313–337.

Ehnvall, A., & Agren, H. (2002). Patterns of sensitisation in the course of affective illness: A life-charting study of treatment-refractory depressed patients. *Journal of Affective Disorders, 70,* 67–75.

Eley, T. C., Sugden, K., Corsico, A., Gregory, A. M., Sham, P., McGuffin, P., et al. (2004). Gene-environment interaction analysis of serotonin system markers with adolescent depression. *Molecular Psychiatry, 9,* 908–915.

Elkin, I., Gibbons, R. D., Shea, M. T., & Shaw, B. F. (1996). Science is not a trial (but it can sometimes be a tribulation). *Journal of Consulting and Clinical Psychology, 64,* 92–103.

Elkin, I., Parloff, M. B., Hadley, S. W., & Autry, J. H. (1985). National Institute of Mental Health treatment of depression collaborative research program: Background and research plan. *Archives of General Psychiatry, 42,* 305–316.

Elkin, I., Shea, M. T., Watkins, J. T., Imber, S. D., Sotsky, S. M., Collins, J. F., et al. (1989). National Institute of Mental Health treatment of depression collaborative research program: General effectiveness of treatments. *Archives of General Psychiatry, 46,* 971–982.

Emanuels-Zuurveen, I., & Emmelkamp, P. M. G. (1996). Individual behavioral-cognitive therapy v. marital therapy for depression in maritally distressed couples. *British Journal of Psychiatry, 169,* 181–188.

Emslie, G. J., Rush, A. J., Weinberg, W. A., Kowatch, R. A., Hughes, C. W., Carmody, T., et al. (1997). A double-blind, randomized, placebo-controlled trial of fluoxetine in children and adolescents with depression. *Archives of General Psychiatry, 54,* 1031–1037.

Emslie, G. J., Wagner, K. D., Kutcher, S., Krulewicz, S., Fong, R., Carpenter, D. J., et al. (2006). Paroxetine treatment in children and adolescents with major depressive disorder: A randomized, multicenter, double-blind, placebo-controlled trial. *Journal of the American Academy of Child and Adolescent Psychiatry, 45,* 709–719.

Endicott, J., Amsterdam, J., Eriksson, E., Frank, E., Freeman, E., Hirschfeld, R., et al. (1999). Is premenstrual dysphoric disorder a distinct clinical entity? *Journal of Women's Health & Gender-Based Medicine, 8,* 663–679.

Endicott, J., & Spitzer, R. L. (1978). A diagnostic interview: The Schedule for Affective Disorders and Schizophrenia. *Archives of General Psychiatry, 35,* 837–844.

Enns, M. W., & Cox, B. J. (1997). Personality dimensions and depression: Review and commentary. *Canadian Journal of Psychiatry, 42,* 274–284.

Enns, M. W., Larsen, D. K., & Cox, B. J. (2000). Discrepancies between self and observer ratings of depression: The relationship to demographic, clinical and personality variables. *Journal of Affective Disorders, 60,* 33–41.

Enserink, M. (1999). Can the placebo be the cure? *Science, 284,* 238–240.

Ernst, E., Rand, J. I., & Stevinson, C. (1998). Complementary therapies for depression: An overview. *Archives of General Psychiatry, 55,* 1026–1032.

ESEMeD/MHEDEA 2000 Investigators. (2004). Prevalence of mental disorders in Europe: Results from the European Study of the Epidemiology of Mental Disorders (ESEMeD) project. *Acta Psychiatrica Scandinavica, 109,* 21–27.

Esposito, K., & Goodnick, P. (2003). Predictors of response in depression. *Psychiatric Clinics of North America, 26,* 353–365.

Essex, M. J., Klein, M. H., Cho, E., & Kalin, N. H. (2002). Maternal stress beginning in infancy may sensitize children to later stress exposure: Effects on cortisol and behavior. *Biological Psychiatry, 52,* 776–784.

Evans, D. L., Charney, D. S., Lewis, L., Golden, R. N., Gorman, J. M., Krishnan, K. R. R., et al. (2005). Mood disorders in the medically ill: Scientific review and recommendations. *Biological Psychiatry, 58,* 175–189.

Evans, E., Hawton, K., & Rodham, K. (2004). Factors associated with suicidal phenomena in adolescents: A systematic review of population-based studies. *Clinical Psychology Review, 24,* 957–979.

Evans, M. D., Hollon, S. D., DeRubeis, R. J., Piasecki, J. M., Grove, W. M., Garvey, M. J., et al. (1992). Differential relapse following cognitive therapy and pharmacotherapy for depression. *Archives of General Psychiatry, 49,* 802–808.

Fadden, G., Bebbington, P., & Kuipers, L. (1987). Caring and its burdens: A study of the spouses of depressed patients. *British Journal of Psychiatry, 151,* 660–667.

Fanous, A., Gardner, C. O., Prescott, C. A., Cancro, R., & Kendler, K. S. (2002). Neuroticism, major depression and gender: A population-based twin study. *Psychological Medicine, 32,* 719–728.

Fava, G. A., Grandi, S., Zielezny, M., Canestrari, R., & Morphy, M. A. (1994). Cognitive-behavioral treatment of residual symptoms in primary major depressive disorder. *American Journal of Psychiatry, 151,* 1295–1299.

Fava, G. A., Grandi, S., Zielezny, M., Rafanelli, C., & Canestrari, R. (1996). Four-year outcome for cognitive behavioral treatment of residual symptoms in major depression. *American Journal of Psychiatry, 153,* 945–947.

Fava, G. A., Rafanelli, C., Grandi, S., Canestrari, R., & Morphy, M. A. (1998). Six-year outcome for cognitive behavioral treatment of residual symptoms in major depression. *American Journal of Psychiatry, 155,* 1443–1445.

Fava, G. A., Ruini, C., Rafanelli, C., Finos, L., Conti, S., & Grandi, S. (2004). Six-year outcome of cognitive behavior therapy for prevention of recurrent depression. *American Journal of Psychiatry, 161,* 1872–1876.

Fava, M., Alpert, J. E., Carmin, C. N., Wisniewski, S. R., Trivedi, M. H., Biggs, M. M., et al. (2004). Clinical correlates and symptom patterns of anxious depression among patients with major depressive disorder in STAR*D. *Psychological Medicine, 34,* 1299–1308.

Fava, M., Rush, A. J., Trivedi, M. H., Nierenberg, A. A., Thase, M. E., Sackeim, H. A., et al. (2003). Background and rationale for the Sequenced Treatment Alternatives to Relieve Depression (STAR*D) study. *Psychiatric Clinics of North America, 26,* 457–494.

Fava, M., Uebelacker, L. A., Alpert, J. E., Nierenberg, A. A., Pava, J. A., & Rosenbaum, J. F. (1997). Major depressive subtypes and treatment response. *Biological Psychiatry, 42,* 568–576.

Feeley, M., DeRubeis, R. J., & Gelfand, L. A. (1999). The temporal relation of adherence and alliance to symptom change in cognitive therapy for depression. *Journal of Consulting and Clinical Psychology, 67,* 578–582.

Fergusson, D. M., & Horwood, L. J. (1987). Vulnerability to life events exposure. *Psychological Medicine, 17,* 739–749.

Fergusson, D. M., Horwood, L. J., & Beautrais, A. L. (1999). Is sexual orientation related to mental health problems and suicidality in young people? *Archives of General Psychiatry, 56,* 876–880.

Fergusson, D. M., Swain-Campbell, N. R., & Horwood, L. J. (2002). Does sexual violence contribute to elevated rates of anxiety and depression in females? *Psychological Medicine, 32,* 991–996.

Field, T., Lang, C., Martinez, A., Yando, R., Pickens, J. N., & Bendell, D. (1996). Preschool follow-up of infants of dysphoric mothers. *Journal of Clinical Child Psychology, 25,* 272–279.

Fincham, F. D., Beach, S. R. H., Harold, G. T., & Osborne, L. N. (1997). Marital satisfaction and depression: Different causal relationships for men and women? *Psychological Science, 8,* 351–357.

Fink, M. (2001). Convulsive therapy: A review of the first 55 years. *Journal of Affective Disorders, 63,* 1–15.

Finlay-Jones, R., & Brown, G. W. (1981). Types of stressful life event and the onset of anxiety and depressive disorders. *Psychological Medicine, 11,* 803–815.

Fitzgerald, P. B., Benitez, J., de Castella, A., Daskalakis, Z. J., Brown, T. L., & Kulkarni, J. (2006). A randomized, controlled trial of sequential bilateral repetitive transcranial magnetic stimulation for treatment-resistant depression. *American Journal of Psychiatry, 163,* 88–94.

Fitzgerald, P. B., Brown, T. L., Marston, N. A. U., Daskalakis, Z. J., de Castella, A., & Kulkarni, J. (2003). Transcranial magnetic stimulation in the treatment of depression: A double-blind, placebo-controlled trial. *Archives of General Psychiatry, 60,* 1002–1008.

Fleming, J. E., Boyle, M. H., & Offord, D. R. (1993). The outcome of adolescent depression in the Ontario Child Health Study follow-up. *Journal of the American Academy of Child and Adolescent Psychiatry, 32,* 28–33.

Fleming, J. E., Offord, D. R., & Boyle, M. H. (1989). Prevalence of childhood and adolescent depression in the community: Ontario Child Health Study. *British Journal of Psychiatry, 155,* 647–654.

Fogel, J., Eaton, W. W., & Ford, D. E. (2006). Minor depression as a predictor of the first onset of major depressive disorder over a 15-year follow-up. *Acta Psychiatrica Scandinavica, 113,* 36–43.

Fombonne, E., Wostear, G., Cooper, V., Harrington, R., & Rutter, M. (2001). The Maudsley long-term follow-up of child and adolescent depression. *British Journal of Psychiatry, 179,* 210–217.

Ford, D. E., & Kamerow, D. B. (1989). Epidemiologic study of sleep disturbances and psychiatric disorders: An opportunity for prevention? *Journal of the American Medical Association, 262,* 1479–1484.

Fowler, R. C., Rich, C. L., & Young, D. (1986). San Diego suicide study: II. Substance abuse in young cases. *Archives of General Psychiatry, 43,* 962–965.

Frank, E., Kupfer, D. J., & Perel, J. M. (1989). Early recurrence in unipolar depression. *Archives of General Psychiatry, 46,* 397–400.

Frank, E., Kupfer, D. J., Perel, J. M., Cornes, C., Jarrett, D. B., Mallinger, A. G., et al. (1990). Three-year outcomes for maintenance therapies in recurrent depression. *Archives of General Psychiatry, 47,* 1093–1099.

Frank, E., Kupfer, D. J., Thase, M. E., Mallinger, A. G., Swartz, H. A., Fagiolini, A. M., et al. (2005). Two-year outcomes for interpersonal and social rhythm therapy in individuals with bipolar I disorder. *Archives of General Psychiatry, 62,* 996–1004.

Frasure-Smith, N., & Lesperance, F. (2003). Depression and other psychological risks following myocardial infarction. *Archives of General Psychiatry, 60,* 627–636.

Frasure-Smith, N., Lesperance, F., & Talajic, M. (1993). Depression following myocardial infarction: Impact on 6-month survival. *Journal of the American Medical Association, 270,* 1819–1825.

Freeman, E. W., Sammel, M. D., Lin, H., & Nelson, D. B. (2006). Associations of hormones and menopausal status with depressed mood in women with no history of depression. *Archives of General Psychiatry, 63,* 375–382.

Galbaud du Fort, G., Bland, R. C., Newman, S. C., & Boothroyd, L. J. (1998). Spouse similarity for lifetime psychiatric history in the general population. *Psychological Medicine, 28,* 789–803.

Ganellen, R. J. (1988). Specificity of attributions and overgeneralization in depression and anxiety. *Journal of Abnormal Psychology, 97,* 83–86.

Garber, J., & Flynn, C. (2001). Predictors of depressive cognitions in young adolescents. *Cognitive Therapy and Research, 25,* 353–376.

Garriock, H. A., Delgado, P., Kling, M. A., Carpenter, L. L., Burke, M., Burke, W. J., et al. (2006, July 5). Number of risk genotypes is a risk factor for major depressive disorder: A case control study. *Behavioral and Brain Functions, 2*(24).

Gaynes, B. N., Magruder, K. M., Burns, B. J., Wagner, H. R., Yarnall, K. S. H., & Broadhead, W. E. (1999). Does a coexisting anxiety disorder predict persistence of depressive illness in primary care patients with major depression? *General Hospital Psychiatry, 21,* 158–167.

Ge, X., Lorenz, F. O., Conger, R. D., Elder, G. H., & Simons, R. L. (1994). Trajectories of stressful life events and depressive symptoms during adolescence. *Developmental Psychology, 30,* 467–483.

Geddes, J. R., Carney, S. M., Davies, C., Furukawa, T. A., Kupfer, D. J., Frank, E., et al. (2003). Relapse prevention with antidepressant drug treatment in depressive disorders: A systematic review. *Lancet, 361,* 653–661.

Gelenberg, A. J., & Chesen, C. L. (2000). How fast are antidepressants? *Journal of Clinical Psychiatry, 61,* 712–721.

Gelenberg, A. J., Trivedi, M. H., Rush, A. J., Thase, M. E., Howland, R., Klein, D. N., et al. (2003). Randomized, placebo-controlled trial of nefazodone maintenance treatment in preventing recurrence in chronic depression. *Biological Psychiatry, 54,* 806–817.

Gelfand, D. M., & Teti, D. M. (1990). The effects of maternal depression on children. *Clinical Psychology Review, 10,* 329–353.

Geller, B., Fox, L. W., & Clark, K. A. (1994). Rate and predictors of prepubertal bipolarity during follow-up of 6- to 12-year-old depressed children. *Journal of the American Academy of Child and Adolescent Psychiatry, 33,* 461–468.

Geller, B., Zimerman, B., Williams, M., Bolhofner, K., & Craney, J. (2001). Bipolar disorder at prospective follow-up of adults who had prepubertal major depressive disorder. *American Journal of Psychiatry, 158,* 125–127.

George, M. S., Lisanby, S. H., & Sackeim, H. A. (1999). Transcranial magnetic stimulation: Applications in neuropsychiatry. *Archives of General Psychiatry, 56,* 300–311.

Gemar, M. C., Segal, Z. V., Sagrati, S., & Kennedy, S. J. (2001). Mood-induced changes on the implicit association test in recovered depressed patients. *Journal of Abnormal Psychology, 110,* 282–289.

Gerlsma, C., Emmelkamp, P. M., & Arrindell, W. A. (1990). Anxiety, depression, and perception of early parenting: A meta-analysis. *Clinical Psychology Review, 10,* 251–277.

Gibb, B. E. (2002). Childhood maltreatment and negative cognitive styles: A quantitative and qualitative review. *Clinical Psychology Review, 22,* 223–246.

Gibb, B. E., Alloy, L. B., Abramson, L. Y., Rose, D. T., Whitehouse, W. G., Donovan, P., et al. (2001). History of childhood maltreatment, negative cognitive styles, and episodes of depression in adulthood. *Cognitive Therapy and Research, 25,* 425–446.

Gibb, B. E., Butler, A. C., & Beck, J. S. (2003). Childhood abuse, depression, and anxiety in adult psychiatric outpatients. *Depression and Anxiety, 17,* 226–228.

Gibbons, R. D., Hur, K., Bhaumik, D. K., & Mann, J. J. (2005). The relationship between antidepressant medication use and rate of suicide. *Archives of General Psychiatry, 62,* 165–172.

Giedke, H., & Schwarzler, F. (2002). Therapeutic use of sleep deprivation in depression. *Sleep Medicine Reviews, 6,* 361–377.

Gillham, J. E., Hamilton, J., Freres, D. R., Patton, K., & Gallop, R. (2006). Preventing depression among early adolescents in the primary care setting: A randomized controlled study of the Penn Resiliency Program. *Journal of Abnormal Child Psychology, 34,* 203–219.

Gillham, J. E., Reivich, K. J., Jaycox, L. H., & Seligman, M. E. P. (1995). Prevention of depressive symptoms in schoolchildren: Two-year follow-up. *Psychological Science, 6,* 343–351.

Gladstone, G., & Parker, G. (2006). Is behavioral inhibition a risk factor for depression? *Journal of Affective Disorders, 95,* 85–94.

Gloaguen, V., Cottraux, J., Cucherat, M., & Blackburn, I. M. (1998). A meta-analysis of the effects of cognitive therapy in depressed patients. *Journal of Affective Disorders, 49,* 59–72.

Glowinski, A. L., Bucholz, K. K., Nelson, E. C., Fu, Q., Madden, P. A. F., Reich, W., et al. (2001). Suicide attempts in an adolescent female twin sample. *Journal of the American Academy of Child and Adolescent Psychiatry, 40,* 1300–1307.

Gold, P. W., Goodwin, F. K., & Chrousos, G. P. (1988). Clinical and biochemical manifestations of depression: Relation to the neurobiology of stress. *The New England Journal of Medicine, 319,* 348–419.

Goldberg, J. F., Harrow, M., & Whiteside, J. E. (2001). Risk for bipolar illness in patients initially hospitalized for unipolar depression. *American Journal of Psychiatry, 158,* 1265–1270.

Golden, R. N., Gaynes, B. N., Ekstrom, R. D., Hamer, R. M., Jacobsen, F. M., Suppes, T., et al. (2005). The efficacy of light therapy in the treatment of mood disorders: A review and meta-analysis of the evidence. *American Journal of Psychiatry, 162,* 656–662.

Goldstein, R. B., Black, D. W., Nasrallah, A., & Winokur, G. (1991). The prediction of suicide: Sensitivity, specificity, and predictive value of a multivariate model applied to suicide among 1906 patients with affective disorders. *Archives of General Psychiatry, 48,* 418–422.

Goodman, S., & Gotlib, I. (1999). Risk for psychopathology in the children of depressed mothers: A developmental model for understanding mechanisms of transmission. *Psychological Review, 106,* 458–490.

Goodwin, F. K., & Jamison, K. R. (Eds.). (1990). *Manic-depressive illness.* New York: Oxford University Press.

Goodwin, R. D., Fergusson, D. M., & Horwood, L. J. (2004). Early anxious/withdrawn behaviours predict later internalising disorders. *Journal of Child Psychology and Psychiatry, 45,* 874–883.

Gortner, E. T., Gollan, J. K., Dobson, K. S., & Jacobson, N. S. (1998). Cognitive-behavioral treatment for depression: Relapse prevention. *Journal of Consulting and Clinical Psychology, 66,* 377–384.

Gotlib, I. H., & Asarnow, R. F. (1979). Interpersonal and impersonal problem-solving skills in mildly and clinically depressed university students. *Journal of Consulting and Clinical Psychology, 47,* 86–95.

Gotlib, I. H., & Beatty, M. E. (1985). Negative responses to depression: The role of attributional style. *Cognitive Therapy and Research, 9,* 91–103.

Gotlib, I. H., & Hammen, C. L. (1992). *Psychological aspects of depression: Toward a cognitive-interpersonal integration.* Chichester, UK: Wiley.

Gotlib, I. H., Lewinsohn, P. M., & Seeley, J. R. (1995). Symptoms versus a diagnosis of depression: Differences in psychosocial functioning. *Journal of Consulting and Clinical Psychology, 63,* 90–100.

Gotlib, I. H., Lewinsohn, P. M., Seeley, J. R., Rohde, P., & Redner, J. E. (1993). Negative cognitions and attributional style in depressed adolescents: An examination of stability and specificity. *Journal of Abnormal Psychology, 102,* 607–615.

Gotlib, I. H., & Meltzer, S. J. (1987). Depression and the perception of social skill in dyadic interaction. *Cognitive Therapy and Research, 11,* 41–53.

Grant, B. F., Stinson, F. S., Hasin, D. S., Dawson, D. A., Chou, S. P., & Anderson, K. (2004). Immigration and lifetime prevalence of DSM-IV psychiatric disorders among Mexican Americans and non-Hispanic Whites in the United States. *Archives of General Psychiatry, 61,* 1226–1233.

Greenberg, R. P., Bornstein, R. F., Greenberg, M. D., & Fisher, S. (1992). A meta-analysis of antidepressant outcome under "blinder" conditions. *Journal of Consulting and Clinical Psychology, 60,* 664–669.

Group for the Advancement of Psychiatry (1989). *Suicide and ethnicity in the United States* (No. 128). Philadelphia, PA: Brunner/Mazel.

Haaga, D. A. F., Dyck, M. J. & Ernst, D., (1991). Empirical status of cognitive theory of depression. *Psychological Bulletin, 110,* 215–236.

Haarasilta, L., Marttunen, M., Kaprio, J., & Aro, H. (2001). The 12-month prevalence and characteristics of major depressive episode in a representative nationwide sample of adolescents and young adults. *Psychological Medicine, 31,* 1169–1179.

Hallfors, D. D., Waller, M. W., Ford, C. A., Halpern, C. T., Brodish, P. H., & Iritani, B. (2004). Adolescent depression and suicide risk: Association with sex and drug behavior. *American Journal of Preventive Medicine, 27,* 224–231.

Hamilton, E. W., & Abramson, L. Y. (1983). Cognitive patterns and major depressive disorder: A longitudinal study in a hospital setting. *Journal of Abnormal Psychology, 92,* 173–184.

Hamilton, K. E., & Dobson, K. S. (2002). Cognitive therapy of depression: Pretreatment patient predictors of outcome. *Clinical Psychology Review, 22,* 875–893.

Hamilton, M. (1960). A rating scale for depression. *Journal of Neurology Neurosurgery and Psychiatry, 12,* 56–62.

Hammad, T. A., Laughren, T., & Racoosin, J. (2006). Suicidality in pediatric patients treated with antidepressant drugs. *Archives of General Psychiatry, 63,* 332–339.

Hammen, C. (1991a). *Depression runs in families: The social context of risk and resilience in children of depressed mothers.* New York: Springer-Verlag.

Hammen, C. (1991b). Generation of stress in the course of unipolar depression. *Journal of Abnormal Psychology, 100,* 555–561.

Hammen, C. (2006). Interpersonal vulnerability and depression in young women. In T. Joiner, J. Brown, & J. Kistner (Eds.), *The interpersonal, cognitive, and social nature of depression* (pp. 69–82). Mahwah, NJ: Lawrence Erlbaum Associates, Inc.

Hammen, C., & Brennan, P. A. (2001). Depressed adolescents of depressed and nondepressed mothers: Tests of an Interpersonal Impairment Hypothesis. *Journal of Consulting and Clinical Psychology, 69,* 284–294.

Hammen, C., & Brennan, P. A. (2002). Interpersonal dysfunction in depressed women: Impairments independent of depressive symptoms. *Journal of Affective Disorders, 72,* 145–156.

Hammen, C., & Brennan, P. (2003). Severity, chronicity, and timing of maternal depression and risk for adolescent offspring diagnoses in a community sample. *Archives of General Psychiatry, 60,* 253–258.

Hammen, C., Burge, D., Burney, E., & Adrian, C. (1990). Longitudinal study of diagnoses in children of women with unipolar and bipolar affective disorder. *Archives of General Psychiatry, 47,* 1112–1117.

Hammen, C., Burge, D., Daley, S. E., Davila, J., Paley, B., & Rudolph, K. D. (1995). Interpersonal attachment cognitions and prediction of symptomatic responses to interpersonal stress. *Journal of Abnormal Psychology, 104,* 436–443.

Hammen, C., Ellicott, A., Gitlin, M., & Jamison, K. (1989). Sociotropy/ autonomy and vulnerability to specific life events in patients with unipolar depression and bipolar disorders.

Journal of Abnormal Psychology, 98, 154–160.

Hammen, C., & Goodman-Brown, T. (1990). Self-schemas and vulnerability to specific life stress in children at risk for depression. *Cognitive Therapy and Research, 14,* 215–227.

Hammen, C., Henry, R., & Daley, S. E. (2000). Depression and sensitization to stressors among young women as a function of childhood adversity. *Journal of Consulting and Clinical Psychology, 68,* 782–787.

Hammen, C., Marks, T., Mayol, A., & deMayo, R. (1985). Depressive self-schemas, life stress, and vulnerability to depression. *Journal of Abnormal Psychology, 94,* 308–319.

Hammen, C., & Peters, S. D. (1978). Interpersonal consequences of depression: Responses to men and women enacting a depressed role. *Journal of Abnormal Psychology, 87,* 322–332.

Hammen, C., Shih, J. H., & Brennan, P. A. (2004). Intergenerational transmission of depression: Test of an Interpersonal Stress Model in a community sample. *Journal of Consulting and Clinical Psychology, 72,* 511–522.

Hankin, B. L., & Abramson, L. Y. (1999). Development of gender differences in depression: Description and possible explanations. *Annals of Medicine, 31,* 372–379.

Hankin, B. L., & Abramson, L. Y. (2001). Development of gender differences in depression: An elaborated cognitive vulnerability-transactional stress theory. *Psychological Bulletin, 127,* 773–796.

Hankin, B. L., & Abramson, L. Y. (2002). Measuring cognitive vulnerability to depression in adolescence: Reliability, validity and gender differences. *Journal of Clinical Child and Adolescent Psychology, 31,* 491–504.

Hankin, B. L., Abramson, L. Y., Miller, N.,

& Haeffel, G. J. (2004). Cognitive vulnerability-stress theories of depression: Examining affective specificity in the prediction of depression versus anxiety in three prospective studies. *Cognitive Therapy and Research, 28,* 309–345.

Hankin, B. L., Abramson, L. Y., Moffitt, T. E., Silva, P. A., McGee, R., & Angell, K. E. (1998). Development of depression from preadolescence to young adulthood: Emerging gender differences in a 10-year longitudinal study. *Journal of Abnormal Psychology, 107,* 128–140.

Hariri, A. R., Drabant, E. M., Munoz, K. E., Kolachana, B. S., Mattay, V. S., Egan, M. F., et al. (2005). A susceptibility gene for affective disorders and the response of the human amygdala. *Archives of General Psychiatry, 62,* 146–152.

Harkness, K. L., Bruce, A. E., & Lumley, M. N. (2006). The role of childhood abuse and neglect in the sensitization to stressful life events in adolescent depression. *Journal of Abnormal Psychology, 115,* 730–741.

Harkness, K. L., & Monroe, S. M. (2002). Childhood adversity and the endogenous versus nonendogenous distinction in women with major depression. *American Journal of Psychiatry, 159,* 387–393.

Harrington, R., Fudge, H., Rutter, M., Pickles, A., & Hill, J. (1990). Adult outcomes of childhood and adolescent depression. *Archives of General Psychiatry, 47,* 465–473.

Harris, T., Brown, G. W., & Bifulco, A. (1986). Loss of parent in childhood and adult psychiatric disorder: The role of lack of adequate parental care. *Psychological Medicine, 16,* 641–659.

Hartlage, S. A., & Arduino, K. E. (2002). Toward the content validity of premenstrual dysphoric disorder: Do anger and irritability more than depressed mood represent treatment-seekers' experiences? *Psychological Reports, 90*, 189–202.

Harvey, A. G., Watkins, E., Mansell, W., & Shafran, R. (2004). *Cognitive behavioural processes across psychological disorders.* Oxford: Oxford University Press.

Hashimoto, K., Shimizu, E., & Iyo, M. (2004). Critical role of brain-derived neurotrophic factor in mood disorders. *Brain Research Reviews, 45*, 104–114.

Hasin, D. S., Goodwin, R. D., Stinson, F. S., & Grant, B. F. (2005). Epidemiology of major depressive disorder: Results from the National Epidemiologic Survey on Alcoholism and Related Conditions. *Archives of General Psychiatry, 62*, 1097–1106.

Haslam, N., & Beck, A. T. (1994). Subtyping major depression: A taxometric analysis. *Journal of Abnormal Psychology, 103*, 686–692.

Hayden, E. P., & Klein, D. N. (2001). Outcome of dysthymic disorder at 5-year follow-up: The effect of familial psychopathology, early adversity, personality, comorbidity, and chronic stress. *American Journal of Psychiatry, 158*, 1864–1870.

Hayes, A. M., Harris, M. S., & Carver, C. S. (2004). Predictors of self-esteem variability. *Cognitive Therapy and Research, 28*, 369–385.

Heim, C., & Nemeroff, C. B. (2001). The role of childhood trauma in the neurobiology of mood and anxiety disorders: Preclinical and clinical studies. *Biological Psychiatry, 49*, 1023–1039.

Heim, C., Newport, D. J., Heit, S., Graham, Y. P., Wilcox, M., Bonsall, R., et al. (2000). Pituitary-adrenal and autonomic responses to stress in women after sexual and physical abuse in childhood. *Journal of the American Medical Association, 284*, 592–597.

Henkel, V., Mergl, R., Allgaier, A. K., Kohnen, R., Moller, H. J., & Hegerl, U. (2006). Treatment of depression with

atypical features: A meta-analytic approach. *Psychiatry Research, 141*, 89–101.

Henriksson, M. M., Aro, H. M., Marttunen, M. J., Heikkinen, M. E., Isometsa, E. T., Kuoppasalmi, K. I., et al. (1993). Mental disorders and comorbidity in suicide. *American Journal of Psychiatry, 150*, 935–940.

Hermann, L. L., & Ebmeier, K. P. (2006). Factors modifying the efficacy of transcranial magnetic stimulation in the treatment of depression: A review. *Journal of Clinical Psychiatry, 67*, 1870–1876.

Hertel, P. T. (1998). Relation between rumination and impaired memory in dysphoric moods. *Journal of Abnormal Psychology, 107*, 166–172.

Hertel, P. T. (2000). The cognitive-initiative account of depression-related impairments in memory. *Psychology of Learning and Motivation: Advances in Research and Theory, 39*, 47–71.

Hertel, P. T., & Rude, S. S. (1991). Depressive deficits in memory: Focusing attention improves subsequent recall. *Journal of Experimental Psychology: General, 120*, 301–309.

Hirschfeld, R. M. A., Klerman, G. L., Clayton, P. J., & Keller, M. B. (1983). Personality and depression: Empirical findings. *Archives of General Psychiatry, 40*, 993–998.

Hirschfeld, R. M. A., Montgomery, S. A., Aguglia, E., Amore, M., Delgado, P. L., Gastpar, M., et al. (2002). Partial response and nonresponse to antidepressant therapy: Current approaches and treatment options. *Journal of Clinical Psychiatry, 63*, 826–837.

Hofstra, M. B., van der Ende, J., & Verhulst, F. C. (2000). Continuity and change of psychopathology from childhood into adulthood: A 14-year follow-up study. *Journal of the Academy of Child and Adolescent Psychiatry, 39,* 850–858.

Hokanson, J. E., Hummer, J. T., & Butler, A. C. (1991). Interpersonal perceptions by depressed college students. *Cognitive Therapy and Research, 15,* 443–457.

Hokanson, J. E., Rubert, M. P., Welker, R. A., Hollander, G. R., & Hedeen, C. (1989). Interpersonal concomitants and antecedents of depression among college students. *Journal of Abnormal Psychology, 98,* 209–217.

Hollon, S. D., DeRubeis, R. J. & Evans, M. D., (1987). Causal mediation of change in treatment for depression: Discriminating between nonspecificity and noncausality. *Psychological Bulletin, 102,* 139–149.

Hollon, S. D., DeRubeis, R. J., Evans, M. D., Wiemer, M. J., Garvey, M. J., Grove, W. M., et al. (1992). Cognitive therapy and pharmacotherapy for depression: Singly and in combination. *Archives of General Psychiatry, 49,* 774–781.

Hollon, S. D., DeRubeis, R. J., Shelton, R. C., Amsterdam, J. D., Salomon, R. M., O'Reardon, J. P., et al. (2005). Prevention of relapse following cognitive therapy vs medications in moderate to severe depression. *Archives of General Psychiatry, 62,* 417–422.

Hollon, S. D., Kendall, P. C., & Lumry, A. (1986). Specificity of depressotypic cognitions in clinical depression. *Journal of Abnormal Psychology, 95,* 52–59.

Hollon, S. D., Shelton, R. C., & Davis, D. D. (1993). Cognitive therapy for depression: Conceptual issues and clinical efficacy. *Journal of Consulting and Clinical Psychology, 61,* 270–275.

Hollon, S. D., Shelton, R. C., Wisniewski, S., Warden, D., Biggs, M. M., Friedman, E. S., et al. (2006a). Presenting characteristics of depressed outpatients as a function of recurrence: Preliminary findings from the STAR*D clinical trial. *Journal of Psychiatric Research, 40,* 59–69.

Hollon, S. D., Stewart, M. O., & Strunk, D.

(2006b). Enduring effects for cognitive behavior therapy in the treatment of depression and anxiety. *Annual Review of Psychology, 57,* 285–315.

Holmes, S. J., & Robins, L. N. (1987). The influence of childhood disciplinary experience on the development of alcoholism and depression. *Journal of Child Psychology and Psychiatry, 28,* 399–415.

Holmes, S. J., & Robins, L. N. (1988). The role of parental disciplinary practices in the development of depression and alcoholism. *Psychiatry: Journal for the Study of Interpersonal Processes, 51,* 24–36.

Holsboer, F. (2000). The corticosteroid receptor hypothesis of depression. *Neuropsychopharmacology, 23,* 477–501.

Holsinger, T., Steffens, D. C., Phillips, C., Helms, M. J., Havlik, R. J., Breitner, J. C. S., et al. (2002). Head injury in early adulthood and the lifetime risk of depression. *Archives of General Psychiatry, 59,* 17–22.

Hooley, J. M., Gruber, S. A., Scott, L. A., Hiller, J. B., & Yurgelun-Todd, D. A. (2005). Activation in dorsolateral prefrontal cortex in response to maternal criticism and praise in recovered depressed and healthy control participants. *Biological Psychiatry, 57,* 809–812.

Horowitz, J. L., & Garber, J. (2006). The prevention of depressive symptoms in children and adolescents: A meta-analytic review. *Journal of Consulting and Clinical Psychology, 74,* 401–415.

Horwath, E., Johnson, J., Weissman, M. M., & Hornig, C. D. (1992). The validity of major depression with atypical features based on a community study. *Journal of Affective Disorders, 26,* 117–126.

Howes, M. J., Hokanson, J. E., & Loewenstein, D. A. (1985). Induction of depressive affect after prolonged exposure to a mildly depressed individual. *Journal of Personality and Social Psychology, 49,* 1110–1113.

Husain, M. M., Rush, A. J., Sackeim, H. A., Wisniewski, S. R., McClintock, S. M., Craven, N., et al. (2005). Age-related characteristics of depression: A preliminary STAR*D report. *American Journal of Geriatric Psychiatry, 13,* 852–860.

Imber, S. D., Pilkonis, P. A., Sotsky, S. M., Elkin, I., Watkins, J. T., Collins, J. F., et al. (1990). Mode-specific effects among 3 treatments for depression. *Journal of Consulting and Clinical Psychology, 58,* 352–359.

Ingram, R. E. (1990). Self-focused attention in clinical disorders: Review and a conceptual model. *Psychological Bulletin, 107,* 156–176.

Ingram, R. E., Bernet, C. Z., & Mclaughlin, S. C. (1994). Attentional allocation processes in individuals at risk for depression. *Cognitive Therapy and Research, 18,* 317–332.

Ingram, R. E., Miranda, J., & Segal, Z. V. (1998). *Cognitive vulnerability to depression.* New York: Guilford.

Ingram, R. E., & Ritter, J. (2000). Vulnerability to depression: Cognitive reactivity and parental bonding in high-risk individuals. *Journal of Abnormal Psychology, 109,* 588–596.

Jacobs, N., Kenis, G., Peeters, F., Derom, C., Vlietinck, R., & van Os, J. (2006). Stress-related negative affectivity and genetically altered serotonin transporter function: Evidence of synergism in shaping risk of depression. *Archives of General Psychiatry, 63,* 989–996.

Jacobsen, F. M., Wehr, T. A., Sack, D. A., James, S. P., & Rosenthal, N. E. (1987). Seasonal affective disorder: A review of the syndrome and its public health implications. *American Journal of Public Health, 77,* 57–60.

Jacobson, N. S., Dobson, K. S., Truax, P. A., Addis, M. E., Koerner, K., Gollan, J. K.,

et al. (1996). A component analysis of cognitive-behavioral treatment for depression. *Journal of Consulting and Clinical Psychology, 64,* 295–304.

Jacobson, N. S., Fruzzetti, A. E., Dobson, K., Schmaling, K. B., & Salusky, S. (1991). Marital therapy as a treatment for depression. *Journal of Consulting and Clinical Psychology, 59,* 547–557.

Jacobson, N. S., Fruzzetti, A. E., Dobson, K., Whisman, M., & Hops, H. (1993). Couple therapy as a treatment for depression: II. The effects of relationship quality and therapy on depressive relapse. *Journal of Consulting and Clinical Psychology, 61,* 516–519.

Jaffee, S. R., Moffitt, T. E., Caspi, A., Fombonne, E., Poulton, R., & Martin, J. (2002). Differences in early childhood risk factors for juvenile-onset and adult-onset depression. *Archives of General Psychiatry, 59,* 215–222.

Jahn, H., Schick, M., Kiefer, F., Kellner, M., Yassouridis, A., & Wiedemann, K. (2004). Metyrapone as additive treatment in major depression: A double-blind and placebo-controlled trial. *Archives of General Psychiatry, 61,* 1235–1244.

Jarrett, R. B., Eaves, G. G., Grannemann, B. D., & Rush, A. J. (1991). Clinical, cognitive, and demographic predictors of response to cognitive therapy for depression: A preliminary report. *Psychiatry Research, 37,* 245–260.

Jarrett, R. B., Kraft, D., Doyle, J., Foster, B. M., Eaves, G. G., & Silver, P. C. (2001). Preventing recurrent depression using cognitive therapy with and without a continuation phase: A randomized clinical trial. *Archives of General Psychiatry, 58,* 381–388.

Jarrett, R. B., Schaffer, M., McIntire, D., Witt-Browder, A., Kraft, D., & Risser, R. C. (1999). Treatment of atypical depression with cognitive therapy or phenelzine: A double-blind, placebo-controlled trial. *Archives of General Psychiatry, 56*, 431–437.

Jaycox, L. H., Reivich, K. J., Gillham, J., & Seligman, M. E. P. (1994). Prevention of depressive symptoms in school children. *Behaviour Research and Therapy, 32*, 801–816.

Jindal, R. D., Thase, M. E., Fasiczka, A. L., Friedman, E. S., Buysse, D. J., Frank, E., et al. (2002). Electroencephalographic sleep profiles in single-episode and recurrent unipolar forms of major depression: II. Comparison during remission. *Biological Psychiatry, 51*, 230–236.

Johnson, J., Horwath, E., & Weissman, M. M. (1991). The validity of major depression with psychotic features based on a community study. *Archives of General Psychiatry, 48*, 1075–1081.

Johnson, J., Weissman, M. M., & Klerman, G. (1992). Service utilization and social morbidity associated with depressive symptoms in the community. *Journal of the American Medical Association, 267*, 1478–1483.

Johnson, S. L., & Jacob, T. (1997). Marital interactions of depressed men and women. *Journal of Consulting and Clinical Psychology, 65*, 15–23.

Joiner, T. E., & Schmidt, N. B. (1998). Excessive reassurance-seeking predicts depressive but not anxious reactions to acute stress. *Journal of Abnormal Psychology, 107*, 533–537.

Joyce, P. R., Mulder, R. T., Luty, S. E., McKenzie, J. M., Sullivan, P. F., Abbott, R. M., et al. (2002a). Melancholia: Definitions, risk factors, personality, neuroendocrine markers and differential antidepressant response. *Australian and New Zealand Journal of Psychiatry, 36*, 376–383.

Joyce, P. R., Mulder, R. T., Luty, S. E., Sullivan, P. F., McKenzie, J. M., Abbott, R. M., et al. (2002b). Patterns and predictors of remission, response and recovery in major depression treated with fluoxetine or nortriptyline. *Australian and New Zealand Journal of Psychiatry, 36*, 384–391.

Joyce, P. R., & Paykel, E. S. (1989). Predictors of drug response in depression. *Archives of General Psychiatry, 46*, 89–99.

Judd, L. L. (1997). The clinical course of unipolar major depressive disorders. *Archives of General Psychiatry, 54*, 989–991.

Judd, L. L., Akiskal, H. S., Maser, J. D., Zeller, P. J., Endicott, J., Coryell, W., et al. (1998). A prospective 12-year study of subsyndromal and syndromal depressive symptoms in unipolar major depressive disorders. *Archives of General Psychiatry, 55*, 694–700.

Judd, L. L., Akiskal, H. S., Zeller, P. J., Paulus, M., Leon, A. C., & Maser, J. D. (2000). Psychosocial disability during the long-term course of unipolar major depressive disorder. *Archives of General Psychiatry, 57*, 375–380.

Just, N., Abramson, L. Y., & Alloy, L. B. (2001). Remitted depression studies as tests of the cognitive vulnerability hypotheses of depression onset: A critique and conceptual analysis. *Clinical Psychology Review, 21*, 63–83.

Kabat-Zinn, J. (1990). *Full catastrophe living: Using the wisdom of your body and mind to face stress, pain, and illness.* New York: Dell.

Kahn, J. S., Kehle, T. J., Jenson, W. R., & Clark, E. (1990). Comparison of cognitive-behavioral, relaxation, and self-modeling interventions for depression among middle-school students. *School Psychology Review, 19*, 196–211.

Kane, P., & Garber, J. (2004). The relations among depression in fathers, children's psychopathology, and father–child conflict: A meta-analysis. *Clinical Psychology Review, 24*, 339–360.

Kasen, S., Cohen, P., Chen, H., & Castille, D. (2003). Depression in adult women:

Age changes and cohort effects. *American Journal of Public Health, 93,* 2061–2066.

Kashani, J. H., & Carlson, G. A. (1987). Seriously depressed preschoolers. *American Journal of Psychiatry, 144,* 348–350.

Kaslow, N. J., Deering, C. G., & Racusin, G. R. (1994). Depressed children and their families. *Clinical Psychology Review, 14,* 39–59.

Katon, W. J. (2003). Clinical and health services relationships between major depression, depressive symptoms, and general medical illness. *Biological Psychiatry, 54,* 216–226.

Katon, W. J., Lin, E. H., Russo, J. E., & Unutzer, J. (2003). Increased medical costs of a population-based sample of depressed elderly patients. *Archives of General Psychiatry, 60,* 897–903.

Katz, S. J., Kessler, R. C., Lin, E., & Wells, K. B. (1998). Medication management of depression in the United States and Ontario. *Journal of General Internal Medicine, 13,* 77–85.

Kaufman, J., Martin, A., King, R. A., & Charney, D. (2001). Are child-, adolescent-, and adult-onset depression one and the same disorder? *Biological Psychiatry, 49,* 980–1001.

Kaufman, J., Plotsky, P. M., Nemeroff, C. B., & Charney, D. S. (2000). Effects of early adverse experiences on brain structure and function: Clinical implications. *Biological Psychiatry, 48,* 778–790.

Keitner, G. I., Ryan, C. E., Miller, I. W., Kohn, R., Bishop, D. S., & Epstein, N. B. (1995). Role of the family in recovery and major depression. *American Journal of Psychiatry, 152,* 1002–1008.

Keitner, G. I., Ryan, C. E., Miller, I. W., & Zlotnick, C. (1997). Psychosocial factors and the long-term course of major depression. *Journal of Affective Disorders, 44,* 57–67.

Keller, F., Spiess, M., & Hautzinger, M.

(1996). Static and dynamic predictors of the course of major depression: An analysis using generalized estimating equations. *Zeitschrift für Klinische Psychologie: Forschung und Praxis, 25,* 234–243.

Keller, K. E. (1983). Dysfunctional attitudes and the cognitive therapy for depression. *Cognitive Therapy and Research, 7,* 437–444.

Keller, M. B. (1985). Chronic and recurrent affective disorders: Incidence, course, and influencing factors. *Advances in Biochemical Psychopharmacology, 40,* 111–120.

Keller, M. B. (1988). Diagnostic issues and clinical course of unipolar illness. In A. J. Frances & R. E. Hales (Eds.), *Review of psychiatry* (pp. 188–212). Washington, DC: American Psychiatric Press.

Keller, M. B., Kocsis, J. H., Thase, M. E., Gelenberg, A. J., Rush, A. J., Koran, L., et al. (1998). Maintenance phase efficacy of sertraline for chronic depression: A randomized controlled trial. *Journal of the American Medical Association, 280,* 1665–1672.

Keller, M. B., Lavori, P. W., Endicott, J., Coryell, W., & Klerman, G. L. (1983). "Double depression": Two year follow-up. *American Journal of Psychiatry, 140,* 689–694.

Keller, M. B., McCullough, J. P., Klein, D. N., Arnow, B., Dunner, D. L., Gelenberg, A. J., et al. (2000). A comparison of nefazodone, the cognitive behavioral-analysis system of psychotherapy, and their combination for the treatment of chronic depression. *New England Journal of Medicine, 342,* 1462–1470.

Keller, M. B., Ryan, N. D., Strober, M., Klein, R. G., Kutcher, S. P., Birmaher, B., et al. (2001). Efficacy of paroxetine in the treatment of adolescent major depression: A randomized, controlled trial. *Journal of the American Academy of*

Child and Adolescent Psychiatry, 40, 762–772.

Keller, M. B., Shapiro, R. W., Lavori, P. W., & Wolfe, N. (1982). Recovery in major depressive disorder: Analysis with the life table and regression models. Archives of General Psychiatry, 39, 905–910.

Kendler, K. S. (1997). The diagnostic validity of melancholic major depression in a population-based sample of female twins. Archives of General Psychiatry, 54, 299–304.

Kendler, K. S., Bulik, C. M., Silberg, J., Hettema, J. M., Myers, J., & Prescott, C. A. (2000a). Childhood sexual abuse and adult psychiatric and substance use disorders in women. Archives of General Psychiatry, 57, 953–959.

Kendler, K. S., Eaves, L. J., Walters, E. E., Neale, M. C., Heath, A. C., & Kessler, R. C. (1996). The identification and validation of distinct depressive syndromes in a population-based sample of female twins. Archives of General Psychiatry, 53, 391–399.

Kendler, K. S., Gardner, C. O., & Prescott, C. A. (2002a). Toward a comprehensive developmental model for major depression in women. American Journal of Psychiatry, 159, 1133–1145.

Kendler, K. S., Gardner, C. O., & Prescott, C. A. (2003a). Personality and the experience of environmental adversity. Psychological Medicine, 33, 1193–1202.

Kendler, K. S., Gardner, C. O., & Prescott, C. A. (2006a). Toward a comprehensive developmental model for major depression in men. American Journal of Psychiatry, 163, 115–124.

Kendler, K. S., Gatz, M., Gardner, C. O., & Pedersen, N. L. (2005a). Age at onset and familial risk for major depression in a Swedish national twin sample. Psychological Medicine, 35, 1–7.

Kendler, K. S., Gatz, M., Gardner, C. O., & Pedersen, N. L. (2006b). Personality and

major depression. Archives of General Psychiatry, 63, 1113–1120.

Kendler, K. S., Hettema, J. M., Butera, F., Gardner, C. O., & Prescott, C. A. (2003b). Life event dimensions of loss, humiliation, entrapment, and danger in the prediction of onsets of major depression and generalized anxiety. Archives of General Psychiatry, 60, 789–796.

Kendler, K. S., Karkowski, L. M., Corey, L. A., & Neale, M. C. (1998). Longitudinal population-based twin study of retrospectively reported premenstrual symptoms and lifetime major depression. American Journal of Psychiatry, 155, 1234–1240.

Kendler, K. S., Karkowski, L. M., & Prescott, C. A. (1999). Causal relationship between stressful life events and the onset of major depression. American Journal of Psychiatry, 156, 837–848.

Kendler, K. S., & Karkowski-Shuman, L. (1997). Stressful life events and genetic liability to major depression: Genetic control of exposure to the environment? Psychological Medicine, 27, 539–547.

Kendler, K. S., Kessler, R. C., Neale, M. C., Heath, A. C., & Eaves, L. J. (1993a). The prediction of major depression in women: Toward an integrated etiologic model. American Journal of Psychiatry, 150, 1139–1148.

Kendler, K. S., Kessler, R. C., Walters, E. E., MacLean, C., Neale, M. C., Heath, A. C., et al. (1995). Stressful life events, genetic liability, and onset of an episode of major depression in women. American Journal of Psychiatry, 152, 833–842.

Kendler, K. S., Kuhn, J. W., Vittum, J., Prescott, C. A., & Riley, B. (2005b). The interaction of stressful life events and a serotonin transporter polymorphism in the prediction of episodes of major depression. Archives of General Psychiatry, 62, 529–535.

Kendler, K. S., Myers, J., & Prescott, C. A.

(2005c). Sex differences in the relationship between social support and risk for major depression: A longitudinal study of opposite-sex twin pairs. *American Journal of Psychiatry, 162,* 250–256.

Kendler, K. S., Neale, M. C., Kessler, R. C., Heath, A. C., & Eaves, L. J. (1993b). A twin study of recent life events and difficulties. *Archives of General Psychiatry, 50,* 789–796.

Kendler, K. S., & Prescott, C. A. (1999). A population-based twin study of lifetime major depression in men and women. *Archives of General Psychiatry, 56,* 39–44.

Kendler, K. S., Sheth, K., Gardner, C. O., & Prescott, C. A. (2002b). Childhood parental loss and risk for first-onset of major depression and alcohol dependence: The time-decay of risk and sex differences. *Psychological Medicine, 32,* 1187–1194.

Kendler, K. S., Thornton, L. M., & Gardner, C. O. (2000b). Stressful life events and previous episodes in the etiology of major depression in women: An evaluation of the "Kindling" hypothesis. *American Journal of Psychiatry, 157,* 1243–1251.

Kendler, K. S., Thornton, L. M., & Gardner, C. O. (2001a). Genetic risk, number of previous depressive episodes, and stressful life events in predicting onset of major depression. *American Journal of Psychiatry, 158,* 582–586.

Kendler, K. S., Thornton, L. M., & Prescott, C. A. (2001b). Gender differences in the rates of exposure to stressful life events and sensitivity to their depressogenic effects. *American Journal of Psychiatry, 158,* 587–593.

Kernis, M. H., Brockner, J., & Frankel, B. S. (1989). Self-esteem and reactions to failure: The mediating role of overgeneralization. *Journal of Personality and Social Psychology, 57,* 707–714.

Kernis, M. H., Whisenhunt, C. R., Waschull, S. B., Greenier, K. D., Berry, A. J., Herlocker, C. E., et al. (1998). Multiple facets of self-esteem and their relations to depressive symptoms. *Personality and Social Psychology Bulletin, 24,* 657–668.

Kessing, L. V. (2003). Subtypes of depressive episodes according to ICD-10: Prediction of risk of relapse and suicide. *Psychopathology, 36,* 285–291.

Kessing, L. V., Hansen, M. G., Andersen, P. K., & Angst, J. (2004). The predictive effect of episodes on the risk of recurrence in depressive and bipolar disorders: A life-long perspective. *Acta Psychiatrica Scandinavica, 109,* 339–344.

Kessler, R. C. (1997). The effects of stressful life events on depression. *Annual Review of Psychology, 48,* 191–214.

Kessler, R. C. (2003). Epidemiology of women and depression. *Journal of Affective Disorders, 74,* 5–13.

Kessler, R. C., Berglund, P., Demler, O., Jin, R., Koretz, D., Merikangas, K. R., et al. (2003). The epidemiology of major depressive disorder. *Journal of the American Medical Association, 289,* 3095–3105.

Kessler, R. C., Berglund, P., Demler, O., Jin, R., Merikangas, K. R., & Walters, E. E. (2005a). Lifetime prevalence and age-of-onset distributions of *DSM-IV* disorders in the National Comorbidity Survey Replication. *Archives of General Psychiatry, 62,* 593–602.

Kessler, R. C., Chiu, W. T., Demler, O., & Walters, E. E. (2005b). Prevalence, severity, and comorbidity of 12-month DSM-IV disorders in the National Comorbidity Survey Replication. *Archives of General Psychiatry, 62,* 617–627.

Kessler, R. C., Davis, C. G., & Kendler, K. S. (1997a). Childhood adversity and adult psychiatric disorder in the US National Comorbidity Survey. *Psychological Medicine, 27,* 1101–1119.

Kessler, R. C., Foster, C. L., Saunders, W. B., & Stang, P. E. (1995). Social consequences of psychiatric disorders: I. Educational attainment. *American Journal of Psychiatry, 152,* 1026–1032.

Kessler, R. C., & Magee, W. J. (1993). Childhood adversities and adult depression: Basic patterns of association in a US national survey. *Psychological Medicine, 23,* 679–690.

Kessler, R. C., Nelson, C. B., McGonagle, K. A., Liu, J., Swartz, M., & Blazer, D. G. (1996). Comorbidity of DSM-III-R major depressive disorder in the general population: Results from the US National Comorbidity Survey. *British Journal of Psychiatry, 168,* 17–30.

Kessler, R. C., Olfson, M., & Berglund, P. A. (1998a). Patterns and predictors of treatment contact after first onset of psychiatric disorders. *American Journal of Psychiatry, 155,* 62–69.

Kessler, R. C., Rubinow, D. R., Holmes, C., Abelson, J. M., & Zhao, S. (1997b). The epidemiology of DSM-III-R bipolar I disorder in a general population survey. *Psychological Medicine, 27,* 1079–1089.

Kessler, R. C., & Walters, E. E. (1998). Epidemiology of DSM-III-R major depression and minor depression among adolescents and young adults in the National Comorbidity Survey. *Depression and Anxiety, 7,* 3–14.

Kessler, R. C., Walters, E. E., & Forthofer, M. S. (1998b). The social consequences of psychiatric disorders: III. Probability of marital stability. *American Journal of Psychiatry, 155,* 1092–1096.

Kessler, R. C., Zhao, S. Y., Blazer, D. G., & Swartz, M. (1997c). Prevalence, correlates, and course of minor depression and major depression in the National Comorbidity Survey. *Journal of Affective Disorders, 45,* 19–30.

Khan, A., Detke, M., Khan, S. R. F., & Mallinckrodt, C. (2003). Placebo response and antidepressant clinical trial outcome. *Journal of Nervous and Mental Disease, 191,* 211–218.

Khan, A., Leventhal, R. M., Khan, S. R., & Brown, W. A. (2002). Severity of depression and response to antidepressants and placebo: An analysis of the Food and Drug Administration database. *Journal of Clinical Psychopharmacology, 22,* 40–45.

Khan, A., Warner, H. A., & Brown, W. A. (2000). Symptom reduction and suicide risk in patients treated with placebo in antidepressant clinical trials: An analysis of the Food and Drug Administration database. *Archives of General Psychiatry, 57,* 311–317.

Kim, H. L., Streltzer, J., & Goebert, D. (1999). St. John's wort for depression: A meta-analysis of well-defined clinical trials. *Journal of Nervous and Mental Disease, 187,* 532–538.

Kirsch, I. (2000). Are drug and placebo effects in depression additive? *Biological Psychiatry, 47,* 733–735.

Klein, D. F. (1974). Endogenomorphic depression: Conceptual and terminological revision. *Archives of General Psychiatry, 31,* 447–454.

Klein, D. N. (2003). Patients' versus informants' reports of personality disorders in predicting 7½-year outcome in outpatients with depressive disorders. *Psychological Assessment, 15,* 216–222.

Klein, D. N., & Miller, G. A. (1993). Depressive personality in nonclinical subjects. *American Journal of Psychiatry, 150,* 1718–1724.

Klein, D. N., Santiago, N. J., Vivian, D., Arnow, B. A., Blalock, J. A., Dunner, D. L., et al. (2004a). Cognitive-behavioral analysis system of psychotherapy as a maintenance treatment for chronic depression. *Journal of Consulting and Clinical Psychology, 72,* 681–688.

Klein, D. N., Schatzberg, A. F., McCullough, J. P., Keller, M. B., Dowling, F., Goodman, D., et al. (1999). Early- versus late-onset dysthymic disorder: Comparison in out-patients with superimposed major depressive episodes. *Journal of Affective Disorders, 52*, 187–196.

Klein, D. N., Schwartz, J. E., Rose, S., & Leader, J. B. (2000). Five-year course and outcome of dysthymic disorder: A prospective, naturalistic follow-up study. *American Journal of Psychiatry, 157*, 931–939.

Klein, D. N., Shankman, S. A., Lewinsohn, P. M., Rohde, P., & Seeley, J. R. (2004b). Family study of chronic depression in a community sample of young adults. *American Journal of Psychiatry, 161*, 646–653.

Klein, D. N., Shankman, S. A., & Rose, S. (2006). Ten-year prospective follow-up study of the naturalistic course of dysthymic disorder and double depression. *American Journal of Psychiatry, 163*, 872–880.

Klein, D. N., & Shih, J. H. (1998). Depressive personality: Associations with DSM-III-R mood and personality disorders and negative and positive affectivity, 30-month stability, and prediction of course of Axis I depressive disorders. *Journal of Abnormal Psychology, 107*, 319–327.

Klein, D. N., Taylor, E. B., Dickstein, S., & Harding, K. (1988a). Primary early-onset dysthymia: Comparison with primary nonbipolar nonchronic major depression on demographic, clinical, familial, personality, and socioenvironmental characteristics and short-term outcome. *Journal of Abnormal Psychology, 97*, 387–398.

Klein, D. N., Taylor, E. B., Harding, K., & Dickstein, S. (1988b). Double depression and episodic major depression: Demographic, clinical, familial, personality, and socioenvironmental characteristics and short-term outcome. *American Journal of Psychiatry, 145*, 1226–1231.

Klein, E., Kreinin, I., Christyakov, A.,

Koren, D., Mecz, L., Marmur, S., et al. (1999). Therapeutic efficacy of right prefrontal slow repetitive transcranial magnetic stimulation in major depression: A double-blind controlled study. *Archives of General Psychiatry, 56*, 315–320.

Kleinman, A. (1991). *Culture and DSM-IV: Recommendation for the introduction and for the overall structure.* Paper presented at the National Institute of Mental Health-sponsored Conference on Culture and Diagnosis, Pittsburgh, PA.

Klerman, G. L., & Weissman, M. M. (1989). Increasing rates of depression. *Journal of the American Medical Association, 261*, 2229–2235.

Klerman, G. L., Weissman, M. M., Rounsaville, B. J., & Chevron, E. (1984). *Interpersonal psychotherapy of depression.* New York: Basic Books.

Klinger, E. (1993). Loss of interest. In C. G. Costello (Ed.), *Symptoms of depression* (pp. 43–62). New York: Wiley.

Kobak, R. R., Sudler, N., & Gamble, W. (1991). Attachment and depressive symptoms during adolescence: A developmental pathways analysis. *Development and Psychopathology, 3*, 461–474.

Kocsis, J. H., Friedman, R. A., Markowitz, J. C., Leon, A. C., Miller, N. L., Gniwesch, L., et al. (1996). Maintenance therapy for chronic depression: A controlled clinical trial of desipramine. *Archives of General Psychiatry, 53*, 769–774.

Koponen, S., Taiminen, T., Portin, R., Himanen, L., Isoniemi, H., Heinonen, H., et al. (2002). Axis I and II psychiatric disorders after traumatic brain injury: A 30-year follow-up study. *American Journal of Psychiatry, 159*, 1315–1321.

Kovacs, M. (1985). The Childrens Depression Inventory (CDI). *Psychopharmacology Bulletin, 21*, 995–998.

Kovacs, M. (1996). Presentation and course

of major depressive disorder during childhood and later years of the life span. *Journal of the American Academy of Child and Adolescent Psychiatry, 35,* 705–715.

Kovacs, M., Akiskal, H. S., Gatsonis, C., & Parrone, P. L. (1994). Childhood-onset dysthymic disorder: Clinical features and prospective naturalistic outcome. *Archives of General Psychiatry, 51,* 365–374.

Kovacs, M., Devlin, B., Pollock, M., Richards, C., & Mukerji, P. (1997). A controlled family history study of childhood-onset depressive disorder. *Archives of General Psychiatry, 54,* 613–623.

Kovacs, M., Goldston, D., & Gatsonis, C. (1993). Suicidal behaviors and childhood-onset depressive disorders: A longitudinal investigation. *Journal of the American Academy of Child and Adolescent Psychiatry, 32,* 8–20.

Kraepelin, E. (1921). *Manic-depressive insanity and paranoia.* New York: Arno.

Kuehner, C., & Weber, I. (1999). Responses to depression in unipolar depressed patients: An investigation of Nolen-Hoeksema's response styles theory. *Psychological Medicine, 29,* 1323–1333.

Kupfer, D. J. (1995). Sleep research in depressive illness: Clinical implications—A tasting menu. *Biological Psychiatry, 38,* 391–403.

Kupfer, D. J., Frank, E., Perel, J. M., Cornes, C., Mallinger, A. G., Thase, M. E., et al. (1992). Five-year outcome for maintenance therapies in recurrent depression. *Archives of General Psychiatry, 49,* 769–773.

Kuyken, W., Kurzer, N., DeRubeis, R. J., Beck, A. T., & Brown, G. K. (2001). Response to cognitive therapy in depression: The role of maladaptive beliefs and personality disorders. *Journal of Consulting and Clinical Psychology, 69,* 560–566.

Lafer, B., Nierenberg, A. A., Rosenbaum, J. F., & Fava, M. (1996). Outpatients with DSM-III-R versus DSM-IV melancholic depression. *Comprehensive Psychiatry, 37,* 37–39.

Laidlaw, K. (2001). An empirical review of cognitive therapy for late life depression: Does research evidence suggest adaptations are necessary for cognitive therapy with older adults? *Clinical Psychology & Psychotherapy, 8,* 1–14.

Laidlaw, K., Thompson, L. W., Gallagher-Thompson, D., & Dick-Siskin, L. (2003). *Cognitive behaviour therapy with older people.* New York: Wiley.

Lam, D. H., Green, B., Power, M. J., & Checkley, S. (1996). Dependency, matching adversities, length of survival and relapse in major depression. *Journal of Affective Disorders, 37,* 81–90.

Lam, D. H., Hayward, P., Watkins, E. R., Wright, K., & Sham, P. (2005). Relapse prevention in patients with bipolar disorder: Cognitive therapy outcome after 2 years. *American Journal of Psychiatry, 162,* 324–329.

Lam, D. H., Watkins, E. R., Hayward, P., Bright, J., Wright, K., Kerr, N., et al. (2003). A randomized controlled study of cognitive therapy for relapse prevention for bipolar affective disorder: Outcome of the first year. *Archives of General Psychiatry, 60,* 145–152.

Lam, R. W., Levitt, A. J., Levitan, R. D., Enns, M. W., Morehouse, R., Michalak, E. E., et al. (2006). The can-SAD study: A randomized controlled trial of the effectiveness of light therapy and fluoxetine in patients with winter seasonal affective disorder. *American Journal of Psychiatry, 163,* 805–812.

Landen, M., & Eriksson, E. (2003). How does premenstrual dysphoric disorder relate to depression and anxiety disorders? *Depression and Anxiety, 17,* 122–129.

Laptook, R. S., Klein, D. N., & Dougherty,

L. R. (2006). Ten-year stability of depressive personality disorder in depressed outpatients. *American Journal of Psychiatry, 163,* 865–871.

Lattuada, E., Serretti, A., Cusin, C., Gasperini, M., & Smeraldi, E. (1999). Symptomatologic analysis of psychotic and non-psychotic depression. *Journal of Affective Disorders, 54,* 183–187.

Lawlor, D. A., & Hopker, S. W. (2001). The effectiveness of exercise as an intervention in the management of depression: Systematic review and meta-regression analysis of randomised controlled trials. *British Medical Journal, 322,* 763–767.

Leader, J. B., & Klein, D. N. (1996). Social adjustment in dysthymia, double depression and episodic major depression. *Journal of Affective Disorders, 37,* 91–101.

Lecrubier, Y., Clerc, G., Didi, R., & Kieser, M. (2002). Efficacy of St. John's Wort extract WS 5570 in major depression: A double-blind, placebo-controlled trial. *American Journal of Psychiatry, 159,* 1361–1366.

Lepine, J. P., Caillard, V., Bisserbe, J. C., Troy, S., Hotton, J. M., & Boyer, P. (2004). A randomized, placebo-controlled trial of sertraline for prophylactic treatment of highly recurrent major depressive disorder. *American Journal of Psychiatry, 161,* 836–842.

Lerer, B., Shapira, B., Calev, A., Tubi, N., Drexler, H., Kindler, S., et al. (1995). Antidepressant and cognitive effects of twice- versus 3-times-weekly ECT. *American Journal of Psychiatry, 152,* 564–570.

Leventhal, A. M., & Rehm, L. P. (2005). The empirical status of melancholia: Implications for psychology. *Clinical Psychology Review, 25,* 25–44.

Levinson, D. F. (2006). The genetics of depression: A review. *Biological Psychiatry, 60,* 84–92.

Levinson, D. F., Zubenko, G. S., Crowe, R. P., DePaulo, J. R., Scheftner, W. S., & Weissman, M. M. (2003). Genetics of recurrent early-onset depression (GenRED) design and preliminary clinical characteristics of a repository sample for genetic linkage studies. *American Journal of Medical Genetics. Part B, Neuropsychiatric Genetics, 119,* 118–130.

Lewinsohn, P. M., Allen, N. B., Seeley, J. R., & Gotlib, I. H. (1999a). First onset versus recurrence of depression: Differential processes of psychosocial risk. *Journal of Abnormal Psychology, 108,* 483–489.

Lewinsohn, P. M., & Clarke, G. N. (1984). Group treatment of depressed individuals: The coping with depression course. *Advances in Behaviour Research and Therapy, 6,* 99–114.

Lewinsohn, P. M., Clarke, G. N., Hops, H., & Andrews, J. (1990). Cognitive-behavioral treatment for depressed adolescents. *Behavior Therapy, 21,* 385–401.

Lewinsohn, P. M., Joiner, T. E. J., & Rohde, P. (2001). Evaluation of cognitive diathesis-stress models in predicting major depressive disorder in adolescents. *Journal of Abnormal Psychology, 110,* 203–215.

Lewinsohn, P. M., Olino, T. M., & Klein, D. N. (2005). Psychosocial impairment in offspring of depressed parents. *Psychological Medicine, 35,* 1493–1503.

Lewinsohn, P. M., Pettit, J. W., Joiner, T. E., & Seeley, J. R. (2003). The symptomatic expression of major depressive disorder in adolescents and young adults. *Journal of Abnormal Psychology, 112,* 244–252.

Lewinsohn, P. M., Rohde, P., Klein, D. M., & Seeley, J. R. (1999b). Natural course of adolescent major depressive disorder: I. Continuity into young adulthood.

Journal of the American Academy of Child and Adolescent Psychiatry, 38, 56–63.

Lewinsohn, P. M., Rohde, P., & Seeley, J. R. (1998). Major depressive disorder in older adolescents: Prevalence, risk factors, and clinical implications. *Clinical Psychology Review, 18,* 765–794.

Lewinsohn, P. M., Rohde, P., Seeley, J. R., & Fischer, S. A. (1993). Age-cohort changes in the lifetime occurrence of depression and other mental disorders. *Journal of Abnormal Psychology, 102,* 110–120.

Lewinsohn, P. M., Rohde, P., Seeley, J. R., & Hops, H. (1991). Comorbidity of unipolar depression: I. Major depression with dysthymia. *Journal of Abnormal Psychology, 100,* 205–213.

Lewinsohn, P. M., Steinmetz, J. L., Larson, D. W., & Franklin, J. (1981). Depression-related cognitions: Antecedent or consequence? *Journal of Abnormal Psychology, 90,* 213–219.

Lewy, A. J., Bauer, V. K., Cutler, N. L., Sack, R. L., Ahmed, S., Thomas, K. H., et al. (1998). Morning vs evening light treatment of patients with winter depression. *Archives of General Psychiatry, 55,* 890–896.

Lewy, A. J., Lefler, B. J., Emens, J. S., & Bauer, V. K. (2006). The circadian basis of winter depression. *Proceedings of the National Academy of Sciences of the United States of America, 103,* 7414–7419.

Lieb, R., Isensee, B., Hofler, M., & Wittchen, H.-U. (2002). Parental depression and depression in offspring: Evidence for familial characteristics and subtypes? *Journal of Psychiatric Research, 36,* 237–246.

Liebowitz, M. R., Quitkin, F. M., Stewart, J. W., McGrath, P. J., Harrison, W. M., Markowitz, J. S., et al. (1988). Antidepressant specificity in atypical depression. *Archives of General Psychiatry, 45,* 129–137.

Lin, E. H., Katon, W. J., VonKorff, M., Russo, J. E., Simon, G. E., Bush, T. M., et al. (1998). Relapse of depression in primary care: Rate and clinical predictors. *Archives of Family Medicine, 7,* 443–449.

Linde, K., Ramirez, G., Mulrow, C. D., Pauls, A., Weidenhammer, W., & Melchart, D. (1996). St John's wort for depression: An overview and meta-analysis of randomised clinical trials. *British Medical Journal, 313,* 253–258.

Lindelow, M. (1999). Parent–child interaction and adult depression: A prospective study. *Acta Psychiatrica Scandinavica, 100,* 270–278.

Liotti, M., Mayberg, H. S., McGinnis, S., Brannan, S. L., & Jerabek, P. (2002). Unmasking disease-specific cerebral blood flow abnormalities: Mood challenge in patients with remitted unipolar depression. *American Journal of Psychiatry, 159,* 1830–1840.

Lisanby, S. H., Maddox, J. H., Prudic, J., Devanand, D. P., & Sackeim, H. A. (2000). The effects of electroconvulsive therapy on memory of autobiographical and public events. *Archives of General Psychiatry, 57,* 581–590.

Liu, Y. (2003). The mediators between parenting and adolescent depressive symptoms: Dysfunctional attitudes and self-worth. *International Journal of Psychology, 38,* 91–100.

Lizardi, H., Klein, D. N., Ouimette, P. C., Riso, L. P., Anderson, R. L., & Donaldson, S. K. (1995). Reports of the childhood home environment in early-onset dysthymia and episodic major depression. *Journal of Abnormal Psychology, 104,* 132–139.

Lloyd, C. (1980). Life events and depressive disorders reviewed: 2. Events as precipitating factors. *Archives of General Psychiatry, 37,* 541–548.

Lovejoy, C. M., Graczyk, P. A., O'Hare, E., & Neuman, G. (2000). Maternal depression and parenting behavior: A meta-analytic review. *Clinical Psychology Review, 20,* 561–592.

Luby, J. L., Heffelfinger, A. K., Mrakotsky, C., Brown, K. M., Hessler, M. J., Wallis, J. M., et al. (2003). The clinical picture of depression in preschool children. *Journal of the American Academy of Child and Adolescent Psychiatry, 42*, 340–348.

Luby, J. L., Heffelfinger, A. K., Mrakotsky, C., Hessler, M. J., Brown, K. M., & Hildebrand, T. (2002). Preschool major depressive disorder: Preliminary validation for developmentally modified DSM-IV criteria. *Journal of the American Academy of Child and Adolescent Psychiatry, 41*, 928–937.

Lustberg, L., & Reynolds, C. F. (2000). Depression and insomnia: Questions of cause and effect. *Sleep Medicine Reviews, 4*, 253–262.

Lyubomirsky, S., & Nolen-Hoeksema, S. N. (1995). Effects of self-focused rumination on negative thinking and interpersonal problem solving. *Journal of Personality and Social Psychology, 69*, 176–190.

Lyubomirsky, S., Tucker, K. L., Caldwell, N. D., & Berg, K. (1999). Why ruminators are poor problem solvers: Clues from the phenomenology of dysphoric rumination. *Journal of Personality and Social Psychology, 77*, 1041–1060.

Ma, S. H., & Teasdale, J. D. (2004). Mindfulness-based cognitive therapy for depression: Replication and exploration of differential relapse prevention effects. *Journal of Consulting and Clinical Psychology, 72*, 31–40.

Maciejewski, P. K., Prigerson, H. G., & Mazure, C. M. (2001). Sex differences in event-related risk for major depression. *Psychological Medicine, 31*, 593–604.

MacMillan, H. L., Fleming, J. E., Streiner, D. L., Lin, E., Boyle, M. H., & Jamieson, E. (2001). Childhood abuse and lifetime psychopathology in a community sample. *American Journal of Psychiatry, 158*, 1878–1883.

MacQueen, G. M., Campbell, S., Mcewen, B. S., Macdonald, K., Amano, S., Joffe, R. T., et al. (2003). Course of illness, hippocampal function, and hippocampal volume in major depression. *Proceedings of the National Academy of Sciences of the United States of America, 100*, 1387–1392.

Maier, E. H., & Lachman, M. E. (2000). Consequences of early parental loss and separation for health and well-being in midlife. *International Journal of Behavioral Development, 24*, 183–189.

Manber, R., Arnow, B., Blasey, C., Vivian, D., McCullough, J. P., Blalock, J. A., et al. (2003). Patient's therapeutic skill acquisition and response to psychotherapy, alone or in combination with medication. *Psychological Medicine, 33*, 693–702.

Mann, J. J. (2002). A current perspective of suicide and attempted suicide. *Annals of Internal Medicine, 136*, 302–311.

Manning, M. (1994). *Undercurrents: A therapist's reckoning with her own depression.* San Francisco: Harper.

Manson, S. M. (1991). *Culture and the DSM-IV: Implications for the diagnosis of mood and anxiety disorders.* Paper presented at the National Institute of Mental Health-sponsored Conference on Culture and Diagnosis, Pittsburgh, PA.

March, J., Silva, S., Petrycki, S., Curry, J., Wells, K., Fairbank, J., et al. (2004). Fluoxetine, cognitive-behavioral therapy, and their combination for adolescents with depression: Treatment for adolescents with depression study (TADS) randomized controlled trial. *Journal of the American Medical Association, 292*, 807–820.

Markowitz, J. C. (1994). Psychotherapy of dysthymia. *American Journal of Psychiatry, 151*, 1114–1121.

Markowitz, J. C. (2003). Interpersonal psychotherapy for chronic depression. *Journal of Clinical Psychology, 59*, 847–858.

Markowitz, J. C., Kocsis, J. H., Bleiberg,

K. L., Christos, P. J., & Sacks, M. (2005a). A comparative trial of psychotherapy and pharmacotherapy for "pure" dysthymic patients. *Journal of Affective Disorders, 89*, 167–175.

Markowitz, J. C., Skodol, A. E., Petkova, E., Xie, H., Cheng, J. F., Hellerstein, D. J., et al. (2005b). Longitudinal comparison of depressive personality disorder and dysthymic disorder. *Comprehensive Psychiatry, 46*, 239–245.

Martell, C. R., Addis, M. E., & Jacobson, N. S. (2001). *Depression in context: Strategies for guided action*. New York: Norton.

Martin, J. L. R., Barbanoj, M. J., Schlaepfer, T. E., Thompson, E., Perez, V., & Kulisevsky, J. (2003). Repetitive transcranial magnetic stimulation for the treatment of depression: Systematic review and meta-analysis. *British Journal of Psychiatry, 182*, 480–491.

Mathews, C. A., & Reus, V. I. (2001). Assortative mating in the affective disorders: A systematic review and meta-analysis. *Comprehensive Psychiatry, 42*, 257–262.

Matza, L. S., Revicki, D. A., Davidson, J. R., & Stewart, J. W. (2003). Depression with atypical features in the national comorbidity survey: Classification, description, and consequences. *Archives of General Psychiatry, 60*, 817–826.

Mayberg, H. S., Liotti, M., Brannan, S. K., McGinnis, S., Mahurin, R. K., Jerabek, P. A., et al. (1999). Reciprocal limbic-cortical function and negative mood: Converging PET findings in depression and normal sadness. *American Journal of Psychiatry, 156*, 675–682.

Mazure, C. M. (1998). Life stressors as risk factors in depression. *Clinical Psychology: Science and Practice, 5*, 291–313.

Mazure, C. M., Bruce, M. L., Maciejewski, P. K., & Jacobs, S. C. (2000). Adverse life events and cognitive-personality characteristics in the prediction of major depression and antidepressant response. *American Journal of Psychiatry, 157*, 896–903.

Mazure, C. M., Maciejewski, P. K., Jacobs, S. C., & Bruce, M. L. (2002). Stressful life events interacting with cognitive/personality styles to predict late-onset major depression. *American Journal of Geriatric Psychiatry, 10*, 297–304.

McCabe, S., & Gotlib, I. H. (1995). Selective attention and clinical depression: Performance on a deployment-of-attention task. *Journal of Abnormal Psychology, 104*, 241–245.

McCabe, S., Gotlib, I. H., & Martin, R. A. (2000). Cognitive vulnerability for depression: Deployment-of-attention as a function of history of depression and current mood state. *Cognitive Therapy and Research, 24*, 427–444.

McCabe, S., & Toman, P. E. (2000). Stimulus exposure duration in a deployment-of-attention task: Effects on dysphoric, recently dysphoric, and nondysphoric individuals. *Cognition & Emotion, 14*, 125–142.

McCall, W. V., Reboussin, D. M., Weiner, R. D., & Sackheim, H. A. (2000). Titrated moderately suprathreshold vs fixed high-dose right unilateral electroconvulsive therapy: Acute antidepressant and cognitive effects. *Archives of General Psychiatry, 57*, 438–444.

McCullough, J. P. (2000). *Treatment for chronic depression: Cognitive behavioural analysis system of psychotherapy*. New York: Guilford.

McCullough, J. P., Klein, D. N., Borian, F. E., Howland, R. H., Riso, L. P., Keller, M. B., et al. (2003). Group comparisons of DSM-IV subtypes of chronic depression: Validity of the distinctions, part 2. *Journal of Abnormal Psychology, 112*, 614–622.

McCullough, J. P., Klein, D. N., Keller, M. B., Holzer, C. E., Davis, S., & Komstein, S. G. (2000). Comparison of

DSM-III-R chronic major depression and major depression superimposed on dysthymia (double depression): Validity of the distinction. *Journal of Abnormal Psychology, 109,* 419–427.

McDermut, W., Zimmerman, M., & Chelminski, I. (2003). The construct validity of depressive personality disorder. *Journal of Abnormal Psychology, 112,* 49–60.

McGonagle, K. A., & Kessler, R. C. (1990). Chronic stress, acute stress, and depressive symptoms. *American Journal of Community Psychology, 18,* 681–706.

McGrath, P. J., Stewart, J. W., Janal, M. N., Petkova, E., Quitkin, F. M., & Klein, D. F. (2000). A placebo-controlled study of fluoxetine versus imipramine in the acute treatment of atypical depression. *American Journal of Psychiatry, 157,* 344–350.

McGuffin, P., Katz, R., & Bebbington, P. (1988). The Camberwell Collaborative Depression Study: III. Depression and adversity in the relatives of depressed probands. *British Journal of Psychiatry, 152,* 775–782.

McIntosh, J. L. (1992). Suicide of the elderly. In B. Bonger (Ed.), *Suicide: Guidelines for assessment, management, and treatment* (pp. 106–124). New York: Oxford University Press.

McNeal, E. T., & Cimbolic, P. (1986). Antidepressants and biochemical theories of depression. *Psychological Bulletin, 99,* 361–374.

Melartin, T. K., Rytsala, H. J., Leskela, U. S., Lestela-Mielonen, P. S., Sokero, T. P., & Isometsa, E. T. (2002). Current comorbidity of psychiatric disorders among DSM-IV major depressive disorder patients in psychiatric care in the Vantaa Depression Study. *Journal of Clinical Psychiatry, 63,* 126–134.

Melartin, T. K., Rytsala, H. J., Leskela, U. S., Lestela-Mielonen, P. S., Sokero, T. P., & Isometsa, E. T. (2004). Severity and comorbidity predict episode duration and recurrence of DSM-IV major depressive disorder. *Journal of Clinical Psychiatry, 65,* 810–819.

Melfi, C. A., Chawla, A. J., Croghan, T. W., Hanna, M. P., Kennedy, S., & Sredl, K. (1998). The effects of adherence to antidepressant treatment guidelines on relapse and recurrence of depression. *Archives of General Psychiatry, 55,* 1128–1132.

Messer, S. C., & Gross, A. M. (1995). Childhood depression and family interaction: A naturalistic observation study. *Journal of Clinical Child Psychology, 24,* 77–88.

Meyer, J. H., Houle, S., Sagrati, S., Carella, A., Hussey, D. F., Ginovart, N., et al. (2004). Brain serotonin transporter binding potential measured with carbon 11–labeled DASB positron emission tomography: Effects of major depression episodes and severity of dysfunctional attitudes. *Archives of General Psychiatry, 61,* 1271–1279.

Meyer, S., E., Chrousos, G. P., & Gold, P. W. (2001). Major depression and the stress system: A life span perspective. *Development and Psychopathology, 13,* 565–580.

Mezulis, A. H., Abramson, L. Y., Hyde, J. S., & Hankin, B. L. (2004). Is there a universal positivity bias in attributions? A meta-analytic review of individual, developmental, and cultural differences in the self-serving attributional bias. *Psychological Bulletin, 130,* 711–747.

Michael, K. D., & Crowley, S. L. (2002). How effective are treatments for child and adolescent depression? A meta-analytic review. *Clinical Psychology Review, 22,* 247–269.

Michalak, E. E., Wilkinson, C., Dowrick, C., & Wilkinson, G. (2001). Seasonal affective disorder: Prevalence, detection and current treatment in North Wales. *British Journal of Psychiatry, 179,* 31–34.

Mineka, S., Watson, D., & Clark, L. A. (1998). Comorbidity of anxiety and unipolar mood disorders. *Annual Review of Psychology, 49,* 377–412.

Miranda, J. (1992). Dysfunctional thinking is activated by stressful life events. *Cognitive Therapy and Research, 16,* 473–483.

Miranda, J. (1997). Cognitive vulnerability, depression, and the mood-state dependent hypothesis: Is out of sight out of mind? *Cognition & Emotion, 11,* 585–605.

Miranda, J., Chung, J. Y., Green, B. L., Krupnick, J., Siddique, J., Revicki, D. A., et al. (2003). Treating depression in predominantly low-income young minority women: A randomized controlled trial. *Journal of the American Medical Association, 290,* 57–65.

Miranda, J., Green, B. L., Krupnick, J. L., Chung, J., Siddique, J., Belin, T., et al. (2006). One-year outcomes of a randomized clinical trial treating depression in low-income minority women. *Journal of Consulting and Clinical Psychology, 74,* 99–111.

Miranda, J., Gross, J. J., Persons, J. B., & Hahn, J. (1998). Mood matters: Negative mood induction activates dysfunctional attitudes in women vulnerable to depression. *Cognitive Therapy and Research, 22,* 363–376.

Miranda, J., & Persons, J. B. (1988). Dysfunctional attitudes are mood-state dependent. *Journal of Abnormal Psychology, 97,* 76–79.

Miranda, J., Persons, J. B., & Byers, C. N. (1990). Endorsement of dysfunctional beliefs depends on current mood state. *Journal of Abnormal Psychology, 99,* 237–241.

Mitchell, J., McCauley, E., Burke, P. M., & Moss, S. J. (1988). Phenomenology of depression in children and adolescents. *Journal of the American Academy of Child and Adolescent Psychiatry, 27,* 12–20.

Mogg, K., Bradbury, K. E., & Bradley, B. P. (2006). Interpretation of ambiguous information in clinical depression.

Behaviour Research and Therapy, 44, 1411–1419.

Mohr, D. C., Hart, S. L., Julian, L., Catledge, C., Honos-Webb, L., Vella, L., et al. (2005). Telephone-administered psychotherapy for depression. *Archives of General Psychiatry, 62,* 1007–1014.

Moncrieff, J., Wessely, S., & Hardy, R. (1998). Meta-analysis of trials comparing antidepressants with active placebos. *British Journal of Psychiatry, 172,* 227–231.

Mondimore, F. M., Zandi, P. P., MacKinnon, D. F., McInnis, M. G., Miller, E. B., Crowe, R. P., et al. (2006). Familial aggregation of illness chronicity in recurrent, early-onset major depression pedigrees. *American Journal of Psychiatry, 163,* 1554–1560.

Monroe, S. M., & Hadjiyannakis, K. (2002). The social environment and depression: Focusing on severe life stress. In I. H. Gotlib & C. L. Hammen (Eds.), *Handbook of depression* (pp. 314–340). New York: Guilford.

Monroe, S. M., & Harkness, K. L. (2005). Life stress, the "kindling" hypothesis, and the recurrence of depression: Considerations from a life stress perspective. *Psychological Review, 112,* 417–445.

Montgomery, S. A., Entsuah, R., Hackett, D., Kunz, N. R., & Rudolph, R. L. (2004). Venlafaxine versus placebo in the preventive treatment of recurrent major depression. *Journal of Clinical Psychiatry, 65,* 328–336.

Mor, N., & Winquist, J. (2002). Self-focused attention and negative affect: A meta-analysis. *Psychological Bulletin, 128,* 638–662.

Moreau, D., Mufson, L., Weissman, M. M., & Klerman, G. L. (1991). Interpersonal psychotherapy for adolescent depression: Description of modification and preliminary application. *Journal of the American Academy of Child and Adolescent Psychiatry, 30,* 642–651.

Morse, J. Q., & Robins, C. J. (2005). Personality–life event congruence effects in late-life depression. *Journal of Affective Disorders, 84*, 25–31.

Msetfi, R. M., Murphy, R. A., Simpson, J., & Kornbrot, D. E. (2005). Depressive realism and outcome density bias in contingency judgments: The effect of the context and intertrial interval. *Journal of Experimental Psychology: General, 134*, 10–22.

Mufson, L., Dorta, K. P., Wickramaratne, P., Nomura, Y., Olfson, M., & Weissman, M. M. (2004). A randomized effectiveness trial of interpersonal psychotherapy for depressed adolescents. *Archives of General Psychiatry, 61*, 577–584.

Mufson, L., Weissman, M. M., Moreau, D., & Garfinkel, R. (1999). Efficacy of interpersonal psychotherapy for depressed adolescents. *Archives of General Psychiatry, 56*, 573–579.

Mulder, R. T. (2002). Personality pathology and treatment outcome in major depression: A review. *American Journal of Psychiatry, 159*, 359–371.

Mulder, R. T., Joyce, P. R., Frampton, C. M. A., Luty, S. E., & Sullivan, P. F. (2006). Six months of treatment for depression: Outcome and predictors of the course of illness. *American Journal of Psychiatry, 163*, 95–100.

Mundt, C., Reck, C., Backenstrass, M., Kronmuller, K., & Fiedler, P. (2000). Reconfirming the role of life events for the timing of depressive episodes: A two-year prospective follow-up study. *Journal of Affective Disorders, 59*, 23–30.

Murphy, J. M., Laird, N. M., Monson, R. R., Sobol, A. M., & Leighton, A. H. (2000). A 40-year perspective on the prevalence of depression. *Archives of General Psychiatry, 57*, 209–215.

Murray, C. J., & Lopez, A. D. (1996). *The global burden of disease.* Cambridge, MA: Harvard University Press.

Murray, D., Cox, J. L., Chapman, G., &

Jones, P. (1995). Childbirth—Life event or start of a long-term difficulty: Further data from the Stoke-on-Trent controlled study of postnatal depression. *British Journal of Psychiatry, 166*, 595–600.

Musselman, D. L., Betan, E., Larsen, H., & Phillips, L. S. (2003). The relationship of depression to diabetes-Type 1 and Type 2: Epidemiology, biology, and treatment. *Biological Psychiatry, 54*, 317–329.

Narrow, W. E., Regier, D. A., Rae, D. S., Manderscheid, R. W., & Locke, B. Z. (1993). Use of services by persons with mental and addictive disorders: Findings from the National Institute of Mental Health Epidemiologic Catchment Area Program. *Archives of General Psychiatry, 50*, 95–107.

Nemeroff, C. B., Heim, C. M., Thase, M. E., Klein, D. N., Rush, A. J., Schatzberg, A. F., et al. (2003). Differential responses to psychotherapy versus pharmacotherapy in patients with chronic forms of major depression and childhood trauma. *Proceedings of the National Academy of Sciences of the United States of America, 100*, 14293–14296.

Newman, J., Engel, R., & Jensen, J. (1991). Age differences in depressive symptom experiences. *Journals of Gerontology, 46*, 224–235.

Newton, S. S., Thome, J., Wallace, T. L., Shirayama, Y., Schlesinger, L., Sakai, N., et al. (2002). Inhibition of cAMP response element-binding protein or dynorphin in the nucleus accumbens produces an antidepressant-like effect. *Journal of Neuroscience, 22*, 10883–10890.

Newton-Howes, G., Tyrer, P., & Johnson, T. (2006). Personality disorder and the outcome of depression: Meta-analysis of published studies. *British Journal of Psychiatry, 188*, 13–20.

Nezu, A. M. (1987). A problem-solving formulation of depression: A literature review and proposal of a pluralistic model. *Clinical Psychology Review, 7,* 121–144.

Nezu, A. M., & Perri, M. G. (1989). Social problem-solving therapy for unipolar depression: An initial dismantling investigation. *Journal of Consulting and Clinical Psychology, 57,* 408–413.

Nezu, A. M., & Ronan, G. F. (1985). Life stress, current problems, problem solving, and depressive symptoms: An integrative model. *Journal of Consulting and Clinical Psychology, 53,* 693–697.

NICHD Early Child Care Research Network. (1999). Chronicity of maternal depressive symptoms, maternal sensitivity, and child functioning at 36 months. *Developmental Psychology, 35,* 1297–1310.

Nierenberg, A. A. (2003). Predictors of response to antidepressants: General principles and clinical implications. *Psychiatric Clinics of North America, 26,* 345–352.

Nierenberg, A. A., Alpert, J. E., Pava, J., Rosenbaum, J. F., & Fava, M. (1998). Course and treatment of atypical depression. *Journal of Clinical Psychiatry, 59,* 5–9.

Nierenberg, A. A., Farabaugh, A. H., Alpert, J. E., Gordon, J., Worthington, J. J., Rosenbaum, J. F., et al. (2000). Timing of onset of antidepressant response with fluoxetine treatment. *American Journal of Psychiatry, 157,* 1423–1428.

Nierenberg, A. A., Keefe, B. R., Leslie, V. C., Alpert, J. E., Pava, J. A., Worthington, J. J., et al. (1999). Residual symptoms in depressed patients who respond acutely to fluoxetine. *Journal of Clinical Psychiatry, 60,* 221–225.

Nietzel, M. T., & Harris, M. J. (1990). Relationship of dependency and achievement/autonomy to depression. *Clinical Psychology Review, 10,* 279–297.

Nobler, M. S., Oquendo, M. A., Kegeles, L. S., Malone, K. M., Campbell, C., Sackeim, H. A., et al. (2001). Decreased regional brain metabolism after ECT. *American Journal of Psychiatry, 158,* 305–308.

Nobler, M. S., Sackeim, H. A., Prohovnik, I., Moeller, J. R., Mukherjee, S., Schnur, D. B., et al. (1994). Regional cerebral blood flow in mood disorders: III. Treatment and clinical response. *Archives of General Psychiatry, 51,* 884–897.

Nock, M. K., & Kessler, R. C. (2006). Prevalence of and risk factors for suicide attempts versus suicide gestures: Analysis of the National Comorbidity Survey. *Journal of Abnormal Psychology, 115,* 616–623.

Nolen-Hoeksema, S. N. (1990). *Sex differences in depression*: Stanford: Stanford University Press.

Nolen-Hoeksema, S. N. (1991). Responses to depression and their effects on the duration of depressive episodes. *Journal of Abnormal Psychology, 100,* 569–582.

Nolen-Hoeksema, S. N. (2000). The role of rumination in depressive disorders and mixed anxiety/depressive symptoms. *Journal of Abnormal Psychology, 109,* 504–511.

Nolen-Hoeksema, S. (2002). Gender differences in depression. In I. H. Gotlib & C. L. Hammen (Eds.), *Handbook of depression* (pp. 492–509). New York: Guilford.

Nolen-Hoeksema, S. N., & Girgus, J. S. (1994). The emergence of gender differences in depression during adolescence. *Psychological Bulletin, 115,* 424–443.

Nolen-Hoeksema, S. N., Morrow, J., & Fredrickson, B. L. (1993). Response styles and the duration of episodes of depressed mood. *Journal of Abnormal Psychology, 102,* 20–28.

Nunn, J. D., Mathews, A., & Trower, P. (1997). Selective processing of concern-related information in depression. *British Journal of Clinical Psychology, 36,* 489–503.

O'Hara, M. W., Stuart, S., Gorman, L. L., & Wenzel, A. (2000). Efficacy of interpersonal psychotherapy for postpartum depression. *Archives of General Psychiatry, 57*, 1039–1045.

O'Hara, M. W., & Swain, A. M. (1996). Rates and risk of postpartum depression: A meta-analysis. *International Review of Psychiatry, 8*, 37–54.

O'Hara, M. W., Zekoski, E. M., Philipps, L. H., & Wright, E. J. (1990). Controlled prospective study of postpartum mood disorders: Comparison of childbearing and nonchildbearing women. *Journal of Abnormal Psychology, 99*, 3–15.

Ohayon, M. M., & Schatzberg, A. F. (2002). Prevalence of depressive episodes with psychotic features in the general population. *American Journal of Psychiatry, 159*, 1855–1861.

Oldehinkel, A. J., Wittchen, H.-U., & Schuster, P. (1999). Prevalence, 20-month incidence and outcome of unipolar depressive disorders in a community sample of adolescents. *Psychological Medicine, 29*, 655–668.

Olfson, M., Kessler, R. C., Berglund, P. A., & Lin, E. (1998). Psychiatric disorder onset and first treatment contact in the United States and Ontario. *American Journal of Psychiatry, 155*, 1415–1422.

Olfson, M., Marcus, S. C., Tedeschi, M., & Wan, G. J. (2006). Continuity of antidepressant treatment for adults with depression in the United States. *American Journal of Psychiatry, 163*, 101–108.

Ormel, J., Oldehinkel, A. J., & Brilman, E. I. (2001). The interplay and etiological continuity of neuroticism, difficulties, and life events in the etiology of major and subsyndromal, first and recurrent depressive episodes in later life. *American Journal of Psychiatry, 158*, 885–891.

Ormel, J., VonKorff, M., Ustun, T. B., & Pini, S. (1994). Common mental disorders and disability across cultures: Results from the WHO Collaborative Study on Psychological Problems in General Health Care. *Journal of the American Medical Association, 272*, 1741–1748.

Osby, U., Brandt, L., Correia, N., Ekbom, A., & Sparen, P. (2001). Excess mortality in bipolar and unipolar disorder in Sweden. *Archives of General Psychiatry, 58*, 844–850.

Pacini, R., Muir, F., & Epstein, S. (1998). Depressive realism from the perspective of cognitive-experiential self-theory. *Journal of Personality and Social Psychology, 74*, 1056–1068.

Pampallona, S., Bollini, P., Tibaldi, G., Kupelnick, B., & Munizza, C. (2004). Combined pharmacotherapy and psychological treatment for depression: A systematic review. *Archives of General Psychiatry, 61*, 714–719.

Parker, G., & Gladstone, G. (1996). Parental characteristics as influences on adjustment in adulthood. In G. R. Pierce, B. R. Sarason, & I. G. Sarason (Eds.), *Handbook of social support and the family* (pp. 195–218). New York: Plenum.

Paykel, E. S. (2003). Life events and affective disorders. *Acta Psychiatrica Scandinavica, 108*, 61–66.

Paykel, E. S., Brugha, T., & Fryers, T. (2005). Size and burden of depressive disorders in Europe. *European Neuropsychopharmacology, 15*, 411–423.

Paykel, E. S., & Cooper, Z. (1992). Life events and social stress. In E. S. Paykel (Ed.), *Handbook of affective disorders* (pp. 149–170). New York: Guilford.

Paykel, E. S., Scott, J., Teasdale, J. D., Johnson, A. L., Garland, A., Moore, R., et al. (1999). Prevention of relapse in residual depression by cognitive therapy: A controlled trial. *Archives of General Psychiatry, 56*, 829–835.

Peeters, F., Nicolson, N. A., & Berkhof, J. (2004). Levels and variability of daily life cortisol secretion in major depression. *Psychiatry Research, 126,* 1–13.

Perez, J. E., & Riggio, R. E. (2002). Nonverbal social skills and psychopathology. In P. Philippot, R. S. Feldman, & E. J. Coats (Eds.), *Nonverbal behavior in clinical settings* (pp. 17–44). Oxford: Oxford University Press.

Perlis, M. L., Giles, D. E., Buysse, D. J., Tu, X., & Kupfer, D. J. (1997). Self-reported sleep disturbance as a prodromal symptom in recurrent depression. *Journal of Affective Disorders, 42,* 209–212.

Perry, A., Tarrier, N., Morriss, R., McCarthy, E., & Limb, K. (1999). Randomised controlled trial of efficacy of teaching patients with bipolar disorder to identify early symptoms of relapse and obtain treatment. *British Medical Journal, 318,* 149–153.

Persons, J. B., Bostrom, A., & Bertagnolli, A. (1999). Results of randomized controlled trials of cognitive therapy for depression generalize to private practice. *Cognitive Therapy and Research, 23,* 535–548.

Petersen, A. C., Sarigiani, P. A., & Kennedy, R. E. (1991). Adolescent depression: Why more girls? *Journal of Youth and Adolescence, 20,* 247–271.

Philipps, L. H. C., & O'Hara, M. W. (1991). Prospective study of postpartum depression: 4½-year follow-up of women and children. *Journal of Abnormal Child Psychology, 100,* 151–155.

Phillips, K. A., Gunderson, J. G., Triebwasser, J., Kimble, C. R., Faedda, G., Lyoo, I. K., et al. (1998). Reliability and validity of depressive personality disorder. *American Journal of Psychiatry, 155,* 1044–1048.

Pilowsky, D. J., Wickramaratne, P., Rush, A. J., Hughes, C. W., Garber, J., Malloy, E., et al. (2006). Children of currently depressed mothers: A STAR*D ancillary study. *Journal of Clinical Psychiatry, 67,* 126–136.

Pine, D. S., Cohen, P., Gurley, D., Brook, J. S., & Ma, Y. (1998). The risk for early-adulthood anxiety and depressive disorders in adolescents with anxiety and depressive disorders. *Archives of General Psychiatry, 55,* 56–64.

Plomin, R., DeFries, J. C., Craig, I. W., & McGuffin, P. (2003). *Behavioral genetics in the postgenomic era.* Washington, DC: American Psychological Association.

Plomin, R., Lichtenstein, P., Pedersen, N. L., McClearn, G. E., & Nesselroade, J. R. (1990). Genetic influence on life events during the last half of the life span. *Psychology and Aging, 5,* 25–30.

Plotsky, P. M., Owens, M. J., & Nemeroff, C. B. (1998). Psychoneuroendocrinology of depression. *Psychoneuroendocrinology, 21,* 293–307.

Posener, J. A., DeBattista, C., Williams, G. H., Kraemer, H. C., Kalehzan, B. M., & Schatzberg, A. F. (2000). 24–hour monitoring of cortisol and corticotropin secretion in psychotic and nonpsychotic major depression. *Archives of General Psychiatry, 57,* 755–760.

Post, R. M. (1992). Transduction of psychosocial stress into the neurobiology of recurrent affective disorder. *American Journal of Psychiatry, 149,* 999–1010.

Post, R. M., Rubinow, D. R., & Ballenger, J. C. (1984). Conditioning, sensitization, and kindling: Implications for the course of affective illness. In R. M. Post & J. C. Ballenger (Eds.), *Neurobiology of mood disorders.* Baltimore, MD: Williams & Wilkins.

Posternak, M. A., & Zimmerman, M. (2005). Is there a delay in the antidepressant effect? A meta-analysis. *Journal of Clinical Psychiatry, 66,* 148–158.

Potthoff, J. G., Holahan, C. J., & Joiner, T. E. (1995). Reassurance seeking, stress generation and depressive symptoms:

An integrative model. *Journal of Personality and Social Psychology, 68,* 664–670.

Poulton, R. G., & Andrews, G. (1992). Personality as a cause of adverse life events. *Acta Psychiatrica Scandinavica, 85,* 35–38.

Powers, D. V., Thompson, L., Futterman, A., & Gallagher-Thompson, D. (2002). Depression in later life: Epidemiology, assessment, impact, and treatment. In C. Hammen & I. H. Gotlib (Eds.), *Handbook of depression* (pp. 560–580). New York: Guilford.

Proudfoot, J., Goldberg, D., Mann, A., Everitt, B., Marks, I., & Gray, J. A. (2003). Computerized, interactive, multimedia cognitive-behavioural program for anxiety and depression in general practice. *Psychological Medicine, 33,* 217–227.

Pyszczynski, T., & Greenberg, J. (1987). Self-regulatory perseveration and the depressive self-focusing style: A self-awareness theory of reactive depression. *Psychological Bulletin, 102,* 122–138.

Quitkin, F. M., Rabkin, J. G., Gerald, J., Davis, J. M., & Klein, D. F. (2000). Validity of clinical trials of antidepressants. *American Journal of Psychiatry, 157,* 327–337.

Quitkin, F. M., Stewart, J. W., McGrath, P. J., Tricamo, E., Rabkin, J. G., Ocepekwelikson, K., et al. (1993). Columbia Atypical Depression: A subgroup of depressives with better response to MAOI than to tricyclic antidepressants or placebo. *British Journal of Psychiatry, 163,* 30–34.

Raes, F., Hermans, D., Williams, J. M. G., Beyers, W., Brunfaut, E., & Eelen, P. (2006). Reduced autobiographical memory specificity and rumination in predicting the course of depression. *Journal of Abnormal Psychology, 115,* 699–704.

Rao, U., Dahl, R. E., Ryan, N. D., Birmaher, B., Williamson, D. E., Giles, D. E., et al. (1996). The relationship between longitudinal clinical course and sleep and cortisol changes in adolescent depression. *Biological Psychiatry, 40,* 474–484.

Rao, U., Dahl, R. E., Ryan, N. D., Birmaher, B., Williamson, D. E., Rao, R., et al. (2002). Heterogeneity in EEG sleep findings in adolescent depression: Unipolar versus bipolar clinical course. *Journal of Affective Disorders, 70,* 273–280.

Rao, U., Hammen, C., & Daley, S. E. (1999). Continuity of depression during the transition to adulthood: A 5-year longitudinal study of young women. *Journal of the American Academy of Child and Adolescent Psychiatry, 38,* 908–915.

Rau, T., Wohlleben, G., Wuttke, H., Thuerauf, N., Lunkenheimer, J., Lanczik, M., et al. (2004). CYP2D6 genotype: Impact on adverse effects and nonresponse during treatment with antidepressants—a pilot study. *Clinical Pharmacology & Therapeutics, 75,* 386–393.

Rausch, J. L., Johnson, M. E., Fei, Y. J., Li, J. Q., Shendarkar, N., Hobby, H. M., et al. (2002). Initial conditions of serotonin transporter kinetics and genotype: Influence on SSRI treatment trial outcome. *Biological Psychiatry, 51,* 723–732.

Reilly-Harrington, N. A., Alloy, L. B., Fresco, D. M., & Whitehouse, W. G. (1999). Cognitive styles and life events interact to predict bipolar and unipolar symptomatology. *Journal of Abnormal Psychology, 108,* 567–578.

Reimherr, F. W., Amsterdam, J. D., Quitkin, F. M., Rosenbaum, J. F., Fava, M., Zajecka, J., et al. (1998). Optimal length of continuation therapy in depression: A prospective assessment during long-term fluoxetine treatment. *American Journal of Psychiatry, 155,* 1247–1253.

Reinecke, M. A., Ryan, N. E., & Dubois, D. L. (1998). Cognitive-behavioral therapy of depression and depressive symptoms during adolescence: A review and meta-analysis. *Journal of the American Academy of Child and Adolescent Psychiatry, 37*, 26–34.

Rende, R., & Plomin, R. (1992). Diathesis-stress models of psychopathology: A quantitative genetic perspective. *Applied and Preventive Psychology, 1*, 177–182.

Reynolds, C. F., Frank, E., Perel, J. M., Imber, S. D., Cornes, C., Miller, M. D., et al. (1999). Nortriptyline and interpersonal psychotherapy as maintenance therapies for recurrent major depression: A randomized controlled trial in patients older than 59 years. *Journal of the American Medical Association, 281*, 39–45.

Ribeiro, S. C. M., Tandon, R., Grunhaus, L., & Greden, J. F. (1993). The DST as a predictor of outcome in depression: A meta-analysis. *American Journal of Psychiatry, 150*, 1618–1629.

Riemann, D., Berger, M., & Voderholzer, U. (2001). Sleep and depression—results from psychobiological studies: An overview. *Biological Psychology, 57*, 67–103.

Riemann, D., & Voderholzer, U. (2003). Primary insomnia: A risk factor to develop depression? *Journal of Affective Disorders, 76*, 255–259.

Riolo, S. A., Nguyen, T. A., Greden, J. F., & King, C. A. (2005). Prevalence of depression by race/ethnicity: Findings from the national health and nutrition examination survey III. *American Journal of Public Health, 95*, 998–1000.

Riso, L. P., du Toit, P. L., Blandino, J. A., Penna, S., Dacey, S., Duin, J. S., et al. (2003). Cognitive aspects of chronic depression. *Journal of Abnormal Psychology, 112*, 72–80.

Riso, L. P., Miyatake, R. K., & Thase, M. E. (2002). The search for determinants of chronic depression: A review of six factors. *Journal of Affective Disorders, 70*, 103–115.

Roberts, C., Kane, R., Thomson, H., Bishop, B., & Hart, B. (2003). The prevention of depressive symptoms in rural school children: A randomized controlled trial. *Journal of Consulting and Clinical Psychology, 71*, 622–628.

Roberts, J. E., & Gotlib, I. H. (1997). Temporal variability in global self-esteem and specific self-evaluation as prospective predictors of emotional distress: Specificity in predictors and outcome. *Journal of Abnormal Psychology, 106*, 521–529.

Roberts, J. E., & Kassel, J. D. (1997). Labile self-esteem, life stress, and depressive symptoms: Prospective data testing a model of vulnerability. *Cognitive Therapy and Research, 21*, 569–589.

Roberts, J. E., Kassel, J. D., & Gotlib, I. H. (1995a). Level and stability of self-esteem as predictors of depressive symptoms. *Personality and Individual Differences, 19*, 217–224.

Roberts, J. E., Lewinsohn, P. M., & Seeley, J. R. (1995b). Symptoms of DSM-III-R major depression in adolescence: Evidence from an epidemiologic survey. *Journal of the American Academy of Child and Adolescent Psychiatry, 34*, 1608–1617.

Roberts, J. E., & Monroe, S. M. (1994). A multidimensional model of self-esteem in depression. *Clinical Psychology Review, 14*, 161–181.

Robertson, E., Grace, S., Wallington, T., & Stewart, D. E. (2004). Antenatal risk factors for postpartum depression: A synthesis of recent literature. *General Hospital Psychiatry, 26*, 289–295.

Robins, C. J. (1990). Congruence of personality and life events in depression. *Journal of Abnormal Psychology, 99*, 393–397.

Robins, L. N., Wing, J., Wittchen, H. U., Helzer, J. E., Babor, T. F., Burke, J., et al.

(1988). The Composite International Diagnostic Interview: An epidemiologic instrument suitable for use in conjunction with different diagnostic systems and in different cultures. *Archives of General Psychiatry, 45,* 1069–1077.

Robinson, L. A., Berman, J. S., & Neimeyer, R. A. (1990). Psychotherapy for the treatment of depression: A comprehensive review of controlled outcome research. *Psychological Bulletin, 108,* 30–49.

Robinson, M. S., & Alloy, L. B. (2003). Negative cognitive styles and stress-reactive rumination interact to predict depression: A prospective study. *Cognitive Therapy and Research, 27,* 275–291.

Rockett, I. R. H., & Smith, G. S. (1989). Homicide, suicide, motor vehicle crash, and fall mortality: United States' experience in comparative perspective. *American Journal of Public Health, 79,* 1396–1400.

Rohde, P., Clarke, G. N., Mace, D. E., Jorgensen, J. S., & Seeley, J. R. (2004). An efficacy/effectiveness study of cognitive-behavioral treatment for adolescents with comorbid major depression and conduct disorder. *Journal of the American Academy of Child and Adolescent Psychiatry, 43,* 660–668.

Rohde, P., Lewinsohn, P. M., & Seeley, J. R. (1991). Comorbidity of unipolar depression: II. Comorbidity with other mental disorders in adolescents and adults. *Journal of Abnormal Psychology, 100,* 214–222.

Rose, D. T., Abramson, L. Y., Hodulik, C. J., Halberstadt, L., & Leff, G. (1994). Heterogeneity of cognitive style among depressed inpatients. *Journal of Abnormal Psychology, 103,* 419–429.

Rosenfarb, I. S., Becker, J., & Khan, A. (1994). Perceptions of parental and peer attachments by women with mood disorders. *Journal of Abnormal Psychology, 103,* 637–644.

Rosenthal, N. E., Sack, D. A., Gillin, J. C., Lewy, A. J., Goodwin, F. K., Davenport, Y., et al. (1984). Seasonal affective disorder: A description of the syndrome and preliminary findings with light therapy. *Archives of General Psychiatry, 41,* 72–80.

Roses, A. D. (2000). Pharmacogenetics and future drug development and delivery. *Lancet, 355,* 1358–1361.

Rossello, J., & Bernal, G. (1999). The efficacy of cognitive-behavioral and interpersonal treatments for depression in Puerto Rican adolescents. *Journal of Consulting and Clinical Psychology, 67,* 734–745.

Rossi, A., Marinangeli, M. G., Butti, G., Scinto, A., Di Cicco, L., Kalyvoka, A., et al. (2001). Personality disorders in bipolar and depressive disorders. *Journal of Affective Disorders, 65,* 3–8.

Rossum van, E. F. C., Binder, E. B., Majer, M., Koper, J. W., Ising, M., Modell, S., et al. (2006). Polymorphisms of the glucocorticoid receptor gene and major depression. *Biological Psychiatry, 59,* 681–688.

Rudolph, K. D. (2002). Gender differences in emotional responses to interpersonal stress during adolescence. *Journal of Adolescent Health, 30,* 3–13.

Rudolph, K. D., & Hammen, C. (1999). Age and gender as determinants of stress exposure, generation, and reactions in youngsters: A transactional perspective. *Child Development, 70,* 660–677.

Rudolph, K. D., Hammen, C., & Daley, S. E. (2006). Mood disorders. In D. A. Wolfe & E. J. Mash (Eds.), *Behavioral and emotional disorders in adolescents: Nature, assessment, and treatment* (pp. 300–342). New York: Guilford.

Rugulies, R. (2002). Depression as a predictor for coronary heart disease: A review and meta-analysis. *American Journal of Preventive Medicine, 23,* 51–61.

Rush, A. J., Beck, A. T., Kovacs, M., Weissenburger, J., & Hollon, S. D. (1982). Comparison of the effects of cognitive therapy and pharmacotherapy on hopelessness and self-concept. *American Journal of Psychiatry, 139*, 862–866.

Rush, A. J., Fava, M., Wisniewski, S. R., Lavori, P. W., Trivedi, M. H., Sackeim, H. A., et al. (2004). Sequenced treatment alternatives to relieve depression (STAR*D): Rationale and design. *Controlled Clinical Trials, 25*, 119–142.

Rush, A. J., Giles, D. E., Schlesser, M. A., Orsulak, P. J., Weissenburger, J. E., Fulton, C. L., et al. (1997). Dexamethasone response, thyrotropin-releasing hormone stimulation, rapid eye movement latency, and subtypes of depression. *Biological Psychiatry, 41*, 915–928.

Rush, A. J., Trivedi, M. H., Wisniewski, S. R., Nierenberg, A. A., Stewart, J. W., Warden, D., et al. (2006a). Acute and longer-term outcomes in depressed outpatients requiring one or several treatment steps: A STAR*D report. *American Journal of Psychiatry, 163*, 1905–1917.

Rush, A. J., Trivedi, M. H., Wisniewski, S. R., Stewart, J. W., Nierenberg, A. A., Thase, M. E., et al. (2006b). Bupropion-SR, sertraline, or venlafaxine-XR after failure of SSRIs for depression. *New England Journal of Medicine, 354*, 1231–1242.

Rush, A. J., & Weissenburger, J. E. (1994). Melancholic symptom features and DSM-IV. *American Journal of Psychiatry, 15*, 489–498.

Rush, A. J., Zimmerman, M., Wisniewski, S. R., Fava, M., Hollon, S. D., Warden, D., et al. (2005). Comorbid psychiatric disorders in depressed outpatients: Demographic and clinical features. *Journal of Affective Disorders, 87*, 43–55.

Russell, J. M., Kornstein, S. G., Shea, M. T., McCullough, J. P., Harrison, W. M., Hirschfeld, R. M. A., et al. (2003). Chronic depression and comorbid personality disorders: Response to sertraline versus imipramine. *Journal of Clinical Psychiatry, 64*, 554–561.

Russo-Neustadt, A. A., & Chen, M. J. (2005). Brain-derived neurotrophic factor and antidepressant activity. *Current Pharmaceutical Design, 11*, 1495–1510.

Ryan, N. D., Puig-Antich, J., Ambrosini, P., Rabinovich, H., Robinson, D., Nelson, B., et al. (1987). The clinical picture of major depression in children and adolescents. *Archives of General Psychiatry, 44*, 854–861.

Sackeim, H. A. (2004). Convulsant and anticonvulsant properties of electroconvulsive therapy: Towards a focal form of brain stimulation. *Clinical Neuroscience Research, 4*, 39–57.

Sackeim, H. A., Haskett, R. F., Mulsant, B. H., Thase, M. E., Mann, J. J., Pettinati, H. M., et al. (2001). Continuation pharmacotherapy in the prevention of relapse following electroconvulsive therapy: A randomized controlled trial. *Journal of the American Medical Association, 285*, 1299–1307.

Sackeim, H. A., Prudic, J., Devanand, D. P., Nobler, M. S., Lisanby, S. H., Peyser, S., et al. (2000). A prospective, randomized, double-blind comparison of bilateral and right unilateral electroconvulsive therapy at different stimulus intensities. *Archives of General Psychiatry, 57*, 425–434.

Sanathara, V. A., Gardner, C. O., Prescott, C. A., & Kendler, K. S. (2003). Interpersonal dependence and major depression: Aetiological inter-relationship and gender differences. *Psychological Medicine, 33*, 927–931.

Sanderson, W. C., Beck, A. T., & Beck, J. S. (1990). Syndrome comorbidity in patients with major depression or dysthymia: Prevalence and temporal relationships. *American Journal of Psychiatry, 147,* 1025–1028.

Santarelli, L., Saxe, M., Gross, C., Surget, A., Battaglia, F., Dulawa, S., et al. (2003). Requirement of hippocampal neurogenesis for the behavioral effects of antidepressants. *Science, 301,* 805–809.

Santor, D. A., Bagby, R. M., & Joffe, R. T. (1997). Evaluating stability and change in personality and depression. *Journal of Personality and Social Psychology, 73,* 1354–1362.

Sanz, J., & Avia, M. D. (1994). Cognitive specificity in social anxiety and depression: Self-statements, self-focused attention, and dysfunctional attitudes. *Journal of Social and Clinical Psychology, 13,* 105–137.

Sapolsky, R. M. (1996). Why stress is bad for your brain. *Science, 273,* 749–750.

Sargent, J. T., Crocker, J., & Luhtanen, R. K. (2006). Contingencies of self-worth and depressive symptoms in college students. *Journal of Social and Clinical Psychology, 25,* 628–646.

Sargent, P. A., Kjaer, K. H., Bench, C. J., Rabiner, E. A., Messa, C., Meyer, J. H., et al. (2000). Brain serotonin(1A) receptor binding measured by positron emission tomography with [C-11]WAY-100635: Effects of depression and antidepressant treatment. *Archives of General Psychiatry, 57,* 174–180.

Saudino, K. J., Pedersen, N. L., Lichtenstein, P., McClearn, G. E., & Plomin, R. (1997). Can personality explain genetic influences on life events? *Journal of Personality and Social Psychology, 72,* 196–206.

Scher, C. D., Ingram, R. E., & Segal, Z. V. (2005). Cognitive reactivity and vulnerability: Empirical evaluation of construct activation and cognitive diatheses in unipolar depression. *Clinical Psychology Review, 25,* 487–510.

Schildkraut, J. J. (1965). The catecholamine hypothesis of affective disorders: A review of supporting evidence. *American Journal of Psychiatry, 122,* 509–522.

Schmitz, N., Kugler, J., & Rollnik, J. (2003). On the relation between neuroticism, self-esteem, and depression: Results from the national comorbidity survey. *Comprehensive Psychiatry, 44,* 169–176.

Scott, J., Garland, A., & Moorhead, S. (2001). A pilot study of cognitive therapy in bipolar disorders. *Psychological Medicine, 31,* 459–467.

Segal, Z. V., Gemar, M., & Williams, S. (1999). Differential cognitive response to a mood challenge following successful cognitive therapy or pharmacotherapy for unipolar depression. *Journal of Abnormal Psychology, 108,* 3–10.

Segal, Z. V., Kennedy, S., Gemar, M., Hood, K., Pedersen, R., & Buis, T. (2006). Cognitive reactivity to sad mood provocation and the prediction of depressive relapse. *Archives of General Psychiatry, 63,* 749–755.

Segal, Z. V., Shaw, B. F., Vella, D. D., & Katz, R. (1992). Cognitive and life stress predictors of relapse in remitted unipolar depressed patients: Test of the congruency hypothesis. *Journal of Abnormal Psychology, 101,* 26–36.

Segal, Z. V., Williams, J. M. G., & Teasdale, J. D. (2002). *Mindfulness-based cognitive therapy for depression: A new approach to preventing relapse.* New York: Guilford.

Segrin, C. (2000). Social skills deficits associated with depression. *Clinical Psychology Review, 20,* 379–403.

Segrin, C., & Abramson, L. Y. (1994). Negative reactions to depressive behaviors: A communication theories analysis. *Journal of Abnormal Psychology, 103,* 655–668.

Seligman, M. E. P., Abramson, L. Y., Semmel, A., & Baeyer, C. V. (1979). Depressive attributional style. *Journal of Abnormal Psychology, 88,* 242–247.

Seligman, M. E. P., Reivich, K., Jaycox, L.,

& Gillham, J. (1995). *The optimistic child.* New York: Houghton Mifflin.

Selmi, P. M., Klein, M. H., Greist, J. H., Sorrell, S. P., & Erdman, H. P. (1990). Computer-administered cognitive-behavioral therapy for depression. *American Journal of Psychiatry, 147,* 51–56.

Shankman, S. A., & Klein, D. N. (2002). The impact of comorbid anxiety disorders on the course of dysthymic disorder: A 5-year prospective longitudinal study. *Journal of Affective Disorders, 70,* 211–217.

Shankman, S. A., & Klein, D. N. (2003). The relation between depression and anxiety: An evaluation of the tripartite, approach-withdrawal and valence-arousal models. *Clinical Psychology Review, 23,* 605–637.

Shapiro, D. A., Barkham, M., Rees, A., Hardy, G. E., Reynolds, S., & Startup, M. (1994). Effects of treatment duration and severity of depression on the effectiveness of cognitive-behavioral and psychodynamic-interpersonal psychotherapy. *Journal of Consulting and Clinical Psychology, 62,* 522–534.

Shea, M. T., Pilkonis, P. A., Beckham, E., Collins, J. F., Elkin, I., Sotsky, S. M., et al. (1990). Personality disorders and treatment outcome in the NIMH treatment of depression collaborative research program. *American Journal of Psychiatry, 147,* 711–718.

Shea, M. T., Widiger, T. A., & Klein, M. H. (1992). Comorbidity of personality disorders and depression: Implications for treatment. *Journal of Consulting and Clinical Psychology, 60,* 857–868.

Sheeber, L., & Sorenson, E. (1998). Family relationships of depressed adolescents: A multimethod assessment. *Journal of Clinical Child Psychology, 27,* 268–277.

Sheffield, J. K., Spence, S. H., Rapee, R. M., Kowalenko, N., Wignall, A., Davis, A., et al. (2006). Evaluation of universal, indicated and combined cognitive-behavioral approaches to the prevention of depression among adolescents. *Journal of Consulting and Clinical Psychology, 74,* 66–79.

Sheline, Y. I. (2003). Neuroimaging studies of mood disorder effects on the brain. *Biological Psychiatry, 54,* 338–352.

Sheline, Y. I., Sanghavi, M., Mintun, M. A., & Gado, M. H. (1999). Depression duration but not age predicts hippocampal volume loss in medically healthy women with recurrent major depression. *Journal of Neuroscience, 19,* 5034–5043.

Shelton, R. C. (2000). Intracellular mechanisms of antidepressant drug action. *Harvard Review of Psychiatry, 8,* 161–174.

Shelton, R. C., Hollon, S. D., Purdon, S. E., & Loosen, P. T. (1991). Biological and psychological aspects of depression. *Behavior Therapy, 22,* 201–228.

Shelton, R. C., Keller, M. B., Gelenberg, A., Dunner, D. L., Hirschfeld, R., Thase, M. E., et al. (2001). Effectiveness of St John's Wort in major depression: A randomized controlled trial. *Journal of the American Medical Association, 285,* 1978–1986.

Sheppard, L. C., & Teasdale, J. D. (1996). Depressive thinking: Changes in schematic mental models of self and world. *Psychological Medicine, 26,* 1043–1051.

Sherbourne, C. D., Hays, R. D., & Wells, K. B. (1995). Personal and psychosocial risk factors for physical and mental health outcomes and course of depression among depressed patients. *Journal of Consulting and Clinical Psychology, 63,* 345–355.

Shih, J. H., Eberhart, N. K., Hammen, C., & Brennan, P. A. (2006). Differential exposure and reactivity to interpersonal stress predict sex differences in adolescent depression. *Journal of Clinical Child and Adolescent Psychology, 35,* 103–115.

Shimizu, E., Hashimoto, K., Okamura, N., Koike, K., Komatsu, N., Kumakiri, C., et al. (2003). Alterations of serum levels of brain-derived neurotrophic factor (BDNF) in depressed patients with or without antidepressants. *Biological Psychiatry, 54,* 70–75.

Silberg, J. L., Pickles, A., Rutter, C. M., Hewitt, J., Simonoff, E., Maes, H., et al. (1999). The influence of genetic factors and life stress on depression among adolescent girls. *Archives of General Psychiatry, 56,* 225–232.

Silberg, J. L., Rutter, M., & Eaves, L. (2001). Genetic and environmental influences on the temporal association between earlier anxiety and later depression in girls. *Biological Psychiatry, 49,* 1040–1049.

Simon, G. E., Heiligenstein, J. H., Grothaus, L., Katon, W., & Revicki, D. (1998). Should anxiety and insomnia influence antidepressant selection: A randomized comparison of fluoxetine and imipramine. *Journal of Clinical Psychiatry, 59,* 49–55.

Simon, G. E., Ormel, J., VonKorff, M., & Barlow, W. (1995). Health care costs associated with depressive and anxiety disorders in primary care. *American Journal of Psychiatry, 152,* 352–357.

Simon, G. E., Savarino, J., Operskalski, B., & Wang, P. S. (2006). Suicide risk during antidepressant treatment. *American Journal of Psychiatry, 163,* 41–47.

Simons, A. D., Garfield, S. L., & Murphy, G. E. (1984). The process of change in cognitive therapy and pharmacotherapy for depression: Changes in mood and cognition. *Archives of General Psychiatry, 41,* 45–51.

Smith, A. L., & Weissman, M. M. (1992). Epidemiology. In E. S. Paykel (Ed.), *Handbook of affective disorders* (pp. 111–129). New York: Guilford.

Smith, J. M., Grandin, L. D., Alloy, L. B., & Abramson, L. Y. (2006). Cognitive vulnerability to depression and axis II personality dysfunction. *Cognitive Therapy and Research, 30,* 609–621.

Sobin, C., & Sackeim, H. A. (1997). Psychomotor symptoms of depression. *American Journal of Psychiatry, 154,* 4–17.

Solomon, A., Haaga, D. A. F., Brody, C., Friedman, D. G., & Kirk, L. (1998). Priming irrational beliefs in recovered-depressed people. *Journal of Abnormal Psychology, 107,* 440–449.

Solomon, D. A., Keller, M. B., Leon, A. C., Mueller, T. I., Lavori, P. W., Shea, M. T., et al. (2000). Multiple recurrences of major depressive disorder. *American Journal of Psychiatry, 157,* 229–233.

Sommers-Flanagan, J., & Sommers-Flanagan, R. (1996). Efficacy of antidepressant medication with depressed youth: What psychologists should know. *Professional Psychology: Research and Practice, 27,* 145–153.

Sotsky, S. M., Glass, D. R., Shea, M. T., Pilkonis, P. A., Collins, J. F., Elkin, I., et al. (1991). Patient predictors of response to psychotherapy and pharmacotherapy: Findings in the NIMH Treatment of Depression Collaborative Research Program. *American Journal of Psychiatry, 148,* 997–1008.

Spangler, D. L., Simons, A. D., Monroe, S. M., & Thase, M. E. (1996). Gender differences in cognitive diathesis-stress domain match: Implications for differential pathways to depression. *Journal of Abnormal Psychology, 105,* 653–657.

Spasojevic, J., & Alloy, L. B. (2001). Rumination as a common mechanism relating depressive risk factors to depression. *Emotion, 1,* 25–37.

Spence, S. H., Sheffield, J. K., & Donovan, C. L. (2003). Preventing adolescent depression: An evaluation of the problem solving for life program. *Journal of Consulting and Clinical Psychology, 71,* 3–13.

Spence, S. H., Sheffield, J. K., & Donovan, C. L. (2005). Long-term outcome of a school-based, universal approach to prevention of depression in adolescents. *Journal of Consulting and Clinical Psychology, 73*, 160–167.

Spijker, J., de Graaf, R., Bijl, R. V., Beekman, A. T., Ormel, J., & Nolen, W. A. (2002). Duration of major depressive episodes in the general population: Results from the Netherlands Mental Health Survey and Incidence Study (NEMESIS). *British Journal of Psychiatry, 181*, 208–213.

Spijker, J., de Graaf, R., Bijl, R. V., Beekman, A. T., Ormel, J., & Nolen, W. A. (2004). Determinants of persistence of major depressive episodes in the general population: Results from the Netherlands Mental Health Survey and Incidence Study (NEMESIS). *Journal of Affective Disorders, 81*, 231–240.

Spitzer, R. L., Williams, J. B. W., Gibbon, M., & First, M. B. (1992). The Structured Clinical Interview for DSM-III-R (SCID): 1. History, rationale, and description. *Archives of General Psychiatry, 49*, 624–629.

Spitzer, R. L., Williams, J. B. W., Gibbon, M., & First, M. B. (1996). *Structured Clinical Interview for DSM-IV (SCID)*. Washington, DC: American Psychiatric Association.

Squire, L. R. (1977). ECT and memory loss. *American Journal of Psychiatry, 134*, 997–1001.

Stark, K. D., Reynolds, W. M., & Kaslow, N. J. (1987). A comparison of the relative efficacy of self-control therapy and a behavioral problem-solving therapy for depression in children. *Journal of Abnormal Child Psychology, 15*, 91–113.

Stark, K. D., Rouse, L., & Kurowski, C. (1994). Psychological treatment approaches for depression in children. In W. M. Reynolds & H. Johnston (Eds.), *Handbook of depression in children and adolescents* (pp. 275–307). New York: Plenum.

Stark, K. D., Rouse, L., & Livingston, R. (1991). Treatment of depression during childhood and adolescence: Cognitive-behavioral procedures for the individual and family. In P. C. Kendall (Ed.), *Child and Adolescent Therapy* (pp. 165–206). New York: Guilford.

Steffens, D. C., Skoog, I., Norton, M. C., Hart, A. D., Tschanz, J. T., Plassman, B. L., et al. (2000). Prevalence of depression and its treatment in an elderly population. *Archives of General Psychiatry, 57*, 601–607.

Stein, M. B., Fuetsch, M., Muller, N., Hofler, M., Lieb, R., & Wittchen, H.-U. (2001). Social anxiety disorder and the risk of depression: A prospective community study of adolescents and young adults. *Archives of General Psychiatry, 58*, 251–256.

Steiner, M. (2000). Premenstrual syndrome and premenstrual dysphoric disorder: Guidelines for management. *Journal of Psychiatry & Neuroscience, 25*, 459–468.

Steiner, M., & Born, L. (2000). Advances in the diagnosis and treatment of premenstrual dysphoria. *CNS Drugs, 13*, 286–304.

Steiner, M., Dunn, E., & Born, L. (2003). Hormones and mood: From menarche to menopause and beyond. *Journal of Affective Disorders, 74*, 67–83.

Stephens, R. S., Hokanson, J. E., & Welker, R. A. (1987). Responses to depressed interpersonal behavior: Mixed reactions in a helping role. *Journal of Personality and Social Psychology, 52*, 1274–1282.

Stewart, W. F., Ricci, J. A., Chee, E., Hahn, S. R., & Morganstein, D. (2003). Cost of lost productive work time among US workers with depression. *Journal of the American Medical Association, 289*, 3135–3144.

Storosum, J. G., van Zwieten, B. J., van den Brink, W., Gersons, B. P. R., &

Broekmans, A. W. (2001). Suicide risk in placebo-controlled studies of major depression. *American Journal of Psychiatry, 158*, 1271–1275.

Strack, S., & Coyne, J. C. (1983). Social confirmation of dysphoria: Shared and private reactions to depression. *Journal of Personality and Social Psychology, 44*, 798–806.

Strunk, D. R., Lopez, H., & DeRubeis, R. J. (2006). Depressive symptoms are associated with unrealistic negative predictions of future life events. *Behaviour Research and Therapy, 44*, 861–882.

Stuart, S., Wright, J. H., Thase, M. E., & Beck, A. T. (1997). Cognitive therapy with inpatients. *General Hospital Psychiatry, 19*, 42–50.

Styron, W. (1990). *Darkness visible: A memoir of madness*. New York: Random House.

Sullivan, P. F., Neale, M. C., & Kendler, K. S. (2000). Genetic epidemiology of major depression: Review and meta-analysis. *American Journal of Psychiatry, 157*, 1552–1562.

Suls, J., & Bunde, J. (2005). Anger, anxiety, and depression as risk factors for cardiovascular disease: The problems and implications of overlapping affective dispositions. *Psychological Bulletin, 131*, 260–300.

Swendsen, J. D., & Merikangas, K. R. (2000). The comorbidity of depression and substance use disorders. *Clinical Psychology Review, 20*, 173–189.

Tarbuck, A. F., & Paykel, E. S. (1995). Effects of major depression on the cognitive function of younger and older subjects. *Psychological Medicine, 25*, 285–295.

Taylor, M. J., Freemantle, N., Geddes, J. R., & Bhagwagar, Z. (2006). Early onset of selective serotonin reuptake inhibitor antidepressant action: Systematic review and meta-analysis. *Archives of General Psychiatry, 63*, 1217–1223.

Teasdale, J. D. (1983). Negative thinking in depression: Cause, effect, or reciprocal relationship. *Advances in Behaviour Research and Therapy, 5*, 3–25.

Teasdale, J. D. (1988). Cognitive vulnerability to persistent depression. *Cognition and Emotion, 2*, 247–274.

Teasdale, J. D., & Barnard, P. J. (1993). *Affect, cognition, and change: Re-modelling depressive thought*. Hove, UK: Lawrence Erlbaum Associates Ltd.

Teasdale, J. D., & Dent, J. (1987). Cognitive vulnerability to depression: An investigation of two hypotheses. *British Journal of Clinical Psychology, 26*, 113–126.

Teasdale, J. D., & Fennell, M. J. V. (1982). Immediate effects on depression of cognitive therapy interventions. *Cognitive Therapy and Research, 6*, 343–352.

Teasdale, J. D., Lloyd, C. A., & Hutton, J. M. (1998). Depressive thinking and dysfunctional schematic mental models. *British Journal of Clinical Psychology, 37*, 247–257.

Teasdale, J. D., Moore, R. G., Hayhurst, H., Pope, M., Williams, S., & Segal, Z. V. (2002). Meta-cognitive awareness and prevention of relapse in depression: Empirical evidence. *Journal of Consulting and Clinical Psychology, 70*, 275–287.

Teasdale, J. D., Scott, J., Moore, R. G., Hayhurst, H., Pope, M., & Paykel, E. S. (2001). How does cognitive therapy prevent relapse in residual depression? Evidence from a controlled trial. *Journal of Consulting and Clinical Psychology, 69*, 347–357.

Teasdale, J. D., Segal, Z., & Williams, J. M. G. (1995a). How does cognitive therapy prevent depressive relapse and why should attentional control (mindfulness) training help. *Behaviour Research and Therapy, 33*, 25–39.

Teasdale, J. D., Segal, Z. V., Williams, J. M. G., Ridgeway, V. A., Soulsby, J. M.,

& Lau, M. A. (2000). Prevention of relapse/recurrence in major depression by mindfulness-based cognitive therapy. *Journal of Consulting and Clinical Psychology, 68,* 615–623.

Teasdale, J. D., Taylor, M. J., Cooper, Z., Hayhurst, H., & Paykel, E. S. (1995b). Depressive thinking: Shifts in construct accessibility or in schematic mental models. *Journal of Abnormal Psychology, 104,* 500–507.

Teicher, M. H., Glod, C. A., Magnus, E., Harper, D., Benson, G. E., Krueger, K., et al. (1997). Circadian rest–activity disturbances in seasonal affective disorder. *Archives of General Psychiatry, 54,* 124–130.

Tennant, C. (2002). Life events, stress and depression: A review of the findings. *Australian and New Zealand Journal of Psychiatry, 36,* 173–182.

Terman, J. S., Terman, M., Lo, E. S., & Cooper, T. B. (2001). Circadian time of morning light administration and therapeutic response in winter depression. *Archives of General Psychiatry, 58,* 69–75.

Thakur, M., Hays, J., & Krishnan, K. R. R. (1999). Clinical, demographic and social characteristics of psychotic depression. *Psychiatry Research, 86,* 99–106.

Thase, M. E., Fasiczka, A. L., Berman, S. R., Simons, A. D., & Reynolds, C. F. (1998). Electroencephalographic sleep profiles before and after cognitive behavior therapy of depression. *Archives of General Psychiatry, 55,* 138–144.

Thase, M. E., Jindal, R. D., & Howland, R. (2002a). Biological aspects of depression. In I. H. Gotlib & C. L. Hammen (Eds.), *Handbook of depression* (pp. 192–218). New York: Guilford.

Thase, M. E., & Kupfer, D. J. (1996). Recent developments in the pharmacotherapy of mood disorders. *Journal of Consulting and Clinical Psychology, 64,* 646–659.

Thase, M. E., Kupfer, D. J., Buysse, D. J., Frank, E., Simons, A. D., Mceachran, A. B., et al. (1995). Electroencephalographic sleep profiles in single-episode and recurrent unipolar forms of major depression:1. Comparison during acute depressive states. *Biological Psychiatry, 38,* 506–515.

Thase, M. E., Kupfer, D. J., Fasiczka, A. J., Buysse, D. J., Simons, A. D., & Frank, E. (1997). Identifying an abnormal electroencephalographic sleep profile to characterize major depressive disorder. *Biological Psychiatry, 41,* 964–973.

Thase, M. E., Nierenberg, A. A., Keller, M. B., & Panagides, J. (2001). Efficacy of mirtazapine for prevention of depressive relapse: A placebo-controlled double-blind trial of recently remitted high-risk patients. *Journal of Clinical Psychiatry, 62,* 782–788.

Thase, M. E., Rush, A. J., Howland, R. H., Kornstein, S. G., Kocsis, J. H., Gelenberg, A. J., et al. (2002b). Double-blind switch study of imipramine or sertraline treatment of antidepressant-resistant chronic depression. *Archives of General Psychiatry, 59,* 233–239.

Thase, M. E., Simons, A. D., Mcgeary, J., Cahalane, J. F., Hughes, C., Harden, T., et al. (1992). Relapse after cognitive behavior therapy of depression: Potential implications for longer courses of treatment. *American Journal of Psychiatry, 149,* 1046–1052.

Thase, M. E., & Wright, J. H. (1991). Cognitive behavior therapy manual for depressed inpatients: A treatment protocol outline. *Behavior Therapy, 22,* 579–595.

Thompson, L. W., Coon, D. W., Gallagher-Thompson, D., Sommer, B. R., & Koin, D. (2001). Comparison of desipramine and cognitive/behavioral therapy in the treatment of elderly outpatients with mild-to-moderate depression. *American Journal of Geriatric Psychiatry, 9,* 225–240.

Timko, C., Cronkite, R. C., Berg, E. A., & Moos, R. H. (2002). Children of parents with unipolar depression: A comparison of stably remitted, partially remitted, and nonremitted parents and nondepressed controls. *Child Psychiatry & Human Development, 32,* 165–185.

Treynor, W., Gonzalez, R., & Nolen-Hoeksema, S. (2003). Rumination reconsidered: A psychometric analysis. *Cognitive Therapy and Research, 27,* 247–259.

Trivedi, M. H., Fava, M., Wisniewski, S. R., Thase, M. E., Quitkin, F., Warden, D., et al. (2006a). Medication augmentation after the failure of SSRIs for depression. *New England Journal of Medicine, 354,* 1243–1252.

Trivedi, M. H., Rush, A. J., Wisniewski, S. R., Nierenberg, A. A., Warden, D., Ritz, L., et al. (2006b). Evaluation of outcomes with citalopram for depression using measurement-based care in STAR*D: Implications for clinical practice. *American Journal of Psychiatry, 163,* 28–40.

Trivedi, M., Rush, A. J., Wisniewski, S. R., Warden, D., McKinney, W., Downing, M., et al. (2006). Factors associated with health-related quality of life among outpatients with major depressive disorder: A STAR*D report. *Journal of Clinical Psychiatry, 67,* 185–195.

Tse, W. S., & Bond, A. J. (2004). The impact of depression on social skills. *The Journal of Nervous and Mental Disease, 192,* 260–268.

Tsuno, N., Besset, A., & Ritchie, K. (2005). Sleep and depression. *Journal of Clinical Psychiatry, 66,* 1254–1269.

Van den Berg, M. D., Oldehinkel, A. J., Bouhuys, A. L., Brilman, E. I., Beekman, A. T., & Ormel, J. (2001). Depression in later life: Three etiologically different subgroups. *Journal of Affective Disorders, 65,* 19–26.

Van Os, J., & Jones, P. B. (1999). Early risk factors and adult person–environment relationships in affective disorder. *Psychological Medicine, 29,* 1055–1067.

Vythilingam, M., Chen, J., Bremner, J. D., Mazure, C. M., Maciejewski, P. K., & Nelson, J. C. (2003). Psychotic depression and mortality. *American Journal of Psychiatry, 160,* 574–576.

Wade, T. D., & Kendler, K. S. (2000). Absence of interactions between social support and stressful life events in the prediction of major depression and depressive symptomatology in women. *Psychological Medicine, 30,* 965–974.

Wallace, J., & O'Hara, M. W. (1992). Increases in depressive symptomatology in the rural elderly: Results from a cross-sectional and longitudinal study. *Journal of Abnormal Psychology, 101,* 398–404.

Wampold, B. E., Minami, T., Baskin, T. W., & Tierney, S. C. (2002). A meta-(re)analysis of the effects of cognitive therapy versus "other therapies" for depression. *Journal of Affective Disorders, 68,* 159–165.

Wang, P. S., Beck, A. L., Berglund, P., McKenas, D. K., Pronk, N. P., Simon, G. E., et al. (2004). Effects of major depression on moment-in-time work performance. *American Journal of Psychiatry, 161,* 1885–1891.

Wang, P. S., Berglund, P., & Kessler, R. C. (2000). Recent core of common mental disorders in the United States: Prevalence and conformance with evidence-based recommendations. *Journal of General Internal Medicine, 15,* 284–292.

Wang, P. S., & Kessler, R. C. (2005). Global burden of mood disorders. In D. Stein, D. Kupfer, & A. Schatzberg (Eds.), *Textbook of mood disorders* (pp. 55–67). Washington, DC: American Psychiatric Publishing.

Wang, P. S., Lane, M., Olfson, M., Pincus, H. A., Wells, K. B., & Kessler, R. C. (2005). Twelve-month use of mental health services in the United States: Results from the National Comorbidity

Survey Replication. *Archives of General Psychiatry, 62*, 629–640.

Watkins, E., & Moulds, M. (2005). Distinct modes of ruminative self-focus: Impact of abstract versus concrete rumination on problem solving in depression. *Emotion, 5*, 319–328.

Watkins, E., & Teasdale, J. D. (2001). Rumination and over-general memory in depression: Effects of self-focus and analytic thinking. *Journal of Abnormal Psychology, 110*, 353–357.

Watson, D. (2005). Rethinking the mood and anxiety disorders: A quantitative hierarchical model for DSM-V. *Journal of Abnormal Psychology, 114*, 522–536.

Watson, D., Gamez, W., & Simms, L. J. (2005). Basic dimensions of temperament and their relation to anxiety and depression: A symptom-based perspective. *Journal of Research in Personality, 39*, 46–66.

Watts, F. N. (1993). Problems of memory and concentration. In C. G. Costello (Ed.), *Symptoms of depression* (pp. 113–140). New York: Wiley.

Wehr, T. A., Duncan, W. C., Sher, L., Aeschbach, D., Schwartz, P. J., Turner, E. H., et al. (2001). A circadian signal of change of season in patients with seasonal affective disorder. *Archives of General Psychiatry, 58*, 1108–1114.

Weiss, B., & Garber, J. (2003). Developmental differences in the phenomenology of depression. *Development and Psychopathology, 15*, 403–430.

Weiss, E. L., Longhurst, J. G., & Mazure, C. M. (1999). Childhood sexual abuse as a risk factor for depression in women: Psychosocial and neurobiological correlates. *American Journal of Psychiatry, 156*, 816–828.

Weissman, M. M. (1979). Psychological treatment of depression: Evidence for the efficacy of psychotherapy alone, in comparison with, and in combination with pharmacotherapy. *Archives of General Psychiatry, 36*, 1261–1269.

Weissman, M. M., Fendrich, M., Warner, V., & Wickramaratne, P. (1992). Incidence of psychiatric disorder in offspring at high and low risk for depression. *Journal of the American Academy of Child and Adolescent Psychiatry, 31*, 640–648.

Weissman, M. M., & Klerman, G. L. (1990). Interpersonal psychotherapy for depression. In B. B. Wolman & G. Stricker (Eds.), *Depressive disorders: Facts, theories, and treatment methods* (pp. 379–395). New York: Wiley.

Weissman, M. M., Klerman, G. L., Prusoff, B. A., Sholomskas, D., & Padian, N. (1981). Depressed outpatients: Results one year after treatment with drugs and/or interpersonal psychotherapy. *Archives of General Psychiatry, 38*, 51–55.

Weissman, M. M., & Olfson, M. (1995). Depression in women: Implications for health care research. *Science, 269*, 799–801.

Weissman, M. M., & Paykel, E. S. (1974). *The depressed woman: A study of social relationships*. Oxford, UK: University of Chicago Press.

Weissman, M. M., Wickramaratne, P., Nomura, Y., Warner, V., Pilowsky, D., & Verdeli, H. (2006). Offspring of depressed parents: 20 years later. *American Journal of Psychiatry, 163*, 1001–1008.

Weissman, M. M., Wolk, S., Goldstein, R. B., Moreau, D., Adams, P., Greenwald, S., et al. (1999a). Depressed adolescents grown up. *Journal of the American Medical Association, 281*, 1707–1713.

Weissman, M. M., Wolk, S., Wickramaratne, P., Goldstein, R. B., Adams, P., Greenwald, S., et al. (1999b). Children with prepubertal-onset major depressive disorder and anxiety grown up. *Archives of General Psychiatry, 56*, 794–801.

Weisz, J. R., McCarty, C. A., & Valeri, S. M. (2006). Effects of psychotherapy for depression in children and adolescents: A meta-analysis. *Psychological Bulletin, 132,* 132–149.

Weisz, J. R., Thurber, C. A., Sweeney, L., Proffitt, V. D., & LeGagnoux, G. L. (1997). Brief treatment of mild-to-moderate child depression using Primary and Secondary Control Enhancement Training. *Journal of Consulting and Clinical Psychology, 65,* 703–707.

Wells, K. B., Katon, W., Rogers, B., & Camp, P. (1994). Use of minor tranquilizers and antidepressant medications by depressed outpatients: Results from the medical outcomes study. *American Journal of Psychiatry, 151,* 694–700.

Wells, K. B., Stewart, A., Hays, R. D., Burnam, A., Rogers, W., Daniels, M., et al. (1989). The functioning and well-being of depressed patients. *Journal of the American Medical Association, 262,* 914–919.

Wenzlaff, R. M., & Grozier, S. A. (1988). Depression and the magnification of failure. *Journal of Abnormal Psychology, 97,* 90–93.

Whiffen, V. E., & Gotlib, I. H. (1993). Comparison of postpartum and nonpostpartum depression: Clinical presentation, psychiatric history, and psychosocial functioning. *Journal of Consulting and Clinical Psychology, 61,* 485–494.

Whisman, M. A. (2001). The association between depression and marital dissatisfaction. In S. R. H. Beach (Ed.), *Marital and family processes in depression: A scientific foundation for clinical practice.* Washington, DC: American Psychological Association.

Whisman, M. A., & Bruce, M. L. (1999). Marital dissatisfaction and incidence of major depressive episode in a community sample. *Journal of Abnormal Psychology, 108,* 674–678.

Whisman, M. A., Miller, I. W., Norman, W. H., & Keitner, G. I. (1991). Cognitive therapy with depressed inpatients: Specific effects on dysfunctional cognitions. *Journal of Consulting and Clinical Psychology, 59,* 282–288.

Whisman, M. A., Uebelacker, L. A., & Weinstock, L. M. (2004). Psychopathology and marital satisfaction: The importance of evaluating both partners. *Journal of Consulting and Clinical Psychology, 72,* 830–838.

WHO World Mental Health Survey Consortium. (2004). Prevalence, severity, and unmet need for treatment of mental disorders in the World Health Organization World Mental Health Surveys. *Journal of the American Medical Association, 291,* 2581–2590.

Widiger, T. A., & Samuel, D. B. (2005). Diagnostic categories or dimensions? A question for the diagnostic and statistical manual of mental disorders—fifth edition. *Journal of Abnormal Psychology, 114,* 494–504.

Wilhelm, K., Mitchell, P. B., Niven, H., Finch, A., Wedgwood, L., Scimone, A., et al. (2006). Life events, first depression onset and the serotonin transporter gene. *British Journal of Psychiatry, 188,* 210–215.

Williams J. (1998). A structured clinical interview guide for the Hamilton Depression Rating Scale. *Archives of General Psychiatry, 45,* 742–747.

Williams, J. M. G. (1996). Depression and the specificity of autobiographical memory. In D. C. Rubin (Ed.), *Remembering our past: Studies in autobiographical memory* (pp. 244–267). Cambridge, UK: Cambridge University Press.

Williams, J. M. G., Barnhofer, T., Crane, C., Hermans, D., Raes, F., Watkins, E., et al. (2007). Autobiographical memory

specificity and emotional disorder.
Psychological Bulletin, 133, 122–148.

Winkler, D., Pjrek, E., Praschak-Rieder, N.,
Willeit, M., Pezawas, L., Konstantinidis,
A., et al. (2005). Actigraphy in patients
with seasonal affective disorder and
healthy control subjects treated with
light therapy. *Biological Psychiatry, 58,*
331–336.

Winokur, A., Gary, K. A., Rodner, S., Rae-
Red, C., Fernando, A. T., & Szuba, M. R.
(2001). Depression, sleep physiology,
and antidepressant drugs. *Depression
and Anxiety, 14,* 19–28.

Wirz-Justice, A., & Van den Hoofdakker,
R. H. (1999). Sleep deprivation in
depression: What do we know, where
do we go? *Biological Psychiatry, 46,*
445–453.

Wittchen, H.-U., Becker, E., Lieb, R., &
Krause, P. (2002). Prevalence, incidence
and stability of premenstrual dysphoric
disorder in the community.
Psychological Medicine, 32, 119–132.

Wittchen, H.-U., Beesdo, K., Bittner, A., &
Goodwin, R. D. (2003). Depressive
episodes: Evidence for a causal role of
primary anxiety disorders? *European
Psychiatry, 18,* 384–393.

Wolkowitz, O. M., & Reus, V. I. (1999).
Treatment of depression with
antiglucocorticoid drugs. *Psychosomatic
Medicine, 61,* 698–711.

Wolkowitz, O. M., Reus, V. I., Keebler, A.,
Nelson, N., Friedland, M., Brizendine,
L., et al. (1999). Double-blind treatment
of major depression with
dehydroepiandrosterone. *American
Journal of Psychiatry, 156,* 646–649.

World Health Organization (1993). *The
ICD-10 classification of mental and
behavioural disorders: Diagnostic criteria
for research.* Geneva, Switzerland: World
Health Organization.

Wright, J. H. (2003). Cognitive behavior
therapy for chronic depression.
Psychiatric Annals, 33, 777–784.

Wright, J. H., Wright, A. S., Albano, A. M.,

Basco, M. R., Goldsmith, L. J., Raffield,
T., et al. (2005). Computer-assisted
cognitive therapy for depression:
Maintaining efficacy while reducing
therapist time. *American Journal of
Psychiatry, 162,* 1158–1164.

Yatham, L. N., Liddle, P. F., Shiah, I. S.,
Scarrow, G., Lam, R. W., Adam, M. J., et
al. (2000). Brain serotonin(2) receptors
in major depression: A positron
emission tomography study. *Archives of
General Psychiatry, 57,* 850–858.

Yehuda, R., Teicher, M. H., Trestman, R. L.,
Levengood, R. A., & Siever, L. J. (1996).
Cortisol regulation in posttraumatic
stress disorder and major depression: A
chronobiological analysis. *Biological
Psychiatry, 40,* 79–88.

Yorbik, O., Birmaher, B., Axelson, D.,
Williamson, D. E., & Ryan, N. D. (2004).
Clinical characteristics of depressive
symptoms in children and adolescents
with major depressive disorder. *Journal
of Clinical Psychiatry, 65,* 1654–1659.

Zimmerman, M., Chelminski, I., &
McDermut, W. (2002). Major depressive
disorder and axis I diagnostic
comorbidity. *Journal of Clinical
Psychiatry, 63,* 187–193.

Zimmerman, M., Coryell, W., Stangl, D., &
Pfohl, B. (1987). Validity of an
operational definition for neurotic
unipolar major depression. *Journal of
Affective Disorders, 12,* 29–40.

Zisook, S., Rush, A. J., Albala, A., Alpert, J.,
Balasubramani, G. K., Fava, M., et al.
(2004). Factors that differentiate early
vs. later onset of major depression
disorder. *Psychiatry Research, 129,*
127–140.

Zlotnick, C., Kohn, R., Keitner, G., & Della
Grotta, S. A. (2000). The relationship
between quality of interpersonal
relationships and major depressive
disorder: Findings from the National
Comorbidity Survey. *Journal of Affective
Disorders, 59,* 205–215.

Zonderman, A. B., Herbst, J. H., Schmidt,

C., Costa, P. T., & McCrae, R. R. (1993). Depressive symptoms as a nonspecific, graded risk for psychiatric diagnoses. *Journal of Abnormal Psychology, 102,* 544–552.

Zubenko, G. S., Hughes, H. B., Stiffler, J. S., Zubenko, W. N., & Kaplan, B. B. (2002). Genome survey for susceptibility loci for recurrent, early-onset major depression: Results at 10cM resolution. *American Journal of Medical Genetics (Neuropsychiatric Genetics), 114,* 413–422.

Zuroff, D. C., Mongrain, M., & Santor, D. A. (2004). Conceptualizing and measuring personality vulnerability to depression: Comment on Coyne and Whiffen (1995). *Psychological Bulletin, 130,* 489–511.

Zuroff, D. C., Santor, D. A., & Mongrain, M. (2005). Dependency, self-criticism, and maladjustment. In J. Auerbach, K. Levy, & C. Schaffer (Eds.), *Relatedness, self-definition and mental representation* (pp. 75–90). New York: Routledge/ Taylor & Francis.

Author index

Index compiled by L. N. Derrick

Subject index

Note: Page numbers in *italics* refer to figures; those in **bold** to tables.

cortex
  activation of 85
  blood flow in 84
corticotrophin releasing hormone (CRH) 77–9, 88
cortisol 78–80, 88, 145
couples, and CBT 173
criminality 37
cultural differences 62–4

death 122
delinquency 37
delusions 8, 19–20, 88
dementia 6, 39–40
dependency 137–9
depressed persons, social behaviours of 135–42
depression
  adolescent onset 38
  adoption studies in 70–1
  and age 51–6
    at onset 29–30, 36, 70
  assessment of 24–8
  and attachment 125–6
  atypical 7, 17, 153
    features of 18
  biological 16–17
  biological aspects of 67–90
    causality vs. correlation 68
    conceptual issues 67–9
    static vs. transactional models 68–9
  biological differences 57–8
  bipolar 9
    see also bipolar disorder
    and brain structure/functioning 83–5
  CBT treatment of 161–76
  childhood onset 36–8
  chronicity of 32–5
  and circadian rhythms 80–3
  and close relationships 131–2
  cognitive approach to 91–118
  cognitive models of 5, 92–7, 174–5
    evaluation 104–5
  comorbidity in 15, 21–4, 50
  consequences of 40–7
  continuum of 24–5
  course and consequences of 29–47
  and death 44–7
  definition of 1–28
  demographics of 34
  diagnosis of 1–28
    in children and adolescents 13–16
    other 12–13
  diagnostic specifiers 17–20
  and disease 45–6
  diurnal variation 17, 80
  double 12, 32, 34–5, 37
  duration of episodes 302
  early onset 30
  effects on work 42–3
  endogenous 16–17
  epidemiology, in children and adolescents 54–5
  experience of 1–3
  and family relationships 120–35
    studies in 69–70

  and female hormones 85–90
  four domains of 4–7
  four groups of 35
  gender differences in 56–65
  genetic aspects 71–5
    research in 69–75
  global burden of 41
  and health 44–7
  implications of 7–8
  increase among young 52–4
  information-processing models of 92–7
  Kraepelin's description of 2
  late life 39–40
  level of severity and CBT 168–9
  life stress approach to 91–118
  lifetime diagnoses 50–1
  major 24–5, 50–1, 53, 88
    course of 29–35
  and marital relationships 43–4, 130–1
  and marital status 65
  melancholic 17
    features of 17–18
  and menopause 89–90
  mild
    chronic 35
    impairing effects of 41–2
    nonchronic 35
  minor 24–5
  moderate–severe chronic 35
  moderate–severe nonchronic 35
  and negative cognitions 97–8
  and negative life events 106–11
  and negative thinking 98–100
  neuroendocrine functioning in 77–80
  and neurotransmitters 75–7
  in older adults 55–6
  and parent–child relations 43, 61, 79, 114, 121,
    126–8
  people affected by 49–66
  and physical exercise 159–60
  and PMDD 87–8
  postpartum 20–1, 88, 178
    psychotic 21, 88
  poststroke 83
  predictors 33
    of recurrence 34
  prevalence of 49–51
    twelve-month 50
  prevention, in children and adolescents 182–4
  psychological 16–17
  with psychotic features 19–20
  and puberty 86–7
  recurrence of 32–5, 33
  recurrent brief 13
  relapse 32
    prevention of 169–72
  residual 149
  response of others to 135–6
  as risk factor 45–6
  seasonal pattern 18–19
  and self-concept 96–7
  severity of 26–8
  and sleep disturbance 7, 14, 80–3, 158

hypercortisolism 78
Hypericum perforatum 154
hyperphagia 7
hypersomnia 7, 15, 18
hypertension 78
hypomania 8–10, 37
hypothalamic–pituitary–adrenal (HPA) axis 77–80,
   83–4, 87–8, 115
hypothalamus 75, 78

imipramine 76, 164, 167
immigrants 63–4
impaired functioning 40–7
impulsive behaviour disorders 16
infanticide 88
information processing, faulty 92
information-processing models 92–7
International Classification of Disorders–Version 10
   (ICD-10) 10, **11**, 25
International Consortium of Psychiatric
   Epidemiology Surveys 29
interpersonal characteristics 135–8
interpersonal deficits, and IPT/IPT-A 177, 182
interpersonal difficulties, mechanisms of 136–7
interpersonal psychotherapy (IPT) 167–8,
   176–9
   for adolescents (IPT-A) 180, 182
   evaluating the outcome of 178–9
   treatment methods 177–8
introversion 137–8
irritability, in children 14–15

Kiddie-SADS 26
kindling model 112–13

late life depression 39–40
learning models 121
life event types, and personality 108–10
life events, negative 95
life stress, approach to depression 91–118
light therapy *see* phototherapy
limbic system 75
listlessness 4
lithium 149
locus coeruleus–norepinephrine (LC-NE) system
   77, 79
loss, concept of 108

major depression 24–5, 50–1, 53, 88
major depressive episodes (MDE) 10, 32
mania 8, 10, 37, 76
marital difficulties, and depression 130–1
marital dysfunction, mechanisms of 132–3
marital relationships 122
marital status 65
markers 68
marriage, relations within 43–4
matching hypothesis 110
Medical Outcomes Study 41
Medicine and Healthcare Products Regulatory
   Agency (MHRA) 154
melancholic depression 17
  features of 17–18

melatonin 19, 80, 83
memory, autobiographical 104
memory dysfunction 84
memory problems 6
men, symptom repression in 57
menopause, and depression 89–90
menstruation 12, 87
metacognitive awareness 176
mild depression, impairing effects of 41–2
mindfulness-based cognitive therapy (MBCT) 171
minor depressive disorder 13
mirtazapine 150
monoamine 159
monoamine oxidase inhibitors (MAOIs) 18, 145,
   147, 151, 153
mood, change in 175
mood disorders 23
  adults with **51**
motor behaviour, changes in 6
myocardial infarction 46

National Comorbidity Study (NCS) 21, 31
   Replication (NCS-R) 50, 52, 63
National Health Service (NHS) 169
National Institute for Clinical Excellence (NICE)
   169
National Institute of Mental Health (NIMH) 31
   Collaborative Program (TDRCP) 31, 164, 168,
   178
nefazodone 145, 150, 167
negative affect 23
negative cognitions, and depression 97–8
negative explanatory style 94
negative life events 91
  and depression 106–11
negative thinking 5, 92, 162–3
  and depression 98–100
Netherlands Mental Health Survey and Incidence
   Study 31
neurogenesis 148
neuroticism 23, 72–3, 138
  and stress 114
neurotransmitters 72, 75–7
neurotrophic factors 148
noncompliance 152–3
nondirective supportive therapy (NST) 182
noradrenaline *see* norepinephrine
norepinephrine 75–6, 83, 145, 147

obesity 45–6, 78
object loss 120
object relations theory 120
Oregon Coping with Depression (CWD-A)
   program 181
   parent program (CWD-a+P) 181
overgeneralization 104–5

panic disorder 21
paranoid beliefs 173
parent training 180
parenting styles
  affectionless and controlling 126–8
  negative 127

social relationships 119–42
social skills, deficits in 136–7
social support 139–41
social withdrawal 15, 137
socio-demographic factors 62–5
sociotropy 137, 139
somatic symptoms 15
state-dependent cognitions 99–100
static models 68–9
stress 34, 54, 58–60, 68–9, *74*
    autonomy 113
    coping factors 59–60
    and depression 34, 54, 58–60, *74*, 105–17
        models of mechanisms in 115–17
    effects of type 108
    and environmental factors 79
    and the family 122
    and gender differences 111
    generation 113–15
    HPA response 145
    interpersonal 62, 87, 113–14, 141–2
    and neuroticism 114
    rates of *107*
    response to 77
    sensitivity 113, 124, *125*
    and social functioning 138–42
    temporal aspects 111–13
stressful experiences 106
stressors 61, 75, 77, 108–9, 112, 115
    and blame 115
    interpersonal 62, 87, 113–14, 141–2
stroke 39, 45–6, 83
Structured Clinical Interview for DSM (SCID) 26, 112
students 43
substance abuse 22, 37
substance use disorders 15–16, 26
suicidal ideation 5, 15–16, 44, 132
    and culture 63
suicide 40–2, 53, 88
    and antidepressants 152
    in children and adolescents 154
    and depression 44–5
    in the elderly 56
symptoms
    alternate causes for 10
    reporting of 28
    residual 170
systemic behaviour family therapy (SBFT) 182

Temple-Wisconsin Cognitive Vulnerability to
    Depression (CVD) Study 98–9, 110
testosterone 86
thalamus 83
thought catching, in CBT 162–3

tranquillizers 42
transactional models 68–9
transcranial magnetic stimulation (TMS) 157–8
    repetitive (rTMS) 85, 157–8
transcription factors 148
transdiagnostic processes 23
trauma, exposure to 59
treatment
    acute 146
    acute phase 164–5
    as-usual (TAU) 170–1, 174
    biological 143–60
    CBT 161–76
    continuation 147, 149–50
    failure to seek 143–4
    maintenance 147, 150
    nonpharmacological biological 155–60
    placebo 150–1
    psychological 161–85
Treatment for Adolescents with Depression Study
    (TADS) 181–2
tricyclic antidepressants 18, 76, 145, 149–50, 153–4
    in children and adolescents 154
twin studies 70–1, 108, 112–13
tyramine 151

unipolar depression 8–9, 21, 37, 112
    childhood-onset 37
    course of 29–35
    familial transmission of 70
    and sleep disturbance 82
    three forms of 10

venlafaxine 145, 150
victimization, sexual 59
violence, in family 123–4
vulnerability 94, 109–10, 115–16, 121, 124, 129, 132, 134
    to interpersonal life events 139

weight changes 15
    loss 7, 17
withdrawal 132, 138
women
    depression in 56–60
    from ethnic minorities 173
    and marital dissatisfaction 129
    and stress 58–60, 113
work, effects of depression on 42–3
World Health Organization (WHO) 41
worry 15, 132
worthlessness 128

youth, increasing depression among 52–4

Index compiled by L. N. Derrick